DECONSTRUCTION IN A NUTSHELL

John D. Caputo, *series editor*

PERSPECTIVES IN
CONTINENTAL
PHILOSOPHY

DECONSTRUCTION IN A NUTSHELL

A Conversation with
JACQUES DERRIDA

Edited with a Commentary by John D. Caputo

With a new Introduction

FORDHAM UNIVERSITY PRESS
New York   2021

Visit us online at www.fordhampress.com.

Library of Congress Cataloging-in-Publication Data available online
at https://catalog.loc.gov.

Printed in the United States of America
23 22 21   5 4 3 2 1
First edition

In Memoriam
Lawrence C. Gallen, O.S.A. (1929–1995)
For his love of Villanova

Contents

Acknowledgments

I would like to thank the administration of Villanova University, Rev. Edmund J. Dobbin, O.S.A., President; Dr. Helen Lafferty, University Vice President; and Dr. Daniel Ziegler, Dean of the Graduate School of Arts and Sciences, for their financial and moral support of this Roundtable and of the doctoral program in philosophy. Their kindness and support, along with the loving encouragement of the late Rev. Lawrence C. Gallen, O.S.A., former Academic Vice President, to whom this volume is dedicated, has been invaluable to us all.

I would like to thank my colleagues, Professors Walter Brogan, Thomas Busch, and Dennis Schmidt for their help in planning this conference and for their contributions to the "Roundtable."

I wish to thank Barbara Romano for her help in the preparation of the index.

Finally, I am deeply grateful to Jacques Derrida for his participation in this Roundtable, which provided everyone at Villanova with a very special day, for his help with the transcript of the "Roundtable," for his inspiring and groundbreaking work, and, above all, for his friendship.

Abbreviations

Note: I cite Derrida's works in parentheses in the body of the text, using the following system of abbreviations, referring first to the French and then, after the slash, to the English translation where such is available. I have adapted this system of abbreviations from the one that I first devised for *The Prayers and Tears of Jacques Derrida* (Bloomington: Indiana University Press, 1997).

AC   *L'autre cap.* Paris: Éditions de Minuit, 1991. Eng. trans. OH.

AL   *Jacques Derrida: Acts of Literature.* Ed. Derek Attridge. New York: Routledge, 1992.

Circon.   *Circonfession: Cinquante-neuf périodes et périphrases.* In Geoffrey Bennington and Jacques Derrida, *Jacques Derrida.* Paris: Éditions du Seuil, 1991. Eng. trans. *Circum.*

Circum.   *Circumfession: Fifty-nine Periods and Periphrases.* In Geoffrey Bennington and Jacques Derrida, *Jacques Derrida.* Chicago: The University of Chicago Press, 1993.

DDP   *Du droit à la philosophie.* Paris: Galilée, 1990. Eng. trans. Pp. 461–498: PR; pp. 577–618: "Sendoffs."

DiT   *Difference in Translation.* Ed. Joseph F. Graham. Ithaca, N.Y.: Cornell University Press, 1985.

DLE   *De l'esprit: Heidegger et la question.* Paris: Galilée, 1987. Eng. trans. OS.

DLG   *De la grammatologie.* Paris: Éditions de Minuit, 1967. Eng. trans. OG.

DM   "Donner la mort." In *L'Éthique du don: Jacques Derrida et la pensée du don.* Paris: Métailié-Transition, 1992. Eng. trans. GD.

DNT   *Derrida and Negative Theology.* Ed. Howard Coward and Toby Foshay. Albany: State University of New York Press, 1992.

DPJ   *Deconstruction and the Possibility of Justice.* Ed. Drucilla Cornell et al. New York: Routledge, 1992.

DT   *Donner le temps.* I. *La fausse monnaie.* Paris: Galilée, 1991. Eng. trans. GT.

ED   *L'écriture et la différence.* Paris: Éditions de Seuil, 1967. Eng. trans. WD.

FL   *Force de loi: Le "Fondement mystique de l'autorité."* Paris: Galilée, 1994. Eng. trans. "The Force of Law: 'The Mystical Foundation of Authority.' " Trans. Mary Quaintance. In DPJ, pp. 68–91.

Foi   "Foi et Savoir: Les deux sources de la 'religion' aux limites de la simple raison." In *La Religion.* Ed. Jacques Derrida and Gianni Vattimo. Paris: Seuil, 1996. Pp. 9–86.

GD   *The Gift of Death.* Trans. David Wills. Chicago: The University of Chicago Press, 1995.

Glas   *Glas.* Paris: Galilée, 1974. Eng. trans. *Glas.* Trans. Richard Rand and John Leavey. Lincoln: University of Nebraska Press, 1986.

GT   *Given Time.* I. *Counterfeit Money.* Trans. Peggy Kamuf. Chicago: The University of Chicago Press, 1991.

HOdG   *Husserl: L'origine de la géométrie.* 2nd. ed. Paris: Presses Universitaires de France, 1974.

HOG   *Edmund Husserl's Origin of Geometry.* Trans. John Leavey. Boulder: John Hays, 1978.

Khôra   *Khôra.* Paris: Galilée, 1993. Eng. trans. *Khôra.* Trans. Ian McLeod, in ON, 87–127.

LO   "Living On/Border Lines," Trans. James Hulbert. In Harold Bloom et al. *Deconstruction and Criticism.* New York: Continuum, 1979. Pp. 75–176.

MB   *Memoirs of the Blind: The Self-Portrait and Other Ruins.* Trans. Pascale-Anne Brault and Michael Naas. Chicago: The University of Chicago Press, 1993.

MdA   *Memoirs d'aveugle: L'autobiographie et autres ruines.* Paris: Éditions de la Réunion des musées nationaux, 1990. Eng. trans. MB.

MdP   *Marges de philosophie.* Paris: Éditions de Minuit, 1967. Eng. trans. MoP.

MfPdM   *Memoires: For Paul de Man.* Trans. Cecile Lindsay, Jona-

	than Culler, and Eduardo Cadava. New York: Columbia University Press, 1986.
MpPdM	*Mémoires: Pour Paul de Man*. Paris: Galilée, 1988.
MoP	*Margins of Philosophy*. Trans. Alan Bass. Chicago: The University of Chicago Press, 1982.
Number	"A Number of Yes." Trans. Brian Holmes. *Qui Parle*, 2 (1988), 120–133.
OCP	"On Colleges and Philosophy," Interview with Geoffrey Bennington, in *Postmodernism: ICA Documents*. Ed. Lisa Appignanesi. London: Free Association Books, 1989. Pp. 209–228.
OG	*Of Grammatology*. Trans. Gayatri Spivak. Baltimore: The Johns Hopkins University Press, 1974.
OH	*The Other Heading: Reflections on Today's Europe*. Trans. Pascale-Anne Brault and Michael Naas. Bloomington: Indiana University Press, 1992.
ON	*On the Name*. Ed. Thomas Dutoit. Stanford: Stanford University Press, 1995.
OS	*Of Spirit: Heidegger and the Question*. Trans. Geoffrey Bennington and Rachel Bowlby. Chicago: The University of Chicago Press, 1989.
Parages	*Parages*. Paris: Galilée, 1986. Eng. trans. pp. 118–218: LO; pp. 250–287: "The Law of Genre." Trans. Avital Ronell. In AL, pp. 221–252.
Pass.	*Passions*. Paris: Galilée, 1993. Eng. trans. "Passions: 'An Oblique Offering.'" Trans. David Wood. In ON, pp. 3–31.
PdS	*Points de suspension: Entretiens*. Ed. Elisabeth Weber. Paris: Galilée, 1992. Eng. trans. *Points*.
Points	*Points . . . Interviews, 1974–94*. Ed. Elisabeth Weber. Trans. Peggy Kamuf et al. Stanford: Stanford University Press, 1995.
Pol.	*Politiques de l'amitié*. Paris: Galilée, 1995.
PR	"The Principle of Reason: The University in the Eyes of Its Pupils." Trans. Catherine Porter and Edward Morris. *Diacritics*, 13 (1983), 3–20.
PSJ	*Post-Structuralist Joyce: Essays from the French*. Ed. Derek Attridge and Daniel Ferrer. New York: Cambridge University Press, 1984.

Psy.   *Psyché: Inventions de l'autre.* Paris: Galilée, 1987. Eng.
            trans. Pp. 11–62: "Psyche: Inventions of the Other." Trans.
            Catherine Portert, in RDR, pp. 25–65. Pp. 203–235: "Des
            Tour de Babel." Eng. trans. DiT 165–207; Pp. 535–596:
            "How to Avoid Speaking: Denials," trans. Ken Frieden, in
            DNT, pp. 73–142. Pp. 639–650: Number.

PTC   *Politics, Theory, and Contemporary Culture.* Ed. Mark
            Poster. New York: Columbia University Press, 1993.

RDR   *Reading De Man Reading.* Ed. Lindsay Waters and Wlad
            Godzich. Minneapolis: University of Minnesota Press,
            1989.

RTP   *Raising the Tone of Philosophy: Late Essays by Immanuel
            Kant, Transformative Critique by Jacques Derrida.* Ed.
            Peter Fenves. Baltimore: The Johns Hopkins University
            Press, 1993.

Sauf   *Sauf le nom.* Paris: Galilée, 1993. Eng. trans. "*Sauf le nom
            (Post-Scriptum).*" Trans. John Leavey, Jr. In ON, pp.
            33–85.

Schib.   *Schibboleth: pour Paul Celan.* Paris: Galilée, 1986. Eng.
            trans. "Shibboleth: For Paul Celan." Trans. Joshua
            Wilner. In WT, pp. 3–72.

SdM   *Spectres de Marx: État de la dette, le travail du deuil, et la
            nouvelle Internationale.* Paris: Galilée, 1993. Eng. trans.
            SoM.

Sendoffs   "Sendoffs." Trans. Thomas Peper. In *Yale French Studies,*
            77 (1990), 7–43.

SoM   *Specters of Marx: The State of the Debt, the Work of
            Mourning, and the New International.* Trans. Peggy
            Kamuf. New York: Routledge, 1994.

SP   *Speech and Phenomena and Other Essays on Husserl's The-
            ory of Signs.* Trans. David Allison. Evanston, Ill.: North-
            western University Press, 1973.

Ton   *D'un ton apocalyptique adopté naguère en philosophie.*
            Paris: Galilée, 1983. Eng. trans. "On a Newly Arisen
            Apocalyptic Tone in Philosophy." Trans. John Leavey, Jr.
            In RTP, pp. 117–171.

UG   *Ulysse gramophone: Deux Mots pour Joyce.* Paris: Galilée,
            1987. Eng. trans. Pp. 15–53: "Two Words for Joyce,"
            trans. Geoff Bennington, in PSJ. Pp. 145–59. Pp. 57–143:

"Ulysses Gramophone: Hear Say Yes in Joyce," trans. Tina Kendall and Shari Benstock, in AL, pp. 256–309.

VP   *La voix et le phénomène*. Paris: Presses Universitaires de France, 1967. Eng. trans. SP.

WD   *Writing and Difference*. Trans. Alan Bass. Chicago: The University of Chicago Press, 1978.

WT   *Word Traces: Readings of Paul Celan*. Ed. Aris Fioretos. Baltimore: The Johns Hopkins University Press, 1994.

Introduction (2020)

Specters of Derrida

John D. Caputo

I made him an offer he couldn't refuse.

I asked him to come to Villanova University, an institution run by *les Catholiques*—which is, he told me, how the Jews of colonial Algeria referred to the powers that be when he was growing up—to celebrate the launch of our new doctoral program in philosophy in the fall of 1994. Villanova University, I said, is not just Catholic; it is conducted by the Order of St. Augustine—the very same, the one he called his "compatriot," upon whose *Confessions* he had written a gloriously obscure and fetching riff called "Circumfession." There he exposed not only his circumcision, saints preserve us, but his "religion about which no one knew anything," not even his mother (Georgette/Monica), who should have known better, he being the son of her tears (*filius istarum lacrymarum*).[1] I asked him, what could be more perfect? What better place to make this unknown religion better known? What more fitting place in all the world to talk about his "Circumfession"?[2]

Of course, "religion" was the wrong word, but it was not necessarily the worst word, one he himself sometimes teasingly enter-

---

1 Jacques Derrida, "Circumfession: Fifty-Nine Periods and Periphrases," in *Jacques Derrida*, by Geoffrey Bennington and Jacques Derrida (Chicago: University of Chicago Press, 1993), 154–56.

2 That is what we did in a conference we held September 2001, just days after "9/11"; see John D. Caputo and Michael Scanlon, eds., *Augustine and Postmodernism: Confessions and Circumfession* (Bloomington: Indiana University Press, 2005).

tained. Where Augustine had once written, "What do I love when I love my God?," he had commented, can I do anything other than translate this question into my own life?[3] Jaws dropped, eyeballs bulged, secular jaws and eyeballs, I mean. God? Loving God, a.k.a. the transcendental signified? Was he kidding? Is this another jest, a sophisticated joke that only readers of *Of Grammatology* would get? This was really spooky. What is he thinking? What is he after? What does he mean by "translate"? What is he talking about? A specter, he said, but not a Holy Spirit, hauntological but not ontological, he quipped. Maybe something religious, or like religion, or at least not unlike religion.

I was secretly counting on the fact that, like an earlier Jewish apostle who spent himself traveling around the known world spreading the good news about Messiah Jesus, he too was willing to go anywhere, risking shipwreck and jet lag, writing furiously on airplanes and in hotel rooms, losing count of the number of lecture invitations, interviews, roundtables, conferences, and visiting professorships, all in the name of getting out the good news of deconstruction, of a new messianic, but this time without a Messiah.

My closer was this. I said to him that in my opinion there had been up to then two waves of deconstruction in the United States; the first, the original landing on the shores of the New World (Baltimore, 1966, to be specific),[4] was its widespread success in English literature and comparative literature departments, which swept over the academic landscape in the 1970s. The philosophy departments took a little longer to catch on to the philosophical seriousness of deconstruction, which came of age among American continental philosophers in the 1980s. My proposal, my premonition, my promise, my prognostication, was that there was a third wave in the making in the 1990s, a swell of people in the divinity schools and departments of religion who, ever since the late 1980s, have come to realize that they have something to learn from deconstruction.

He couldn't refuse.

---

3   Derrida, "Circumfession," 122.

4   Richard Macksey and Eugenio Donato, eds., *The Languages of Criticism and the Sciences of Man: The Structuralist Controversy* (Baltimore: Johns Hopkin University Press, 1967). Derrida's contribution, "Structure, Sign and Play in the Discourse of the Human Sciences," is found in *Writing and Difference*, trans. Alan Bass (Chicago: University of Chicago Press, 1978), 278–94.

1. "Religion and Postmodernism"

The "Roundtable" we held that day (October 3, 1994) was a huge success.[5] The auditorium was overflowing, standing room only. He was a philosophical celebrity, a rock star, and the topic could have been medieval logic or ancient Roman coins, anything. Elvis is in the building, we joked. But there was something else. He attracted the interest of a great range of people, from professional theologians and academic philosophers of religion to the growing number of "nones" and various religious activists—like the then emerging "Emergent Church"[6]—who were influential in progressive theology and leftist religion in the United States. To this day, people come up to me and tell me they were there and report the lasting impact it made on them. As I witnessed it all unfolding that day, I realized it deserved to be published. Accompanied by a commentary, this would make a splendid introduction to deconstruction and a perfect way to launch "Perspectives in Continental Philosophy," a new series we were inaugurating at Fordham University Press. So *Deconstruction in a Nutshell* was itself a bit of an event because I had no intention of publishing the "Roundtable"—until I heard it! It was Derrida at his most crystal clear.

I had heard him speak often enough to know that the key was to not let him read a paper, which could go on for hours, testing the patience of even the most faithful, and would be too subtle by half for even the specialists in the audience to simply sit and listen. The thing to do was to sit down with him around a table and talk. So I said all he had to do was show up and people with religion and theology on their mind would ask him about his work, about things like justice, the gift, hospitality, literature, and the pure messianic—which is pretty much the table of contents of *Deconstruction in a Nutshell*. I promised him: no questions about the *Filioque* debate, Double Predestination, or Didymus the Blind. Forced to extemporize in English, deprived of the complex somersaults of which he was the master when he spoke in French—anyone who has tried to communicate in a foreign language knows to avoid subjunctives

---

5   The mention of October 2, 1994, in Derrida and Caputo, *Deconstruction in a Nutshell* (New York: Fordham University Press, 1996), 3, is a mistake.

6   See Katharine Sarah Moody, *Radical Theology and Emerging Christianity: Deconstruction, Materialism and Religious Practices* (Surrey, UK: Ashgate, 2015).

and complicated sentences—he was usually the clearest speaker in the room. That was the most effective, not to mention the most merciful, way to treat an American audience, many of whom would be hearing him for the first time. His interviews and roundtables are the best place for beginners to start with his work, and the "Villanova Roundtable," as clear and compact as can be, has proven to be one of the best. Like any good teacher, he had a knack for serving up difficult ideas with clarity, along with a sparkling wit. He had a genius for answering questions, a capacity to hold an audience spellbound, a charming accent and a command of English for which he had no need to apologize, although he constantly did. He also had the devil in his eye, and what could be better than that if you were going to talk about religion? He reminded me of a devilish knight of faith.[7] Good Lord, is this the man? Why, he looks like a grammatologist!

The success of the "Roundtable" gave rise to the subsequent "Religion and Postmodernism" conferences. I knew very well that he had no time for the title "Religion and Postmodernism." He was not wrong. Whatever deconstruction is, if it is, whatever its name is, if it has a name, it is neither religion nor postmodernism. He objected to the periodization, the oversimplification of both "modernity" and its "post-"—and he was not simply opposed to the Enlightenment; he just wanted a new one.[8] He was also wary of the word "religion," not only because it was a Christian Latin word caught up in a history of violence, colonialism, patriarchy, superstition, anti-Semitism, and Islamophobia, but also because he did not want to pass himself off as a philosopher or scholar or practitioner of religion. I did not argue. I assured him the title was mainly intended to draw a crowd, and he knew he would be among friends. In an entry in *Counter-Paths* entitled "Villanova, 26 September 1997," referring to the conference that brought him together with Jean-Luc Marion on the question of God and the gift,[9] he wrote to Catherine Malabou:[10]

---

7 Caputo, "Like a Devilish Knight of Faith," *Oxford Literary Review* 36, no. 2 (2014): 188–90; reprinted in Caputo, *In Search of Radical Theology: Expositions, Explorations, Exhortations* (New York: Fordham University Press, 2020), 203–205.

8 Derrida and Caputo, *Deconstruction in a Nutshell*, 49–60.

9 Caputo and Michael J. Scanlon, eds., *God, the Gift and Postmodernism* (Bloomington: Indiana University Press, 1999).

10 Catherine Malabou, *Counter-Path: Traveling with Jacques Derrida*, trans. David Wills (Stanford, Calif.: Stanford University Press, 2004), 95. See Caputo and Scanlon, *God, the*

Leave tomorrow for New York, after a meeting on "Postmodernism and Religion" (two things that are foreign to me, as you know, one had to get used to it, resist, it all goes too quickly). My atheism develops in the churches, all the churches, can you understand that, can you? Here it's an Augustinian university. Feel better here than in certain other philosophy departments, my friend Caputo has something to do with that. . . .

I did have something to do with that, and I had a hunch that I understood why his atheism played well in the churches, definitely not all of them, but certainly some. I had a theory that he had a theory for this, that his atheism was of irreducible importance to any possible religion or theology. Paul Tillich put it thus: to traditional theistic religion "atheism is the right religious and theological reply," and it is central to "the most intensive piety of all times."[11] By making trouble for theism, atheism opens the doors to a radical post-theism (Tillich), to a "completely different story" about God and theology and religion (Derrida). How so? That is what I wanted to work out.

Third-Wave Deconstruction

In speaking of third-wave deconstruction, I hasten to point out that I mean three waves of the American reception of deconstruction. I am not speaking of three stages of his thought. Although I have been falsely accused of it, I never held to the idea of a religious, ethical, or political "turn" in his thought, which would be anything more than a turn of attention. I have always thought that the main lines staked out in the early work, especially in the three books of 1967, his *annus mirabilis*, were a consistent point of departure for him, a basic matrix. What had changed over the years was the context, which demanded the progressive growth, re-elaboration, reintroduction, and reinvention of deconstruction under the force of different circumstances and in response to different questions. He could say with Husserl, in deconstruction we are always just beginning. If someone is in search of the coming of what he cannot see coming, of the event, how could it be otherwise? What can this development

---

Gift and Postmodernism.

11 Paul Tillich, *Theology of Culture* (London: Oxford University Press, 1959), 25.

be other than the unfolding deconstruction of deconstruction, the
auto-verification of deconstruction by its own auto-deconstruction,
exposing deconstruction to its own future?

To be specific, what had happened, I think, is this. Based on his
interest in literature and the fact that, although always a man of the
left, he was not a card-carrying member of the French Communist
Party,[12] he had early on acquired the popular image of an anomic
apolitical aesthete.[13] As a result of this misperception, he was concerned to show that and how deconstruction can be brought to bear
on the ethical and political questions of the day, which cannot be
separated from religion. This issue came to a head in 1988 with the
irruption of the National Socialist controversy surrounding Heidegger
(by whom, along with Husserl, Derrida was deeply influenced) and
the discovery of anti-Semitic essays by the young Paul de Man (a close
friend and supporter of Derrida at Yale). In October 1989 Drucilla
Cornell held a symposium at the Cardoza Law School that afforded
him an opportunity to show the link between deconstruction and
justice—whence the landmark essay "The Force of Law."[14] Just so,
my intention was to provide him a forum at Villanova to show that
deconstruction was not the archenemy of ethics, religion, and institutions[15]—we were, after all, inaugurating a new doctoral "program."

We had been together at a phenomenology conference in Perugia
in July 1987, which he attended accompanied by his wife, Margue-
rite, at which he made a presentation on undecidability. After the session I said to him that the whole thing reminded me of Kierkegaard:
undecidability is not the opposite of a decision but the condition of
possibility of a genuine one. Of course, he said. That was all I needed
to hear. What must be shown is that the exceptionality and alterity
that are valorized in deconstruction do not fall below the universal,

---

12   Derrida and Caputo, *Deconstruction in a Nutshell*, 182–200.

13   In fact, Derrida was personally very close to Louis Althusser and gave a year-long
seminar in 1976–77 on Althusser's interpretation of Marx. This course is now available in
Derrida, *Theory and Practice*, trans. David Wills, ed. Geoffrey Bennington and Peggy Kamuf
(Chicago: University of Chicago Press, 2019). His personal relationship with Althusser
is discussed in Benoît Peeters, *Derrida: A Biography*, trans. Andrew Brown (Cambridge:
Polity Press, 2013).

14   Derrida, "The Force of Law: 'The Mystical Foundation of Authority,'" trans. Mary
Quantaince, in *Acts of Religion*, ed. Gil Anidjar (New York and London: Routledge, 2002),
228–98.

15   Derrida and Caputo, *Deconstruction in a Nutshell*, 4–8, 60–69.

into aestheticism (which is not to be confused with art), but rise above the universal, on an analogy with the teleological suspension of the universal in *Fear and Trembling*. This was what Kierkegaard called "the religious" and Levinas called "ethics." As soon as I got home, I wrote a piece entitled, "Beyond Aestheticism: Derrida's Responsible Anarchy," which was the most crisp formulation I could give to the religious element in deconstruction in the 1980s.[16]

That was before Derrida came to my rescue with a rush of new and surprising work—more than I could have hoped for—in the final decade and a half of his life. It started in 1989 with the Cardoza lecture and "Circumfession" and continued with *The Gift of Death* (1992),[17] which was his book on Kierkegaard's *Fear and Trembling*, "Faith and Knowledge" (1994),[18] and other often quasi-autobiographical works.[19] Mark C. Taylor and I had both been independently urging him to write something about *Fear and Trembling*. Impatient, I wrote my own book, *Against Ethics* (1991), which, inspired by Derrida and Lyotard, was meant to be my deconstructive "repetition" of *Fear and*

---

16   Caputo, "Beyond Aestheticism: Derrida's Responsible Anarchy," *Research in Phenomenology* 18 (1988): 59–73; reprinted in *The Essential Caputo: Selected Writings*, ed. B. Keith Putt (Bloomington: Indiana University Press, 2018), 184–94. In 1990, I called it not "responsible" but "Sacred Anarchy" in a conference presentation that was never published until Keith Putt included it in *Essential Caputo*, 287–304; it is an early sketch of what would become *The Prayers and Tears of Jacques Derrida: Religion without Religion* (Bloomington: Indiana University Press, 1997).

17   Derrida, "*Donner la mort*," in *L'Éthique du don: Jacques Derrida et la pensée du don* (Paris: Métailié-Transition, 1992); *The Gift of Death*, trans. David Wills (Chicago: University of Chicago Press, 1995).

18   Derrida, "Faith and Knowledge: The Two Sources of Faith and Knowledge at the Limits of 'Reason' Alone," trans. Samuel Weber, in *Religion*, ed. Derrida and Gianni Vattimo (Stanford, Calif.: Stanford University Press, 1998), 1–78. This is an extremely difficult text, and we are very fortunate to have the magisterial commentary of Michael Naas, *Miracle and Machine: Jacques Derrida and the Two Sources of Religion, Science and the Media* (New York: Fordham University Press, 2012), to lead us through it. In its terms, I treat religion as a matter of faith beyond belief and of contaminating itself with the impure, the nothings and nobodies of the world (auto-immunity).

19   Derrida, *Memoirs of the Blind: The Self-Portrait and Other Ruins*, trans. Pascale-Anne Brault and Michael Naas (Chicago: University of Chicago Press, 1993); and Derrida, *Monolingualism of the Other; or, The Prosthesis of Origin*, trans. Patrick Mensah (Stanford, Calif.: Stanford University Press, 1998), not to mention, of course, the treatment of the messianic in the hauntology book, Derrida, *Specters of Marx: The State of the Debt, the Work of Mourning, and the New International*, trans. Peggy Kamuf (New York: Routledge, 1994), which is my inspiring specter here, my go-to text.

Trembling.[20] A year later, he published *The Gift of Death*, which I read with some fear and trembling, fearful that my anticipation of what his book on Kierkegaard would look like would be contradicted by its actual appearance. It was not. Of course, no one could predict what he would come up with, but its central thesis, that the paradox (exception) of the binding of Isaac is the paradigm (universal) of any genuine ethical decision, is pretty much what I meant by "against ethics."

What Is Deconstruction in a Nutshell — Today?

In the "Roundtable" Derrida mentions that a journalist asked him at a talk he was giving at the time of the Cambridge crisis,[21] "Tell me, in a nutshell, what is deconstruction?" That is impossible, he said, but then he added, "Sometimes it may be useful to try."[22] So, in an effort to update this little book, let us pose once again the question "What is deconstruction in a nutshell — today?" In the third decade of the twenty-first century, ninety years after he was born, let us seek out the word, the name, that sums up deconstruction. If not religion, if not postmodernism, what then? What comes after religion? What comes after postmodernism?

Why is finding a nutshell impossible, today just as much as before? Because, whatever it is, deconstruction by definition resists reduction to a single principle, a *principium*, for that would decisively decide the undecidability in things and thereby flatten the deconstruction. As a theory of the undecidability of our most assured names and propositions, deconstruction could never be condensed into an X, capitalized and in the singular, like Religion, or an X-ism, like Atheism or Marxism or Postmodernism. For any such X would amount to a "master name," a "transcendental signified," that would "arrest the play of signifiers," as we used to say back in the day. It would bring peace to all the restlessness, order to the chaos, locate the center of its eccentricity. Finding the value of this variable X would write the "program" by which everything Derrida has to say could be

---

20   Caputo, *Against Ethics: Contributions to a Poetics of Obligation with Constant Reference to Deconstruction* (Bloomington: Indiana University Press, 1993).

21   Derrida and Caputo, *Deconstruction in a Nutshell*, 38–40.

22   Derrida and Caputo, *Deconstruction in a Nutshell*, 16.

generated.[23] Any such X would prevent the event. It would organize everything in deconstruction around a particular "construction," a particular "effect" of the play.

Nonetheless, against all these warnings, against the advice of counsel, in what follows I am going to walk right into this trap and say that today, after the death of Derrida, after postmodernism, after he has become a ghost, deconstruction in a nutshell is a *hauntology*! Why would I do such a foolish thing? Because sometimes it is useful to try. Sometimes, to stay in motion requires that we go where it is impossible to go. In saying this I am not saying that I know the secret—because the secret is, there is no Secret. Nor am I saying that I have found the value of X, where X is a *specter*. Or better still, I am saying that, but watch out, because I am also unsaying it. In saying that deconstruction is hauntology, and that X is a specter, I am in truth saying that anything that dares to pose as *the* value of X—justice or democracy, hospitality or the gift—is haunted, that the value of the variable is always to-come.

Hauntology is a kind of philosophical X-Files of spooky unsolved cases. I am making a meta-statement about deconstruction. Hauntology means that X is in principle spooked—that is, endlessly translatable, endlessly substitutable—that every time we translate X one way and then attempt to grasp it in a concept (from *con + capere*, in German: *begreifen*) it slips between our conceptual fingers. X does not represent the unknown thing in itself, the infinite depth of the ground of being, or the *Deus absconditus*, but infinite translatability, substitutability, replaceability, recontextualizability. X does not signify depth, but drift. It we try to intuit it clearly and distinctly in an *Anschauung*, it immediately shifts its shape and demands to be retranslated otherwise. You cannot measure both its velocity and its position at the same time. Very spooky.

As to the specter *itself*, if it has a self, *s'il y en a*, it is next to nothing. It does not even exist, but flits incessantly between existence and nonexistence. So what? Lots of things that do not exist can cause quite a disturbance. If the only choice we have is between existence

---

23   That is the literary conceit of Derrida, "Circumfession," 1. Above the dotted line, occupying the omniscient theological position, Geoffrey Bennington writes a commentary "on" the *corpus* of Derrida's work, which purports to be a program that anticipates everything that will be said by Derrida, writing down below the dotted line and trying to surprise Bennington.

and nonexistence, we will never understand anything and never get anything done. The specter does not exist; it *insists*.[24] That's the spooky thing.

Do You Believe in Ghosts?

In a hauntology, the basic question is, even and especially if ghosts do not exist, "Do you believe in ghosts?" That is the question that is put to Derrida in 1982 in a film entitled "Ghost Dance." In the film, in which he plays himself, he is interviewed by an actress (Pascale Ogier) who asks him this question directly. He answers that by "appearing" in this film he has himself become a ghost, a cinematic specter, capable of multiple apparitions in other times and places long after he is dead. "I think that the future belongs to ghosts," he continues, "that technology increases greatly the power of ghosts (*fantômes*)." Derrida asks in turn whether Pascale believes in ghosts, and she says, "Yes, now I do, yes." In 1984 the actress died at the age of twenty-four, and Derrida reports the uncanny experience he had watching the film some years later. She looks him in the eye on the big screen and repeats her answer, yes, she does now. Does she mean *now*, he wonders, now that she is dead?[25]

To be sure, today, a decade and a half after his death, Derrida himself has become a specter, and, as Rev. Ames says in the exquisite letter to his son that opens Marilynne Robinson's *Gilead*, now he knows most of what there is to know about being dead but he is keeping it to himself.[26] Today, we can conjure him up with a touch of our smart phones, with a click of a mouse, carry him around in our pocket, seek his advice like a guardian angel, a prompting spirit still whispering in our ear while we wait out a flight delay. We can, at this very moment, here, *now*, see this film clip from "Ghost Dance" and listen to these dead people speaking about ghosts.[27] He is dead, but he won't stay dead; he has become one of the countless undead, a *revenant*. He looks on at us, with the same sly smile and a twinkle in his eye, in countless photos and videos. A quarter-century after

---

24   This is the point of departure for Caputo, *The Insistence of God: A Theology of Perhaps* (Bloomington: Indiana University Press, 2013).

25   Peeters, *Derrida: A Biography*, 345–46.

26   Marilynne Robinson, *Gilead* (New York: Farrar, Straus, and Giroux, 2004), 3.

27   Visit "'The Science of Ghosts': Derrida in 'Ghost Dance,'" *YouTube*, https://www.youtube.com/watch?v=0nmu3uwqzbI.

the "Roundtable," Derrida lives on, just as he would have hoped, spectrally, inspiringly, still smiling at us—"I love you and I am smiling at you from wherever I am."[28] Today, he haunts the questions we ask ourselves, as the better angels of our nature continue to do battle with our demons.

Itinerary

Up to now, in Section 1 of this introduction, I have been describing the original setting of the "Villanova Roundtable" and of the conferences that ensued upon it bearing the title that made Derrida wince, "Religion and Postmodernism."

In Section 2, I will survey the scene of deconstruction after the death of Derrida (2004). I will describe several spectral appearances, several sightings, not of Elvis or the Blessed Virgin Mary, but of Jacques Derrida today, *now*, several scenes that we will allow him to revisit, like the revenant he has become, to which we will have him put the question, "Do you believe in ghosts?" In the 1990s the air was thick with debates about the "return of religion" and whether postmodernism implied postsecularism. Today, after Derrida's death, a number of other conceptual flying objects are to be observed—not religion but atheism, and not postmodernism but realism and materialism. Continental philosophy is currently experiencing a *return* of the modernity of which postmodernism was meant to be the "post-." We witness today a reprisal, a retaliation, a pendulum-swing back to pre-Kantian early modernist impulses, purporting to undo postmodernism and to "save the name" of materialism and atheism.[29] These new realists, I will maintain, show every sign of being afraid of ghosts.

As I said, Derrida himself had no time for "postmodernism," not because he supported the Enlightenment but because he wanted a *new* one. But this round of realism, I argue, is not the "new Enlightenment" that Derrida had in mind. This one intends to consign deconstruction and the entire generation of the "Sixty-Eighters" dominated by Derrida and Foucault to a bygone day. What Derrida sought was a *reinvention* of the Enlightenment, not a restoration of the old one, not a simple return to modernity. The difference is that

---

28 Words read at his graveside by his son Pierre; see Peeters, *Derrida: A Biography*, 541.

29 Derrida plays with the shift in *sauf* between "save" and "except" in Derrida, *Sauf le nom* (Paris: Galilée, 1993); *On the Name*, ed. Thomas Dutoit (Stanford, Calif.: Stanford University Press, 1995).

a return is a reproduction of modernity, a retrenchment, whereas a reinvention is a new production, a continuation of modernity but in another way. A rein*vention* is focused on the *event*. It has passed through and learned from modernity but then continues its project differently, repeating the event that was going on there in a new way. For example, if modernity means a critique of authoritarianism, a retrenchment doubles down on and becomes ruthless about critique, but a reinvention cultivates a critical attitude about the authoritarianism of pure critique; if modernity makes fun of ghosts, a deconstruction asks what anxiety lies behind such fears. A repetition does not simply reinstate the old name, nor does it stand in simple opposition to it; it writes it differently. A deconstruction of X does not result in an anti-X, the contrary or the contradictory, but a new iteration of X in a surprising form. The laws of deconstruction are not covered by logic's square of opposition; it changes the field, the universe of discourse in which X is at play.

In short, the current wave of atheists, realists, and materialists would greet the hauntological question—do you believe in ghosts?—with scorn. Of hauntology, they would proudly proclaim themselves the learned despisers. So, on this point, in Part II, I hope to show they have, as Derrida says of Marx, chased away one ghost too many.[30] The evidence is everywhere. Derrida's prediction in "Ghost Dance," that in virtue of the new technologies the future belongs to ghosts, has come true. Today, the whole world is spooked.[31] Today, we oppose the (mere) "physical presence" of something—say a business—to its "virtual" or "digital presence" all over the globe. The globe is engulfed by a new atmospheric layer, a cybersphere, an extraordinary proliferation of cyber-spirits darting across the skies like angels of old, of advanced telecommunications, a cyberworld of smart phones and smart watches, of smart cars and smart bombs, eponymously represented by the release of the first iPhone in 2007, three years after Derrida died. In addition, in quantum physics things are afoot of such a strange and extraordinary kind that Einstein himself denounced them as too "spooky" to be physics, and "matter" itself has become a kind of quaint, almost primitive idea, ensuring that the

---

30   Derrida, *Specters of Marx*, 174.

31   Derrida, *Specters of Marx*, 105–6, 136–37. This is a citation from Max Stirner to which I will return later.

embarrassment of the new realists is complete.

This is not to say that the contemporary tide of atheism, materialism, and realism is without importance. Above all, it is a wake-up call that directs our attention to a serious flaw in mainstream continental philosophy—its neglect of the legitimate role of the natural sciences, both biological and physical, on the grounds that "science does not think." The future of continental philosophy, if it is to have one, should look a lot more like the work that is being done today by writers like Bruno Latour and Catherine Malabou.[32] What I insist upon is that the contribution the new atheists, realists, and materialists make stands in need of *spectralization*, apart from which, left in their raw form, posing as pure presence, as master names, as stable positions, they are misleading, dogmatic, strident, reductionistic, antagonistic attacks that not only misunderstand deconstruction but also misunderstand themselves and the natural sciences.

In Section 3, I will conclude with what I describe under the nickname of his "haunto-theology," which displaces ontotheology. This sums up the progressively more theological voice I have assumed since the appearance of *Deconstruction in a Nutshell*; it shows where I have been led by Derrida. Here I will take my point of departure from a fascinating text on the name of God:

> For wherever the name of God would allow us to think
> something else, for example a vulnerable nonsovereignty,
> one that suffers and is divisible, one that is mortal even,
> capable of contradicting itself or of repenting (a thought
> that is neither impossible nor without example), it would
> be a completely different story, perhaps even the story of
> a God who deconstructs himself in his ipseity.[33]

Hauntology opens up "a completely different story" about God told in the spirit/specter of Derrida, who "can do nothing other than try to translate the name of God in my life." I offer this as my chosen spin on this spinning top called deconstruction, my preferred way to stay in play with its elusiveness, my turn on the floor of this ghost

---

32   See Clayton Crockett, B. Keith Putt, and Jeffrey W. Robbins, eds., *The Future of Continental Philosophy of Religion* (Bloomington: Indiana University Press, 2014).

33   Derrida, *Rogues: Two Essays on Reason*, trans. Pascale-Anne Brault and Michael Naas (Stanford, Calif.: Stanford University Press, 2005), 157.

dance. This is my theory about his theory, about why it will play in at least some of the churches, the ones that are willing to engage in the play, and why—beyond religion and the churches, whose future is questionable—it speaks more broadly to anyone who can resonate with Augustine's confession that he has become a great question to himself (*quaestio mihi magna factus sum*), a confession I make every day and in the middle of every night, when I wake with a start, sure that there was someone in the room.

2. THE SPECTRALITY OF ATHEISM

He had given up the practice of his Jewish faith while still a student, and he treated God in *Of Grammatology* as the transcendental signified, a menace to the free play of signifiers. He was plainly and simply, by the standards of any rabbi or pastor, a nonbeliever, an atheist.[34] Or so it seemed. But right from the start, we were not confident that this was the last word. (In deconstruction, there is no last word.) Those of us with a theological ear could hear another melody playing in the background. We were never certain this was just atheism, plain and simple; in deconstruction, nothing is ever plainly this or simply that. Who knows, maybe it was actually a crypto-theology?[35] We were not sure just what it was. That was already the giveaway, the sign that this choice, these binary categories, theist and atheist, religious and secular, would give out, would not hold up, that they were polarizing, ham-fisted, unhelpful, unfit for service in the subtilities of deconstruction. In short, spooked. If, as Paul Tillich had pointed out, atheism has long served an honorable role in theology more deeply considered, why not here?

---

34 Of course, it is far more complicated than that. See Steven Shakespeare, *Derrida and Theology* (London: T. & T. Clark International, 2009), for a careful and rewarding reconstruction of Derrida's "theological" itinerary.

35 Several early authors commented insightfully on the religious and theological resonances in Derrida. See Robert Detweiler, ed., "Derrida and Biblical Studies," *Semeia: An Experimental Journal for Biblical Criticism* 23 (1982); Louis Mackey, "Slouching Towards Bethlehem: Deconstructive Strategies in Theology," *Anglican Theological Review* 65, no. 3 (1983): 255–72; Carl A. Raschke, *Alchemy of the Word* (Missoula, Mont.: Scholars Press, 1979). Among the new generation of scholars, in addition to Shakespeare, *Derrida and Theology*, I highly recommend Clayton Crockett, *Derrida after the End of Writing: Political Theology and the New Materialism* (New York: Fordham University Press, 2018).

Maybe this atheism is mystical, in the vein of Eckhart's prayer to God to rid him of God, an exquisitely deconstructive formulation. It sounded like that. As far back as 1968, the famous *"Différance"* lecture led to the "accusation"—why not congratulation? he asked—of being a negative theology.[36] But as interesting as the kinship of deconstruction to apophatic theology is, I argued, it was misleading. Derrida deeply admired the rhetorical resourcefulness of negative theology, its "detours, locutions and syntax."[37] It provides the very model of the art of speaking under the imperative of the impossible, which requires unsaying something in the very act of saying it, which is a subtle, dark, and spectral art. But deconstruction has nothing to do with its substantive concerns, the Christian Neoplatonic aspiration to become one with the One in an eternal now. If we pressed that "tropic of negativity," then Derrida would opt for the opposite one, not *epekeina tes ousias* but *khora*, which looks a lot more like atheism plain and simple.[38] Christian Neoplatonism is conjuring up the wrong spirit. The right one, I argued, is more Jewish than Christian, more messianic than mystical, and more prophetic than apophatic. He was talking about a specter, not the Holy Spirit, the coming of the *revenants* and *arrivants*, not becoming one with the One. On this point, insightful Jewish commentators like Susan Handelman were on the mark by singling out Derrida's very Jewish thematization of writing, the link between *écriture* and *saint écriture*, and the uncanny Kabbalistic look of texts like *Glas*.[39]

Mark C. Taylor, resonating with the atheism, made a landmark statement in *Erring*, but Taylor tacked too far in the direction of a dissolution of deconstruction into the "death of God," whereas in deconstruction nothing is ever really dead, completely done and over with. Nothing ever simply gives up its ghost. I wanted the "Roundtable" and the conferences to show that deconstruction is affirmative, not negative, a *oui, oui*, not about death but mortal life, *vita mortalis*

---

36 Derrida, "How to Avoid Speaking: Denials," trans. Ken Friedan, in *Derrida and Negative Theology*, ed. Howard Coward and Toby Foshay (Albany: SUNY Press, 1992), 74.

37 Derrida, "Difference," in *Margins of Philosophy*, trans. Alan Bass (Chicago: University of Chicago Press, 1982), 6.

38 Derrida and Caputo, *Deconstruction in a Nutshell*, 71–105.

39 Susan Handelman, *The Slayers of Moses: The Emergence of Rabbinic Interpretation in Modern Literary Theory* (Albany: State University of New York Press, 1982).

et mors vitalis, life/death.[40] In short, I argued, deconstruction is not a "hermeneutics of the *death* of God" but a hermeneutics of the *desire* for God.[41] But watch out. I do not mean a desire for some eternal transcendent deathless supernatural being—that is theism, and whatever this is, it comes after, reiterates, and reinvents the God of theism—but a desire for the *event* that is harbored in the name of God. My idea is that deconstruction, with or without atheism, *s'il y en a*, opens up another approach to God, one where God is thought not in terms of existence or nonexistence but of the very idea of the to-come, *à venir*, of the messianic or quasi-messianic event that is going on in the name of God, where God is "the possibility of *the* impossible."[42]

Lacking a better alternative, I had seized upon what Derrida—speaking of others, not himself—called a "religion without religion" as a way to describe this spectral effect,[43] deconstruction as *his religion*, without the doctrines and dogmas, hierarchies and rituals of the religion he learned growing up in Algeria in his parent's home. For a while, my approach seemed like a stretch, but he made it easy for me with the work he did in the last fifteen years of his life. His religion without religion would not and could not be entirely without relationship to what we ordinarily call religion, even as it would not and could not be unrelated to his atheism. That is because to deconstruct something, according to what he called *iterability*, is not to attack it from without, like the assault of the "new atheists" on religion, but to repeat it *from within*. When he reads Augustine's *Confessions*, he does not install himself within an atheistic standpoint and attack its two-worlds Christian-Neoplatonic dualism. He "translates" it, rewriting it in the voice of a slightly black and Arab Jew, a *pied noir*, who does not speak a language of his own, repeating its religious tropes and moves differently, so the two texts have a kind of eerie likeness.

---

40   Derrida, *Life Death*, ed. Pascale-Anne Brault and Peggy Kamuf, trans. Pascale-Anne Brault and Michael Naas (Chicago: University of Chicago Press, 2020), which is Derrida's 1975–76 seminar.

41   Mark C. Taylor, *Erring: A Postmodern A/theology* (Chicago: University of Chicago Press, 1984); see my review of *Erring*, in *Man and World* 21 (1988): 107–14.

42   See Mark Dooley's interview of Derrida, "The Becoming Possible of the Impossible," which concerns Caputo, *The Prayers and Tears of Jacque Derrida*, in *A Passion for the Impossible: John D. Caputo in Focus*, ed. Mark Dooley (Albany: SUNY Press, 2003), 21–34, and my response, "A Game of Jacks," 34–50.

43   Derrida, *The Gift of Death*, 49; *Deconstruction in a Nutshell*, 47–48. "Religion without Religion" is the subtitle of Caputo, *Prayers and Tears of Jacques Derrida*.

When he comes to Marx, he does not extol his materialism but his spectrality, and he pokes Marx in the ribs for trying to exorcise one ghost too many, the messianic. To deconstruct something is not to strike a counterposition like atheism or materialism. A deconstruction does not strike; it spooks. According to the spectral logic of the *sans*, it writes *sous rature*. It does not strike a thing out but strikes *through* it, *Durchstreichung*, but only in such a way that the legibility of what is struck through is conserved, which is the sense in which he says that deconstruction is a very conservative thing.[44] That means that a religion *without* religion is just as much a religion *within* religion in the ordinary sense, written in between the lines of religion, or even an archi-religion, occupying the distance between the standard-form, worn-out categories of theism and atheism.

By announcing his religion of which no one knew anything,[45] by giving deconstruction a highly idiosyncratic religious modality without giving up his atheism, Derrida succeeded in gaining the attention of theologians and theorists of religion. He opened the doors of theology and religion to a more radical and risky way of conducting its business—not Kabbalistic, not apophatic, not atheology—but a radical haunto-theology with which I will conclude these remarks.

This religious evocativeness was bound to stir some passions and make a lot of people nervous. The proof positive of the success that Derrida's theological opening enjoyed is the negative reactions it provoked among secular intellectuals, the frantic attempt to close the doors Derrida had opened. The Derrida-and-religion work had taken a deep enough root that it began to spook the Derrideans. Efforts were launched to pull it up, root and branch. My friend David Wood, having invited me to Vanderbilt to speak on *The Prayers and Tears of Jacques Derrida*, which had just appeared, introduced me by saying, we are all praying that Caputo is wrong.[46] This reaction was not entirely new. The "theological turn" in phenomenology, centered on Levinas and Marion, had already drawn the fire of Dominique

---

44 Derrida and Caputo, *Deconstruction in a Nutshell*, 8, 37.

45 Derrida, "Circumfession," 155.

46 See Caputo, "The Prayers and Tears of Jacques Derrida," in *Styles of Piety: Practicing Philosophy after the Death of God*, ed. S. Clark Buckler and Matthew Statler (New York: Fordham University Press, 2006), 193–204, followed in the same volume by David Wood, "God: Poison or Cure, A Reply to John D. Caputo," 205–12, and my response, "Weeping before God," 253–69.

Janicaud in 1991.[47]

The reaction reached a peak after Derrida's death in the critique of deconstruction and religion made by Martin Hägglund in 2008 under the name of a "radical atheism." Let there be no mistake. Hägglund's book has something to say but, as I have explained at some length elsewhere,[48] not about religion. Based on a strong-armed reading of Derrida that effectively reduced him to a "logical empiricist," its mistreatment of the Derrida-and-religion question was egregious. On the one hand, Hägglund attempted a rash and baffling reduction of the "quasi-transcendental" to a principle of ontological materialism, according to which only spatiotemporal objects can exist. He made an even more brazen claim that deconstruction is a purely "descriptive" undertaking, without any prescriptive ethical or political content, as if the binarity of prescriptive and descriptive constitutes a clean-cut distinction embraced by deconstruction instead of one more illusion of pure critique that is submitted to deconstruction. On the other hand, this misadventure was pegged to a strong-armed reading of religion, which effectively reduced it to a classical two-worlds, Neoplatonic (eternity vs. time) dualism. It sought to block every opening Derrida had created, even to the point of correcting Derrida whenever Derrida plainly said what Hägglund said Derrida does not say. Hägglund's reading of Derrida and religion, oozing with an *odium theologiae*, attacking religion, is everything a deconstruction is not. Deconstruction is a haunting, not a hammering.

To be sure, there is *an* atheism in Derrida; that is where we start. But under Hägglund's heavy hand Derrida's atheism is *deprived of*

---

47 Dominique Janicaud et al., *Phenomenology and the Theological Turn: The French Debate* (New York: Fordham University Press, 2001).

48 Martin Hägglund, *Radical Atheism: Derrida and the Time of Life* (Stanford, Calif.: Stanford University Press, 2008). For my critique, see Caputo, "The Return of Anti-Religion: From Radical Atheism to Radical Theology," *Journal of Cultural and Religious Theory* 11, no. 2 (Spring 2011): 32–125; a shorter version can be found in "Unprotected Religion: Radical Theology, Radical Atheism, and the Return of Anti-Religion," in *The Trace of God: Derrida and Religion*, ed. Peter E. Gordon and Edward Baring (New York: Fordham University Press, 2015), 151–77; reprinted in Caputo, *In Search of Radical Theology*, chapter 6. For incisive critiques of Hägglund and religion, see Crockett, *Derrida after the End of Writing*, and Neil DeRoo, "The Dangers Of Dealing with Derrida—Revisiting the Caputo-Hägglund Debate on the 'Religious' Reading of Deconstruction," in *Religious Theory: E-Supplement to the Journal for Cultural and Religious Theory* (2018), in three parts, http://jcrt.org/religioustheory/2018/06/26/the-dangers-of-dealing-with-derrida-revisiting-the-caputo-hagglund-debate-on-the-religious-reading-of-deconstruction-part-1-neal-deroo/.

its spectrality—I "rightly pass" (*à juste titre*)—as an atheist, Derrida says. I once asked him, at a huge session we did with him at the American Academy of Religion in Toronto in 2000, why not say, "I am" ("*c'est moi,*" "*je suis*") an atheist?[49] First of all, he answered, this "I" is not him, Jacques, in the flesh; by writing it down, it has become a specter, a trace, a text, iterable by anyone, who can repeat it for himself. Next, he said, even for the faithful, belief in God must pass through atheism. "True believers know they run the risk of being radical atheists." Furthermore, while it is "right" for others to say this about him, he cannot say it about himself:[50]

> It's not a *position.* I cannot say, "I know what I am: I am this and nothing else." I wouldn't say "I am an atheist: and I wouldn't say, "I am a believer" either. I find the statement absolutely ridiculous. Who can say, "I am a believer"? Who *knows* that? . . . And who can say, "I am an atheist?"

It is "right," correct, to say of him that he is a "nonbeliever in God in a certain way," but who knows what he is "in truth"? Hägglund, however, does not believe in ghosts; he does not respect this specter. His atheism is assured and undisturbed, a strong Position, a Counterposition, an Authoritative Translation of X as spatiotemporal matter—which for Derrida is "absolutely ridiculous." Might it not be that matter too is spooked and filled with gods? Hägglund suppresses the really interesting questions about Derrida's atheism, which—unlike Hägglund's—plays well in (some of) the churches? A radical theology begins with and "passes through" atheism; it is the "right theological and religious response" to classical theism, as Tillich said. Hägglund's analysis of a "radical atheism" in Derrida—about the God of classical dualism—was "right" as far as it goes, but it does not go very far. It is a torso. Hägglund's atheism is exorcism; it is afraid of ghosts, whereas Derrida believes in ghosts and conjures them up. Hägglund squandered Derrida's atheism by refusing to allow it its spectrality, by missing the fact that the "radical" in deconstruction is never a destructive closure or reductionistic critique

---

49   "Epoche and Faith: An Interview with Jacques Derrida" [with Yvonne Sherwood and Kevin Hart], in *Derrida and Religion: Other Testaments,* ed. Yvonne Sherwood and Kevin Hart (New York: Routledge, 2005), 46–47.

50   Derrida, "Circumfession," 155–56.

but a reinvention and an iteration. So his atheism is not "true" in the sense of genuinely disclosing what is going on in deconstruction. Derrida is not Diderot.[51]

A deconstruction releases the blocks that have been thrown up against the promptings of the spirits, of spectral figures hitherto held captive by the forces of being, presence, and actuality. A deconstruction does not shut things down; it opens them up. It releases a thing from being riveted to itself. It does not consign a thing to its past; it gives it back its future. In deconstruction, radical atheism does not spell the end of religion but the beginning of a radical rethinking of religion (without religion), of a God beyond or otherwise than the God of classical theology. In deconstruction, the Holy Spirit reappears as a specter, as a spectral God, beyond or otherwise than the subject of the dead-end debate between theism and atheism. After Derrida, theology becomes haunto-theology, conjuring up specters that have provoked many sleepless nights and disturbed the dreams of overwrought theologians and overworked pastors who need their sleep.[52] I will fill in, or flesh out, this phantom inquiry—beyond theism and atheism—later.

The Specter of the Thing Itself

If flitting between existence and nonexistence, as specters are wont to do, is the spooky thing, then to put deconstruction in a pointedly polemical way, we could say that the spooky thing is the thing itself (*Sache selbst*), that the thing in itself (*Ding an sich*), *s'il y en a*, it, *es*, *Ça*, is spooked. Talking like that was bound to create trouble. It is not entirely surprising that, after his death, Derrida's work came under fire by a wave of self-anointed apostles of the real material world, guardians of the thing itself, in which everything spectral has been exorcised. Spurred on by the work of Quentin Meillassoux, the new

---

51 Curiously, in a student exam, Derrida was reprimanded for turning a text of Diderot inside out and making it say what he wanted to say himself; see Edward Baring, *The Young Derrida and French Philosophy: 1945–1968* (Cambridge: Cambridge University Press, 2011), 54.

52 Under names like "radical theology" and "continental philosophy of religion," a great deal of good work done in the wake of Derrida can be found in *Journal of Cultural and Religious Theory* (www.jcrt.org) and the new *Journal for Continental Philosophy of Religion* (Brill). See also *The Palgrave Handbook of Radical Theology*, ed. Christopher D. Rodkey and Jordan E. Miller (Cham, Switzerland: Palgrave Macmillan, 2018).

exorcists, or as I called them elsewhere the "warrior realists,"[53] have criticized continental philosophers from Kant to the poststructuralists under the name of "correlationalism."[54] By this is meant that, under the influence of Kant's Copernican Revolution, they have fallen into an anti-realist subjectivistic reduction of the real thing to its relationship to us. The being-in-itself of the real thing is reduced to its being-for-us, the thinking-speaking subjects, as if deconstruction is like the subjective idealism of Berkeley, where *esse est percipi*, but with a French accent, where *esse est dici.*

I repeat. This movement has not been without its point. Meillassoux touched at least one nerve. A lot of the people flying under the banner of "overcoming ontotheology" are serving up not haunto-theology but what Meillassoux called "fideism," meaning a Kantian apologetics that uses postmodern theory as a way to deny knowledge (limit the natural sciences) in order to make room for Christian faith in eternity and the afterlife. I share this criticism and have made it elsewhere under the name of "postmodernism lite."[55] But if Meillassoux was dead on about fideism, his charge of correlationalism is dead on arrival. Indeed, if Hägglund got off on the wrong foot about religion, he was right to put his foot down on this point. The main merit of Hägglund's book was to demonstrate how deconstruction has to do with clarifying our contact with material reality.[56]

If we are confined to the categories Meillassoux permits, we would have to say that Derrida is neither a realist nor an antirealist, both a realist and an antirealist. That means that there is never a moment in deconstruction where contact with the real is not everything *and* — this is the spectral effect — never a moment in deconstruction where we must not question ourselves about what we are calling real, where we are not prepared to have our assurance about what we claim is real

---

53   Caputo, *Insistence of God*, 197–210.

54   Quentin Meillassoux, *After Finitude: An Essay on the Necessity of Contingency*, trans. Ray Brassier (London: Continuum, 2008).

55   Caputo, "On Not Settling for an Abridged Edition of Postmodernism: Radical Hermeneutics as Radical Theology," in *Reexamining Deconstruction and Determinate Religion: Toward a Religion with Religion*), ed. J. Aaron Simmons and Stephen Minister (Pittsburgh: Duquesne University Press, 2012), 271–353; an excerpt from this text has been reprinted in Caputo, *In Search of Radical Theology*, chapter 5.

56   See Hägglund, "Radical Atheist Materialism: A Critique of Meillassoux," in *The Speculative Turn: Continental Materialism and Realism*, ed. Levi Bryant, Nick Srnicek and Graham Harmon (Melbourne: re.press,), 114–29.

thrown into confusion. In deconstruction, the work the word "real" does for the realists is done by *tout autre*. That is why Derrida can write that deconstruction has "always come forward *in the name of the real*, of the irreducible reality of the real—not the real as an attribute of the *thing* (*res*), objective, present, sense-able or intelligible, but the real as coming or event of the other. . . . In this sense, nothing is more 'realist' than deconstruction."[57] Thus, when it comes to the *tout autre* (the real), we can safely say—in Franco-Latin—two things.

> *First*, everything in deconstruction turns on the *tout autre*, where the *tout autre* is precisely *alter*, other, what is *not* me, not mine, *totaliter*, totally not my doing. When Derrida speaks of the "invention of the other" he means the "in-coming"—the in-venting (*in* + *venire*)—of the event, over which the ego does not preside. In the military, if someone shouts "incoming" what is coming is definitely not their doing. The event is the coming of what the ego cannot see coming. The other does not derive from me; it arrives at my door, as a visitation without a prior invitation.
>
> *Second*, for Derrida, *tout autre est tout autre*, each and everything is like that, like an uninvited guest, equally marked by an irreducible alterity.

On the first point, Derrida is close to Levinas, who, we cannot fail to observe, very significantly gets a pass from the realists.[58] For Levinas, the other person approaches me from an infinite distance. I am related to an absolute that withdraws from my relation to it. I set out for a shore I will never reach. This distance, this nonpresence, is not a lack or a fault; it is *constitutive* of the other. Absent this absence, the alterity of the "other" would evaporate. The distance of the other is not elliptical; it is hyperbolic. Levinas's point of departure is Husserl's *Cartesian Meditations*, V, the analysis of the alter ego, the other person, who is *positively* constituted by the inaccessibility of her or his consciousness. If I were conscious of the consciousness of the other, the other would be the same. In Derridean terms, there is a kind of

---

57   Derrida, *Paper Machine*, trans. Rachel Bowlby (Stanford, Calif.: Stanford University Press, 2005), 96.

58   Ray Brassier, *Nihil Unbound* (London: Palgrave Macmillan, 2007), 230–34. Graham Harman studied with Al Lingis, the Levinas translator, at Pennsylvania State University.

spectrality in *l'autrui*, other persons, a distance in their proximity, an absence in their very presence, something that is not there in their being there. For Levinas, this is ethics and all the religion we will need, which makes the proposal that in Derrida there is nothing but "descriptive" work being done, with no trace of ethics, all the more amusing. The ethics, unless it is religion, or the religion, unless it is ethics, is that the *tout autre* puts me in the accusative, irrecusably, calling for my response, *me voici*, awakening my responsibility. So true is this that, as Derrida puts it, when "I" act, when the "I" poses as self-positing, passes itself off as autarchic and autonomous, that is the action of the other-in-me; that is my response to the address by which I am always already overtaken, surprised (*sur* + *pris*) — or shall we say "possessed"?

But when Derrida presses the second point, *tout autre est tout autre*, he goes further than Levinas. It is not simply the face of the neighbor, the other person, that is wholly other, but *every* other. Like the animal, which I also am/follow (*suis*). Whence the famous analysis of his cat watching him emerge from the shower — what is the cat thinking? he eerily asks, trying to enter the feline mind.[59] Each and every individual thing is marked by this deep alterity and spectrality.[60]

Given these considerations, the claim that deconstruction is a form of what Meillassoux calls correlationalism ranks high on the list of truly uncomprehending things to say about it.[61] What is true is that the *tout autre* is a kind of absolute always absolving itself from the relation (Levinas), always withdrawing in the very movement of giving itself, like Heidegger's *lethe*, which is, we should not forget, the inspiration of Harman's version of object-oriented ontology (discussed later). That is, our access to the real is quasi-transcendental: the real is present (possible) only under the condition that also preserves its absence (impossible). "There is nothing outside the text"

---

59   Derrida, *The Animal That Therefore I Am*, ed. Marie-Louise Mallet, trans. David Wills (New York: Fordham University Press, 2008).

60   A predecessor form of this view can be found in the medieval theory of the transcendental *aliquid*, where, *omne ens est aliquid*, every being is a particular something, a notion made famous by Duns Scotus's doctrine of *haecceitas*, this-ness, and turned into poetry by Gerard Manley Hopkins.

61   I spelled out my objections to Meillassoux in Caputo, *Insistence of God*, 197–222; for the details, see 287–89n5.

means not that signifiers have no reference, but that reference is never possible without difference. Access to the real is always coded and differential, finite and perspectival, historical and socialized, gendered and embodied, revisable and reinventable, which is why laying claim to the real is always both a promise and a threat. Our *relationship* to the world is, in short, always "constituted" (Husserl), always an effect produced by the play of traces, always a construction, which as such is always deconstructible (Derrida).

This view may be described as antirealist only if by realism you mean magic,[62] full presence, naked givenness to a "consciousness" of which nothing is required, as if it were possible to receive something without receiving it in the manner of the received (Aquinas). Unchecked realism is always magical realism, and it is more magical than realistic (practical), a kind of anxious, fist-pounding "it's there, it's really there" realism, as if someone is going to steal the world away from us if we do not keep our eye on it. To think the world that is "really there without us" is, as Derrida puts it, to think the world "as if I were dead," for which the *language* of mathematics is very useful. This accounts for what Meillassoux calls the "ancestral," except that Meillassoux suffers from the illusion that this somehow refutes deconstruction instead of representing one of the points made in deconstruction, that signifiers (fossils) operate in the absence of the signified (the past).[63] Mathematics did not drop from the sky; it is constituted in and by a sophisticated coded-differential system of signifiers. If you do not believe that, ask the Romans, who got nowhere in mathematics because of their maladroit notation.

But it is perverse in the extreme to label the quasi-transcendental view (simply) "antirealist." Realism and antirealism, like theism and atheism, are categories unfit for service in deconstruction. The quasi-transcendental provides an account for our *access* to the givenness of what is there. Meillassoux speaks as if "access" is a bad word, as if it were better to have no access, as if it were better for a drowning man to have no lifeline, as if only aphasia and unconsciousness would insure naked contact with the world. The spectrality of the other, its

---

62   See the interesting discussion of magic and realism in Timothy Morton, *Realist Magic: Objects, Ontology, Causality* (London: Open Humanities, 2013).

63   Meillassoux, *After Finitude*, 10; "As If I Were Dead: An Interview with Jacques Derrida," in *Applying: To Derrida*, ed. John Brannigan, Ruth Robbins, and Julian Wolfreys (New York: Palgrave Macmillan, 1996), 212–26.

haunting alterity, lies in withdrawing from us even as it addresses us, so that our access is always already interrupted by *recess*. That is why the words and deeds of people we have known for years are capable of surprising us. That is also why I like to speak of deconstruction as a form of *hyperrealism*, always exposing what is present to the *arrivants*, the unforeseeable, to what may shatter our horizon of expectation, to something unexpected, something spectral. To affirm the other (read: real) means affirming the real beyond (what we take to be) real; it means to confess the unexpected in what we expect, to say come to the coming of what is always to-come, of what we cannot see coming, including what is coming back (from the dead).

To affirm the real, to really face up to all the force of the real, requires believing in ghosts. It is the most realistic position we could adopt. Deconstruction articulates an access to the world that is marked not by magic but by a logic, or quasilogic, or hauntologic of excess-in-recess, and this in accord with Derrida's axiomatic of the hyperbolic, of the beyond, of the *super, epekeina, hyper, über, au-delà*.[64] We have always to do with the thing itself (*die Sache selbst*), but the thing itself always slips away, always escapes our grasp (*la chose même se dérobe toujours*).[65] The thing about the thing itself is its spectrality. By axiomatic I mean not a deductive system but an axiology, what we treasure and desire, what we love, the value of the variable X, in which case deconstruction in a nutshell is love, a love of the things themselves, where the things themselves always have a spectral quality, a haunting-luring reality that draws us out of ourselves and down dark, unexplored, and unforeseeable paths.[66]

OOO's Obfuscations, Obscurations, and Objectionability

It is in this regard instructive to follow how Derrida today has become the object of criticism of "object-oriented ontology"[67]—OOO—which is based upon the work of two major French thinkers. Michel

64 Derrida, *On the Name*, 64.

65 Derrida, *Speech and Phenomena and Other Essays on Husserl's Theory of Signs*, trans. David Allison. (Evanston, Ill.: Northwestern University Press, 1973), 104.

66 See Caputo, "For Love of the Things Themselves: Derrida's Hyper-Realism," *Journal for Cultural and Religious Theory* 1, no. 3 (August 2000), http://www.jcrt.org.

67 The abbreviation is coined by Levi Bryant, but the concept goes back to Graham Harman; see Harman's *Object-Oriented Ontology: A New Theory of Everything* (London: Pelican, 2018).

Serres (1930–2019) sought to surpass the Cartesian privileging of the subject-object relationship and recommended instead that we think of objects as "quasi-subjects." Objects are not "inert" lumps of matter but active and interactive agents of their own, producing complex systems—like the interactive relationship of the climate and the oceans and today the proliferating information systems. With each passing day we see that so-called lifeless things have a "life of their own." To this end, Bruno Latour (1947–), under the impact of Serres, coined the term "actants," meaning not human agents but the nonhuman actors or agencies Serres described.

In a series of brilliant analyses of what came to be called the "social construction" of science, Latour shows how a scientific theory is the result of a complex concatenation of sociopolitical structures, communities of scientists, communication technologies, sophisticated instruments, and costly laboratories that supply the collective conditions under which microbes or electrons introduce themselves to us. Serres and Latour are describing complex systems in which things, both human and nonhuman, are deeply imbricated in one another. These are *relational* systems, not merely *cor*relational—which suggests only two, a binary subject/object relation—but *multi*relational. Serres and Latour would not exactly deny the relation of what we call objects to what we call subjects or criticize correlationalism, except to say it is an abstraction. They would argue that the relational situation—what I would call the phenomenological situation—is much more complicated than that.

These results, that objects (nonhumans) are much more like human subjects and human subjects are much more like nonhuman objects than we think, that science does not exist in a pure or abstract logocentric vacuum but is socially constructed, under contingent conditions, represent a distinctively deconstructive line of thinking. Work quite like this is found in the mainstream continental tradition, not in Derrida, but in the "phenomenology of technology" done by people like Don Ihde.[68] Ihde tried to engage Latour in dialogue and disabuse Latour of his "naïve belief" in the naivete of phenomenology, which Latour reduces to a philosophy of consciousness à

---

68 Don Ihde, "ANT meets Postphenomenology," 4/S (2008), http://www.4sonline.org. See his critique of Heidegger in Ihde, *Heidegger's Technologie(s): Postphenomenological Perspectives* (New York: Fordham University Press, 2010). See also *Postphenomenology: A Critical Companion to Ihde*, ed. Evan Selinger (Albany: SUNY Press, 2006).

la Husserl. Derrida himself was deeply interested in decentering an-
thropocentric theories by way of the technical order (*technicité*); his
earliest work was to show the historical and material conditions under
which Husserl's "ideal objects" are constituted. He also analyzed
the impact of globalized communication and telecommunication
systems on ethics, politics, and religion. *Différance* is a term of art for
nonhuman differential networks whose elements are constituted by
and are the effects of differential relationships; they are not atomic
entities that subsequently enter into relationships with one another.

So the work of Serres and Latour is completely congenial to careful
readers of the tradition that gradually unfolds from Husserl through
Heidegger and Merleau-Ponty to Foucault, Lyotard, Deleuze, and
Derrida. But OOO—which is *in principle* separable from the phony
correlationalism critique—obscures the important insights of Serres
and Latour by embracing Meillassoux's misguided attack on the con-
coction he calls correlationalism. This perpetuates a philosophical
culture war—and Latour says he seeks peace!—on the continental tradition, including Derrida, which it has deeply distorted. The
philosophical point that Serres and Latour, Foucault and Derrida
embrace, which OOO obscures and obfuscates, is that "construction"
and "reality" are directly proportional to each other, not inversely.
The more constructions—the more instruments, refined theoretical
assumptions, communities of researchers, systems of communicating
results—the more reality! As Heidegger says, the idea is not to be
presupposition-free but to find the right presuppositions that let the
thing appear; the problem is not to assume too much, but too little.
And whatever is constructed is deconstructible. That is how science
moves.

The Future Belongs to Ghosts: Cyborgs, Cyberspirits, and other Spooks

Derrida says in "Ghost Dance" that technology does not drive out
the ancient belief in ghosts—or, I would add, with Michel Serres,
in angels[69]—but enhances it, that the future will be more and more
a matter of ghosts. His point is verified every day, in every way. His
prediction of the rising ascendency of specters and spooks, phantoms

---

69   Michel Serres, *Angels: A Modern Myth*, trans. Francis Cowper, ed. Philippa Hurd
(Paris: Flammarion, 1995).

and virtual realities, is positively eerie. The least out-of-date thing Derrida ever said, the thing that keeps on proving itself more and more timely, even prophetic, is pretty much the first thing he ever said and for which he was most frequently criticized during his life-time — his early work on grammatology and *archi-écriture*.

Meillassoux's charge of correlationalism is old wine in new skins. Long before Meillassoux came along, deconstruction had already been the target of an analogous complaint that went under the name of linguisticism or linguistic idealism, meaning that when Derrida famously (infamously?) remarked that there is nothing outside the text, his intention was to lock us inside what Fredric Jameson called the "prison house of language," of "signifiers," forever barred from making contact with their "signified." To be taken seriously, the complaint here cannot be that language really is an epistemological prison. If it were, aphasia would be freedom, and learning a second language would represent only further confinement, worsening our incarceration, doubling our "sentence." The complaint must be the absolutization of the linguistic model, which would represent an arbitrary decision and its own version of the metaphysics of pres-ence. But, as Jameson points out, Derrida is perfectly aware of this objection and indeed formulates it better than others.[70] According to Derrida, we are always exploring what he calls the "inside/outside," achieving such limited results as we can within a given horizon while always pointing out its limiting presuppositions, or what he calls the "constitutive outside." The inside is co-constituted by its own outside, always already haunted by its outside. Any given horizon both opens up and confines its own achievements, exposing its results structurally to the coming of what it cannot see coming.

Still more fundamentally, deconstruction *is not and never was* about language in any narrow empirical sense but about how our relationship to the world is constituted within coded differential systems in general. The neologisms *différance* and *archi-écriture* are meant to "point" like a finger at the moon to *every* such system, even though these neologisms, once they catch on, become themselves effects of the system. Jameson is right to say that language is an ontic point of departure for a model that is elevated to an ontological status. But Derrida is both aware of this

---

70 Fredric Jameson, *The Prison-House of Language* (Princeton: Princeton University Press, 1975), 186.

move—which is unavoidable—and has very impressively generalized it beyond its linguistic limits. What he means by *différance* is not words or natural language but differential structures found everywhere in the culture, in all our beliefs and practices and institutions, in power structures and turf wars and organizational charts, in race and gender relations—in everything from language, art, and literature to ethics, politics, and religion, to recite Derrida's own particular itinerary. All of these systems, he argued, are open-ended *quasi*-systems, not closed; pliable and repliable, not hard and fast (which is why the word "post-structuralism" is not all that bad). That, to make a very long story short, is another way to sum up deconstruction in a nutshell. The question is not how to avoid giving some ontic point of departure a privileged ontological status. There is no other available point of departure. The alternative is to wait for something to drop from the sky. If we do not construct models consciously, they will get constructed behind our back. The question is how to do it felicitously, provisionally, cautious-ly, strategically, eyes-wide-open, working inside-outside, producing a maximum of insight without being blinded by one's point of view. Models are to be adopted *quasi*-transcendentally, without embracing the transcendental illusion that one has unlocked the mystery of being. That is what deconstruction is, if it is.

Judged by this standard, it is remarkable just how felicitous, how far-reaching, how far-sighted, how clairvoyant this model has prov-en to be. This has been confirmed by the title of Derrida's early masterpiece *Of Grammatology*, which is all about writing programs and, I submit, might have been entitled today *Of Programmatology*. Any attempt to describe Derrida's early work on *écriture* as dated, as a product of and confined to the "linguistic turn" taken back in the 1970s and 1980s, is reduced to silence by the steady drumbeat of the word "program."[71] *Écriture*, admittedly a creature of the Left Bank in the 1960s, is about as out of date as the latest "program" "written" by software engineers in Silicon Valley. Just as Heidegger prescient-ly flagged the word "information" in 1957,[72] the word "program"

---

71 On this point, I disagree with Catherine Malabou, *Plasticity at the Dusk of Writing: Di-alectic, Destruction, Deconstruction*, trans. Carolyn Shread (New York: Columbia University Press, 2009), who argues that "plasticity" has replaced and displaced the model of writing. This is the one question I would put to Clayton Crockett's *Derrida after the End of Writing*.

72 Martin Heidegger, *The Principle of Reason*, trans. Reginald Lilly (Bloomington: Indiana University Press, 1991), 29.

was presciently—dare I say prophetically?—flagged by Derrida in 1967. These words are our hashtags; they define our age, our epoch, our lives. We are everywhere spooked by electronic devices programmed to talk back to us when we ask them questions, to remind us of things on our calendars we might forget, that obey our voice commands and sometimes speak without being asked and overhear what they are not intended to hear. That is very spooky. Among the many pressing problems and urgent questions by which we are beset today—eco-global suicide, nationalist hatred of the stranger, the polarization of rich and poor, of left and right—the question of the program has an assured place. What are the limits of the program? Of programs that will write new programs without us? Can there be programs for the *unprogrammable*? For the undecidable? Does the event elude the program, or is the summit of the program reached when there are programs that program even for events? Is the entire universe describable as a vast information system? Maybe the very world we live in, as some people speculate, is a computer simulation! A matrix, a moving film, a ghost dance.

Différance and *écriture* were introduced back in 1960s as models of culture and were deployed in such a way as to take the air out of the nature/culture divide. They deflate the infatuation of Rousseau and Lévi-Strauss with an imaginary state of nature uncontaminated by culture by showing that the "state of nature" is itself culturally constituted, that it is itself a dream set in motion by culture. If culture "supplements" nature, the supplement goes all the way down and constitutes nature. This is not to say there is no natural world "out there," "without us"; it is to say that there is no way to speak of such a world without coded-differential systems, both cultural and natural-mathematical. But beyond that, what is most striking of all is that nowadays we find ourselves asking, is *everything* programmable, not just in the "culture" but also in "nature"? Far from being a time-bound fashion of the linguistic turn in the humanities, has not "writing" turned out to be the dominant model of the *natural sciences*? The single most decisive breakthrough in the biological sciences is to have worked out the structure of the DNA molecule that issues the written instructions that make up the life of living organisms. We are, all livings things are, composites of bits of information stored up in the language of DNA—our vocabulary, worked out by four letters—and RNA—our syntax. Deep Thought got it wrong. The meaning of life is not 42; it is A, T, G, and C! The biological sciences today speak in terms of genetic information, its replication, genetic codes, processes of transcription and translation, and so forth—up to and including the development of the CRSPR technology in 2015 that allows us now to "edit" the human gene, to issue ever new editions—iterations—of the human species, indeed of any species. How appropriate that the parent company of Google, as of this writing worth about a trillion dollars on Wall Street, is named "Alphabet."

What more fitting figure, what more felicitous formulation, what more efficient model to articulate this, than to say that in the biological sciences today the architecture of organic life is its *archi-écriture*? Ar-chi-écriture does not mean, never did mean, either speaking or writing in the narrow sense but coded-differential systems. The eerie thing today is that we do not *use* information; we *are* information. We do not write with our bodies; our bodies are written in genetic code. The very material bodies championed by the critics of Derrida's "textualism," who anointed themselves lord high defenders of the bricks-and-mortal "real world," have turned out to be governed by the archi-language of the genetic code, which perhaps explains why Derrida had a fondness for biological metaphors (*pharmakon*, parasite, auto-immunity).

When Derrida writes that there is nothing outside the text, those whose interpretation of this passage is not based on conference hotel bar banter understood that he means that nothing happens outside of coded, differential systems, a point whose truth is so pervasive that even he could not have appreciated how well and truly he spoke. His critique of logocentrism is turning out to be right, not only as a critique of ontotheology but because it constitutes a cosmology in its own right. It is not that everything is being reduced to language, but that the structuralist analysis of language and the poststructuralist critique it provoked was the tip of the iceberg, a tip-off, a clue to the workings of open-ended differential systems that are everywhere to be found in culture *and in nature*, a distinction that is become increasingly blurred. It's not that there is some super-intelligent somebody who has designed everything and operates it from above, as in the anthropo-theo-person-alism of classical theism, but that everything is being run by immanent, impersonal, or pre-personal differential coded systems or quasi-systems, up to and including nature itself—*scriptura sive natura!*

We have today been forced to face a very eerie and spectral fact: *we have never been human*—if we may slightly adapt the title of a book by Bruno Latour.[73] The difference between human and nonhuman animals is far more porous than we liked to think; the "spacing" is not species-based but differential. Furthermore, the difference between the natural-human and artificial-technological is far more porous than we are comfortable thinking because, as Derrida said, the impersonal "technology" of *différance* as an impersonal differential meaning-making machine has always already made human intelligence possible and disturbed its self-identity from within. We are cyborgs, cyber-organisms, cyber-spirits, cyber-specters—even "cyber selves," as theologian Jeanine Thweatt-Bates says.[74] To Heidegger's horror, *physis* is always already disturbed by technicity (*Technik*). Just as living bodies are a function of bits of biological information-processing systems, so too are human minds, albeit of an extraordinarily supple and creative—open-ended—sort, that Catherine Malabou, borrowing a word from brain-science, calls "plasticity."[75] That open-endedness is the point of Derrida's argument against the Copenhagen formalists in *Of Grammatology*.

Today we wonder, might it be possible to lift this system off its neurological substrate and reproduce it on silicon, the way the differential structure of chess is played equally well with pieces made of ivory, wood, or pixels? That is the "post-human" dream—unless it is a nightmare or, as Mary Shelly warned long ago, the makings of a monster. In the meantime, we can at least "supplement" our brains by interfacing them with artificial intelligence systems, even as we have supplemented our bodies with artificial joints and organs. We are today already immersed in AI devices—like "Watson"—that help us run everything and vastly extend our intelligence. That is called the "trans-human," as in transitional, in transit to, on the way to the "post-human," and it has already begun. It is all around us and we are daily warned—just as King Thamus warned the Egyptians—that these "supplements" are "dangerous," that these "inventions of writing," the contemporary *pharmakon*, may kill us before they cure us, that they are a promise/threat, a poison/gift.[76]

---

73   Bruno Latour, *We Have Never Been Modern*, trans. Catherine Porter (Cambridge, Mass.: Harvard University Press, 1993).

74   Jeanine Thweatt-Bates, *Cyborg Selves: A Theological Anthropology of the Posthuman* (London: Routledge, 2016).

75   Malabou, *Plasticity at the Dusk of Writing*.

76   Derrida, "Plato's Pharmacy," in *Dissemination*, trans. Barbara Johnson (Chicago: University of Chicago Press, 1981), 95–117.

Hauntological Materialism

If the word "difference" served as the watchword of the last quarter of the twentieth century, the postmodern age, the word "materialism" has now taken its place. Today, if you cannot show your position is materialistic to a coalition of theorists out to "save the name" of materialism, you're living in the wrong century. But "materialism" is a word Derrida steadfastly avoided because the "-ism," any -ism, including deconstructionism, executes an exorcism. An -ism is, by definition, a reduction to a single principle that decisively decides the undecidability and shuts down the translatability and chases away the specters. In hauntology (deconstruction), nothing is less assured than the distinction between matter and spirit. So, when it comes to describing deconstruction, "materialism"—old, new, or middle-aged—is every bit as bad a word as "religion" or "postmodernism," "atheism" or "realism." Matter is just another competing transcendental signified, another *eminence grise*, like God or Spirit, the Will or the One. Deconstruction is not materialism because the very idea of deconstruction is not to endorse materialism but to haunt, disturb, and make questionable the very idea of "matter," *s'il y en a*, as if this were a stable presence and plenitude. Where is it written that "matter" gets a pass, that matter is not spooked? The only excuse for saying deconstruction is materialism is *strategic*: it avoids making deconstruction look dated, an illusion that is artfully dispelled by Clayton Crockett's *Derrida after the End of Writing*, which is an insightful confrontation of Derrida with these contemporary movements. So, if we feel compelled to say it today, we should say it the way the Marranos accepted baptism. While the word is on our lips, in our hearts we really believe that deconstruction is *not* materialism, but that matter is worthy of being deconstructed, indeed that matter is a mystery of increasingly perplexing dimensions. If, under threat of execution at dawn or, worse still, academic excommunication, we are coerced into saying that deconstruction is materialism, then, under our breath, we whisper "hauntological" materialism.

What? What is that? It means that matter too is spooked, and the real materialists believe in ghosts. How can that be?

In his 1929 lecture course Heidegger proposed what we might take to be a kind of canonical formulation of humanism when he said that the rock is world-less (inert, nonsentient), the animal is world-poor (dumb, merely sentient), while Dasein alone constitutes a world (has an understanding of being and world, especially if Dasein speaks German). In a "Manifesto for Cyborgs" in 1985, which haunted humanists everywhere, Donna Haraway showed that this whole Heideggerian schema is spooked. She proposed three "border-breakdowns"—between the human and nonhuman, between the animate and the inanimate, between matter and spirit—that show that Heidegger is indulging in a prescientific impressionistic fiction that is refuted on every level by contemporary research.[77] As Crockett has shown,[78] by affirming an infinite depth of alterity and singularity in each and every thing, and by thinking difference as differential not oppositional, deconstruction too spells the undoing of Heidegger's formula, which Derrida revisited on several occasions. Derrida consistently challenged the humanism of Hegel, Husserl, Heidegger, and Levinas and disturbed the fixed binarity of humans and "animals" (*les animaux, l'ani-mot*).[79] But Derrida did not show much interest in questioning the "thing," the rock or the stone, which is portrayed by Heidegger as a dense, inactive lump of worldlessness.

However, that account of inert things, which was first contested by Schelling and various versions of vitalism influenced by Schelling up to Gilles Deleuze, is strongly contested today by quantum physics, to which, as Karen Barad has argued, Derrida's "hauntology," his concept of the specter, is particularly well-suited. Only prudence and good taste prevent me from suggesting that we might think of this as the spooky action at a distance between Derrida's cat and Schrödinger's cat. Barad's point is that the quantum world is not made up of actual and determinate objects, as in classical physics, but of indeterminate potential events. Matter is not inert but a process of materialization—"spacetimemattering," Barad calls it[80]—and the real is not an inert reified *res* but a process of realization, an event needing to be actualized. This occurs only on the occasion of the interaction of quanta with one another or with an observer, mean-

---

77   Donna Haraway, "A Manifesto for Cyborgs," in *The Haraway Reader*, ed. Donna Haraway (New York and London: Routledge, 2004), 8, 10–13.

78   Crockett, *Derrida after the End of Writing*, 67–73, 81–87.

79   Derrida, *The Animal That Therefore I Am*, ed. Marie-Louise Mallet, trans. David Wills (New York: Fordham University Press, 2008).

80   Karen Barad, "Quantum Entanglements and Hauntological Relations," *Derrida Today*, 3 (2010): 244; see Crockett, *Derrida after the End of Writing*, 121–38, for a superb commentary.

ing us, which suggests that what we call matter, as if it were a solid, stable, self-identical thing, is constituted as an effect of ontological relationships. Not only is deconstruction innocent of what the warrior realists call epistemological correlationalism, it turns out it is highly congenial to the ontological relations, correlations, and multirelations of the so-called things themselves in contemporary physics. This interaction—Barad speaks of "agential realism," which reminds us of Latour's "actants" and Serres's "quasi-subjects"—produces spectral effects, like Schrödinger's cat, which is neither dead nor alive, or either, depending on the course of interactions, which is a very spooky thing to say, as spooky as Einstein's well-known complaint that quantum entanglement is "spooky action at a distance."

The quantum world suggests not an ontology of determinate objects (read: metaphysics of presence) but a hauntology of indeterminate (read: undecidable) ones, not epistemologically uncertain (Heisenberg) but ontologically indeterminate (Bohr). Instead of an object-oriented ontology, we meet up with an event-disoriented hauntology; instead of discrete objects, differential systems. Subatomic particles are not worldless but world-entangled. Without trying to make too much of Barad's "quantum hauntology,"[81] without saying that one logically entails the other, it is not too much to say that they are kindred specters, that there is spectral congeniality between them, a kindred frame of mind. The style of deconstructive thinking, its "imaginary," is congruent with or congenial to the way of thinking about the universe found in contemporary physics (its imaginary). Instead of hard-and-fast distinctions between fixed, self-identical, and discriminate objects connected in linear causal chains, or between objects and the subjects observing them, science today describes the shifting differential relationships and fleeting intermittent effects produced by their intersection. While things are identifiable, in the sense that we can name and refer to them, they are not identical-with-themselves.[82] Quantum computing, still in its nascent stage, is based not upon discrete bits (1, 0) but qubits, units that are either 1 or 0 or some combination of both 1 and 0. Instead of self-identity, indeterminacy and superposition. Instead of presence, an interplay

---

81   We should not forget the Alan Sokal hoax; Derrida and Caputo, *Deconstruction in a Nutshell*, 71–74.

82   Derrida, *The Other Heading: Reflections on Today's Europe*, trans. Pascale-Anne Brault and Michael Naas (Bloomington: Indiana University Press, 1992), 9.

of pres-absence. Instead of an ontology of actual beings, a hauntology of perhaps. Instead of beings and objects, events; instead of closed, determinate, deductive systems, open-ended indeterminate, probabilistic ones. Instead of a classical imaginary of objects governed by hard rules (*cosmos*), a Derridean imaginary open to odd, irregular, and unforeseen events (*chaosmos*). In short, instead of classical materialism, a hauntological materialism.

I would add to Barad's account that many years ago, the young Derrida contested the primacy of intuition over intention in Husserl on the grounds that the real power of signs lay not in their fulfillment by intuition but in their capacity to function in the *absence* of intuition, to carry us into what we today call "virtual" worlds, worlds that are not present but represented, and beyond that to worlds that we can only imagine, and even beyond that, into worlds we cannot imagine, that cannot be imaginatively figured or prefigured, into spooky unimaginable worlds.[83] That not only makes literature possible; it makes mathematics, science, and its "thought experiments" possible. That is exquisitely confirmed today when quantum physicists tell us that, on the one hand, they are just following the math and the experimental evidence but, on the other hand, they increasingly do not know what they are talking about. Not only are they at a loss to adequately explain these phenomena, but they also cannot imaginatively intuit the world, the possible worlds, that the mathematics is, shall we say, conjuring up. They are spooked by the spectral effects they are discovering, for which they lack both an explanation and an intuition; they encounter spectral phenomena generated by the mathematics and the evidence, which do not have perceptual correlates. Their constant fear, their main reservation, is that this is just too spooky to be science!

The world, it turns out, *pace* Wittgenstein, is precisely *not* everything that is the case, the sum total of every worldly item taken one by one and added up. That, as Richard Rorty said, is a world well lost.[84] The world of atomic cases is a casualty of the displacement of classical physics. What is the case is a function of the world, not the other way around. The world is more likely everything that is and

---

83 Caputo, "The Economy of Signs in Husserl and Derrida: From Uselessness to Full Employment," in *Deconstruction and Philosophy*, ed. John Sallis (Chicago: University of Chicago Press, 1987), 99–113.

84 Richard Rorty, "The World Well Lost," *Journal of Philosophy* 69, no. 19 (1972): 649–65.

is not the case; it may be either and may be neither, not to mention that it depends upon which world you are talking about. In deconstruction, we have given up saying that the world is everything that is the case and simply concede, "The whole world is spooked" ("*Es spukt in der ganzen Welt*"), as Max Stirner said.[85] That sums up deconstruction in a nutshell. The case of the world is spectral, and the spectrality is general.

In sum, deconstruction (hauntology) differs from classical philosophy (ontology) in a way that is analogous to the way quantum physics differs from classical physics. It embraces a world of paradox and perplexity, uncertainty, indeterminacy, and undecidability, of quasi-systems and differential relationships, a world of excessively odd effects that are downright spooky, unexpectedly spectral. The two are kindred specters.

What then of materialism? The answer is that the "new materialism" begins by confessing that the word "matter" is spooked, and materialism is as suspicious to quantum physics as it is to Derrida. The quantum physicists believe in ghosts. The Marrano materialists turn out to be the quantum physicists! The last laugh is on the old-time *odium theologiae,* the not-so-new materialist antagonists of theology, the exorcists, who have an embarrassing problem on their hands. It is not God who died but matter, bricks and mortar matter, the old hard rock matter of classical physics. At midnight (1905), their petrological materialism turned into hauntological materialism. The learned despisers of theology have to come to grips with a world of quantum events of quite a different, almost immaterial sort. The quantum world is like a ghost dance, not your great grandfather's Newtonianism! Once you say $e=mc^2$, you cannot go on to speak of "inert" matter. Then matter and materialism, matter and spirit, spirit and Idealism begin to look like very impressionistic, prescientific categories that collapse under closer analysis, the sorts of things the prisoners in Plato's cave were conjuring up, having never visited the real world above. Just so, Michel Serres has explored the remarkable analogies between AI technology and medieval angelology, which was, after all, the first theory of instant messaging among superintelligent immaterial beings.[86] How much information can dance on

85 Derrida, *Specters of Marx*, 105–6, 136–37.
86 That is the argument of Serres, *Angels: A Modern Myth.*

the head of a microchip? Mock that! Having abandoned the assured certainties of being and presence, essence and substance, subjects and objects, matter and spirit, the assured divisions of epistemology and ontology, the fixed boundaries of disciplinary domains; having embraced the heteromorphic, polymorphic, pluralistic provisionality of a multiplicity of positions, points of view, and possible worlds, of systems, frameworks, and contexts, having displaced the old billiard ball model of linear causal chains of objects (*Gegenstand*) with "fields" of events—after all that, what more felicitous way than deconstruction to think the world, if we can think it, and if there is (only) one (world)?

What Is Called Deconstruction

As I said at the start, Derrida disliked the word "postmodernism," and he was nervous about the word "religion," and of course he was right. After his death, we have seen that the atheism that wanted to displace (exorcise) religion and the realism and materialism that wanted to displace (exorcise) postmodernism fare just as poorly, all the more so as they try to immunize themselves from spectralization. Deconstruction is the name that caught on, and while it serves a purpose, I do not think even this is its best name. Although its genealogy across five languages is honorable, even fascinating,[87] its semantic negativity obscures the affirmation that drives it, the *viens, oui, oui*. He was feeling about for something else, something different, in search of something for which there is no one name, no one word, as a stand-in for which, as I have been arguing, hauntology does ironic-comic service of a very serious sort. To say that X is a hauntology is to give it a name without a name; it is to say it must be prepared to live without a name. Hauntology is a way to name something by saying that no name is stable and substantive enough to hold up for long, that any name is spooked and unstable, because deconstruction is not a what but a way, and even then it is not a Way in the way of a Method, but a way of making our way in the dark when the Method has fallen into

---

87 *Déconstruction* is first used by Derrida as a translation of Heidegger's *Destruktion*, which Heidegger has taken from Luther's *destructio* (of medieval metaphysical theology), which is a translation of the Greek *apolo* in 1 Cor 1:19, which is itself a citation of Isaiah 29:14. See Caputo, *Cross and Cosmos: A Theology of Difficult Glory* (Bloomington: Indiana University Press, 2019), 71–76; John Edward van Buren, *The Young Heidegger: Rumor of the Hidden King* (Bloomington: Indiana University Press, 1994) 159–68.

crisis. Hauntology does not call for lapsing into apophatic silence; it calls for a multiplication of names and for having conversations with ghosts. It does not call for mystical unnameability but for omni-nameability. Its real enemy is the exorcists, who think they can come up with something unspooked, some first spooker unspooked. The value of the variable X always slips away.

He was searching not for an overarching ahistorical omniscient omnipotent omni-name but for something historically omni-nameable, which takes different names in different contexts, which is why the history of his thought is the history of various nicknames—from supplement to specter to autoimmunity—which he picked up along the way. He practiced a multicontextual dexterity, a style or way of thinking that specializes in the art of *mutatis mutandis,* an ambiance of thought that stays in play with the elusiveness of things, which does not seek to supervise from above but to join in the dance going on down below. He said he does not trust anything that does not pass through apophatic theology, referring not to its ill-advised romance with the eternal now and its esoteric Gnosticism, but to its roguishness, to an intellectual agility that is allergic to dogmatic definitions, rigidly enforced categories, conceptual grasping, an artfulness that can serve a more general purpose, a more "general apophatic."[88]

The thinking he pursued does not care what we call it so long as it is not inflated, capitalized, and put in the singular—like Religion, Postmodernism, Marxism, Materialism, and so on (including "Deconstruction"). In deconstruction, you could put everything in scare quotes because everything has been scared by spooks. It proceeds with respect for complexity and perplexity, with suspicion of received wisdoms and "-isms" of any sort. It describes a world that fluctuates between steady sense and shocking surprise, between settled conventions and unsettling interventions. It seeks out the eccentric rather than the center, the margins rather than the middle, the ellipsis or the hyperbole rather than the mean, the parasite rather than the host, the subversion rather than the norm, the supplement rather than the original, the copy rather than the exemplar, the representation rather than presence, the impossible rather than the possible, the specter rather than bodily presence. All this is undertaken not from sheer perversity but from a conviction that a true decision requires

---

88   Caputo, *Prayers and Tears,* 41–56.

an antecedent undecidability. It is done not in order to produce enervating confusion or fence-sitting indecision but to keep the undeconstructible safe from being contracted into provisional constructions. Our beliefs and practices, our constitutions and institutions, can flourish only by being spectralized — that is, exposed to a future they themselves resist and disturbed by immemorial memories they would sooner forget. The world can be kept safe only by being kept at risk, the real difficulty being, as Johannes Climacus muses, when everything is made easy.[89] *Sauf le nom*: save the name by saving everything except the name. In the most condensed possible formula, he wants to keep the future open. For what? For the coming of what we cannot see coming, for a Messiah who never shows up.

He sometimes suggests that the thinking he pursued might simply be called *thinking*, on an analogy between thinking the gift beyond the rational calculus of an economy and Kant's distinction between thinking and conceptual knowledge, or Heidegger's distinction between thinking and calculation.[90] Before, during, and after the disciplined work of giving reasons (*rationem reddere*) that takes place inside relatively settled standards, adopted paradigms, and received hermeneutic horizons, there is "what is called thinking," what thinking calls for and recalls, with all the ambiance this is given by Heidegger.[91] Thinking is what is called upon when the framework is shaken, the paradigm falls into crisis, the horizon is crossed, the rules have met an intractable exception, and economies close in on us like traps. Thinking takes place on the margins; it happens in moments of crisis and exceptionality. It is like a kind of "quasi-transcendental illusion," like thinking what is without why, *sine ratione*, which exceeds the whys and wherefores we depend upon, thinking the incalculable, thinking *the* impossible that exceeds the stable orders of the possible, of presence, meaning, knowledge, philosophy, science, reason. This thinking is sometimes summarized

89 Søren Kierkegaard, *Concluding Unscientific Postscript to Philosophical Fragments*, in *Kierkegaard's Writings*, trans., ed. Howard Hong and Edna Hong, vol. 12, part 1 (Princeton: Princeton University Press, 1992), 185–88.

90 Derrida poses this analogy in Derrida, *Given Time*, vol. 1, *Counterfeit Money*, trans. Peggy Kamuf (Chicago: University of Chicago Press, 1991), 29–30.

91 Heidegger, *What Is Called Thinking?* trans. Fred D. Wieck and J. Glenn Gray (New York: Harper and Row, 1968).

by Derrida as "the right to ask any question."[92] Schelling called it "ecstatic reason," where reason encounters the intractable resistance of the "unprethinkable," where thinking meets its match.[93]

The power of thinking itself cannot be regionalized (to philosophy or science), cannot be confined within any disciplinary border, cannot be measured by some method or overarching standard, even as, with waxen wing, it dare not fly too close to the sun. To such thinking, which is undertaken in the name of the open-ended play of the world, of the promise of the world,[94] he attached unconditional importance. Deconstruction arises in response to an imperative that has to do with the "mystery" of the impossible, not merely the "problems" of the possible, to go back to a distinction from Gabriel Marcel in which, as Edward Baring has shown, the (very) young Derrida was once interested.[95] Derrida was feeling around for an elusive style of thinking that allows a cloud of suspicion to settle over the old assurances (including all the old binaries), not in order to explode them but to explore them, adventively, adventurously, to search out what is *going on* in them (*venir*). That is what he called the event, the promise of the to-come, *à venir, l'avenir*, the coming of what we cannot see coming. Thinking is thinking the event, transitively, intensively, affirming the event, unconditionally. That is what we came to call deconstruction, what deconstruction calls for, what it recalls, what deconstruction is, if it is. In a nutshell.

3. RADICAL THEOLOGY

When I first invited Derrida to Villanova it was on the premise, the prognostication, that there was a theology in the making stirring

92   Derrida, "The University without Condition," in *Without Alibi*, ed., trans. Peggy Kamuf (Stanford, Calif.: Stanford University Press, 2002), 202–37.

93   F. W. J. Schelling, *The Grounding of Positive Philosophy: The Berlin Lectures*, trans. Bruce Matthews (Albany: SUNY Press, 2008), 48, 203; *Philosophy of Revelation (1841–42) and Related Texts*, ed. and trans. Klaus Ottmann (Putnam, Conn.: Spring, 2020), 124–44.

94   Caputo, "The Promise of the World," *Transfiguration: Nordic Journal of Christianity and the Arts* (Museum Tusclanum: University of Copenhagen) 10 (2010/11): 13–32.

95   See Baring, *Young Derrida and French Philosophy*, 57–59, and Caputo, "Marcel and Derrida: Christian Existentialism and the Genesis of Deconstruction," in *Living Existentialism: Essays in Honor of Thomas W. Busch*, ed. Joseph C. Berendzen and Gregory Hoskins (Eugene, Ore.: Pickwick, 2017), 3–23.

within deconstruction, a new species of theologians on the horizon, theologians to come. This I have variously nicknamed "weak theology," a "theology of perhaps," a "theology of the event," a theology of the "insistence of God," "theopoetics," and lately "radical theology"[96]—a phrase I found congenial, having started out defending the cause of what I called "radical hermeneutics." Something like that has in fact happened, and deconstruction has been an important part of it. Today we are witness to a new theological constellation grouped loosely under the name of radical theology.

In radical theology the idea is—to put it in Derridean terms—to think the "event" that is harbored by the name (of) "God," to deconstruct the sedimented body of confessional beliefs (*croyances*) in order to release the deeper faith (*foi*) by which we are driven. In phenomenological terms, radical theology represents a suspension of the supernaturalism of confessional theology, an *epochē* of its authoritarianism, effecting a reduction that leads us back (*re + ducere*) to the *Sache selbst*, the core experiences that fund thinking. In Tillichian terms, radical theology is the courage to be in the face of the forces of nonbeing by making contact with matters of unconditional import simmering within the various cultural conditions in which they are both expressed and distorted.

The "radical" in "radical theology" means that, down deep, at the roots, there is a disturbance, instability, uncertainty, even an anonymity. "Radical" does not mean foundational thinking, but the opposite: a thinking that is radically exposed, radically at risk, where the victory may be found in defeat, the faith lodged in the depths of doubt, the hope pitted against hopelessness, the ground threatened by groundlessness. "Radical theology" means thinking radically, moving beyond and digging beneath the classical disciplinary boundaries.

Today this term gathers together a creative coalition of the discontent, a mobile constellation of many voices, drawing upon the diverse streams of poststructuralism, process theology, the new physics, political theology, decolonial studies, race and gender theory,[97] all in the name of telling a completely different story about a God

---

96 I have spelled out in some detail what I mean by this term in Caputo, "What Is Radical Theology?," the Introduction to *In Search of Radical Theology*, 1–28.

97 See Rodkey and Miller, *Palgrave Handbook of Radical Theology*, 3–40, for an impressive survey of the history, leading figures, and major movements in radical theology.

who is vulnerable and nonsovereign, who suffers and is divisible, who is deconstructed in his or her or its ipseity.[98]

Only as Hauntology Is Theology Possible

In the present piece, radical theology is traveling under the name of haunto-theology, so it is fitting to conclude these remarks by saying a bit more about this theology, as this is pretty much my story with Derrida, where I have been led by letting Derrida whisper in my ear. In *Prayers and Tears* I tried to follow what Derrida says about religion as carefully as possible. Afterward, I took what Derrida has to say and put it to work in constructing a theology for which I bear the responsibility.

For it has been my lot in life to be interested in religion. I did not choose it; it chose me before I had a chance to object or appeal my case. It has haunted me my whole life long. For me, for a lot of us who are interested in religion—pastors and their graying-around-the-muzzle congregations, theologians and philosophers alike—religion is not a word we have found easy to live with. It has not been kind to us, and there are more profitable ways to earn a living. We could readily do without it, even without a "religion without religion," which can cause confusion. There is some question as to whether anyone can save the name of religion, or whether anyone should even bother to try. We may be better served by keeping a safe distance from all the baggage of religion. It may have suffered irreparable damage from its authoritarianism, its supernaturalism, its superstition, its fixation on rigidly right beliefs (*orthe* + *doxa*), its mean-spirited, right-wing, reactionary, excommunicatory, anti-modern, anti-scientific belligerence, its bigotry and hypocrisy, its bald aspiration for theocracy, for a nationalized religion, a religious nationalism. Religion keeps making itself more and more unbelievable. The "nones" are waxing, the nuns are waning. It flourishes mostly among the elderly and is greeted with a yawn by the young. It thrives among undereducated rural populations, where it fuels the fires of a destructive reactionary populism and is increasingly held in disdain by the well-educated. It keeps feeding its learned despisers with new material.

That is rather a lot of baggage for any one word to bear, and the damage done may be irreparable. I myself am not sure—it depends

---

98   Derrida, *Rogues*, 157.

on what day you ask me—whether religion is even worth saving, that it has not provoked more trouble than it prevents. But if there is a way to save the name of religion—to save it from itself, to keep the rest of us safe from it, to save everything that we should about religion save (*sauf*, except) the name—deconstruction is the way. The word "religion" makes people squirm, especially people who are interested in religion, some of whom try to squirm out of it by saying that they are spiritual but not religious. Seeing the disaster that religion has made of itself, I think that God on high would claim to be spiritual but not religious. Derrida, with a twinkle in his eye, can add another twist: that he is spectral but not spiritual, hauntological but not ontological.

I worried that my interest in religion would make him nervous, so before I published *The Prayers and Tears of Jacques Derrida* I sent him the manuscript to see if, in his opinion, I had gone too far and, like Bartleby, he would prefer not to have anyone say such things about him. Then I would have retitled it *my* prayers and tears, not his. (This game of jacks has been going on for a while.) To my very great relief he said that I was reading him "the way I love to be read," a point that he elaborated in an interview with Mark Dooley about the book in January 2000.[99] What has held my interest is the odd and eerie communication between deconstruction and (a certain) religion. The two trade in spectral figures, and they both believe in ghosts. Their communication is affirmative: deconstruction is structured like a certain religion (of the impossible) even as religion is always structured like a deconstruction (of idols passing themselves off as the impossible). The best theology, the greatest theologians, have always obeyed an auto-deconstructive imperative, never sure how or even whether to speak of God, much less to speak for God, never speaking without endless qualifications, never trusting their own words. Just so, the best deconstruction is marked by a certain longing, love, or desire—and even a certain prayer—for the undeconstructible, for the impossible, for the unconditional. *Viens, oui, oui.* For better or for worse, deconstruction and religion need each other, even and especially if they think they do not, even and especially if they distrust each other, even and especially if neither of these words will do. These two kindred specters cannot disentangle themselves

---

99   Dooley, "Becoming Possible of the Impossible," 21.

from each other; they mutually act upon each other at a distance. Each one keeps the other safe by exposing it to peril, which is the closest deconstruction gets to soteriology.

The result is haunto-theology—that, at least, is my theory of his theory and my explanation for why it flourishes in some of the churches (and why it is treated as the devil itself in other churches). After all, even if God does not exist, even if religion has become unbelievable, that does not mean we do not believe in ghosts. If, as I argue, "hauntology" is the last word in deconstruction, that means the last word is that there is no Last Word. Religion and deconstruction each arise as a response to the imperative of the impossible, to go where we can never go, which is where we really want to go. They live under a double bind. We must, but we cannot. It is impossible, but that is why it is necessary. It is forbidden, but that is why we desire it so much. We can never talk and never *not* talk about God, about the impossible, the undeconstructible, the unconditional, even and especially if we think we can. We cannot desire what is impossible, and yet the impossible is all we truly desire. It is because it is impossible that we desire it. Since we can never get as far as the impossible, the impossible must happen to us under certain conditions. Since we can never attain the unconditional, the unconditional must visit itself upon us, always taking us by surprise. That is what Derrida calls the "experience of the impossible."[100] The imperative of the impossible, to be "bound back" to the impossible by this double bind, is the subversive way deconstruction conforms to piety's questionable etymology of religion as *re + ligare*.

It is not an accident that, in order to explain their common quandary, both Derrida and the theologians hit upon the word "unconditional," upon the paradox that we seek the unconditional and everywhere meet only conditions.[101] Paul Tillich, my favorite official theologian, who was always trying to put his finger on what is going on *in* religion without being caught in the trap that *is* religion, depicted the unconditional under the figure of depth. Tillich wished to subvert the figure of the omnipotent big guy high in the sky by way of the power of the ground of being deep down below. But Derrida, my

---

100   Derrida, "Force of Law," 243.

101   "Everywhere we search for the unconditioned (*Unbedingte*) but only ever find things (*Dinge*)"; *Novalis Schriften*, ed. P. Kluckhohn and R. Samuel (Stuttgart: Verlag W. Kohlhammer, 1983), 413, B, no. 1.

favorite unofficial, slightly atheistic quasitheologian, favors figures of multiplicity and complexity, not depth but drift and dissemination, not the power of being but the weak force of may-being (*peut-être*), an unconditional without sovereignty, force, or power. The unconditional is not a being or an entity, but neither is it the ground of being or beyond being; it is a call, a solicitation, a disturbance that breaks in upon being. It spooks, but it does not speak in plain English. This call gives no advance warning, leaves no calling card, provides us with no instructions, and its only testimony, its only witness, is a response, exposing us to the ridicule of seeming to answer a call we have not heard. The whole thing is spooky.[102]

What does this really mean? How would a hauntology actually work?

Let us take God, for example. Why do I choose the name of God? Once again, I did not. It chose me. I came into a world in which this word was already up and running, overrunning everything. It had me before I had it. I never had a chance. I have repeatedly prayed God to rid me of God, but that only made it worse.

The Spectrality of God: There Is God

Thesis (hypothesis, prosthesis; postulate, axiom; proposal, promise, provocation; hope, sigh, dream, prayer):[103]

> God does not exist, but there is—*il y a, es gibt*—God.[104] That sentence sums up the strange logic or paralogic of this haunto-theology. It articulates the anarchic *arche*, proposing the *principium sine principio*, the principle without principle, the beginning without beginning, of the spectrality of God. In the beginning, God does not exist; but there is God. In the beginning, God does not exist, but there will have been God. That is our faith, hope, and desire, the three great haunto-theological virtues, these three, the greatest of which is undecidable; it depends.

---

102 See the phenomenology of the call in Heidegger, *Being and Time*, trans. John Macquarrie and Edward Robinson (New York: Harper & Row, 1962), §§56–57, 317–25.

103 See Derrida, "Circumfession," 314.

104 The trope is Heideggerian: Because being itself is not a being, Heidegger says we should say beings exist but "there is" (*es gibt*) being. This trope works better in German or French (*il y a*) where, unlike the English "there is," the verb to be (*sein, être*) is not to be found.

That is the axiomatics of this spectrality, the law of the multiplication of the shifting shapes this phantom assumes, the mad method of this fantastic phenomenology. That is the way to tell "a completely different story . . . of a God who deconstructs himself in his ipseity."[105] That is the formula predicting the spectral apparitions of God, the evidence of the "existance"[106] of God, which does not mean that God exists. After the death of the God of theism comes the spectral apparitions of God, postmortem and prenatal, the *arrivants* and *revenants* of God's comings and goings, which tell a completely different story about God.

Still, we want to know how this hauntological formula works. What does this principle, this axiomatic, look like in practice? Where can we see it in action? To this end I choose a crucial passage from "The Force of Law," where its operations can be observed. Were we so minded, we could retitle this famous lecture "Specters of Justice," because the weak force of justice haunts the strong force of the law. Justice does not exist, but its nonexistence is not all there is to it, for there is justice. Justice does not exist; justice insists. The laws exist, but they do not simply exist (nothing does) because they are spooked by justice (everything is spooked by something). In this lecture, Derrida, who has been challenged by Drucilla Cornell to address the question of deconstruction and (*et*) justice, responds by claiming that deconstruction *is* (*est*) justice, which he explained in three steps.

First, the *interval*:[107]

> Deconstruction takes place in the interval that separates the undeconstructibility of justice from the deconstructibility of law.

The law—the lawmakers, the courts, the police, the prisons—exist, but justice in itself, if there is such a thing, does not exist. Justice insists; the laws exist. Laws can only guarantee legality, not justice. Justice is not an existing thing, and it cannot guarantee anything;

---

105   Derrida, *Rogues*, 157

106   Baring, *Young Derrida and French Philosophy*, 75, found the neologism "existance" in writings of the young (eighteen-year-old) Derrida, who proposed it as a French translation of Heidegger's *Dasein*.

107   Derrida, "Force of Law," 243. For a fuller commentary, see Derrida, *Deconstruction in a Nutshell*, 129–40.

it can only call. Justice calls, justice is what is called for, justice is recalled. Justice is possible because the law is deconstructible, because it can be amended and interpreted, repealed and appealed; otherwise the law would be a monster, pure terror. But justice in itself, if there is such a thing, is not deconstructible. The rule of law has real and present force, but the rule, the regime, the reign (*basileia*) of justice is a weak force; it has not arrived and is not to be found, not yet. The day of justice is not a future date on a calendar; it does not belong to calendar time but to messianic time, where it is always coming, always calling, and always being recalled. By opening up the interval, the spectral distance, between what exists and what does not exist, between insistence and existence, between what is possible and *the* impossible, between the deconstructible and the undeconstructible, there is justice, there is deconstruction. *Ubi justitia, ibi deconstructio.*[108]

Second, the *event*:

> Deconstruction is possible as an experience of the impossible, there where, even if it does not exist, if it is not *present*, not yet or never, there is justice [*il y a la justice*].

Justice does not exist, but there is, *il y a, es gibt*, justice. Justice happens when the impossible happens, when the impossible becomes possible, when what does not exist or subsist eventuates. Justice takes place in singular instances, in idiosyncratic exceptions to the universal, in transient moments, in particular acts, in circumstantial judgments so unique that we could never say that a law is just, or even that a person is just, but only that here justice comes about, occurs, arrives, arises. Deconstruction is situated at that point where justice breaks out. Justice is situated just at that point in which deconstruction is at work. Justice happens in the space between the insistence of justice and the existence of the law. The event of justice is released when the weak force of justice is made strong by the force of law and when the rigid power of the law is bent by the winds of justice. There is justice when justice breaks through the accumulated crust of the law, interrupting it, disrupting it, disjoining it, intermittently,

---

108   Where there is justice, there is deconstruction, which is my substitution of the Roman Church's (self-congratulatory) self-assurance: *ubi ecclesia, ibi Spiritus*. Maybe we could say, *ubi spectrum, ibi deconstructio*.

momentarily, eventively, kairotically. Justice happens in the disjuncture, when the time is out of joint.

Third, the *translatability*. The passage concludes with a generalizing gesture, which creates the space for the open-ended translatability or substitutability of the event that is taking place in justice:

> Wherever one can replace, translate, determine the X of justice, one would have to say: deconstruction is possible, as impossible, to the extent (there) where there is X (undeconstructible), thus to the extent (there) where there is (the undeconstructible).

Justice can happen under many names, in many ways, and in every such case, under whatever name, deconstruction is at work. Justice is not the master name, and it cannot guarantee anything. The worst evils can be and are committed under the name of justice. There is no master name, no name at the sound of which *every* knee should bend, but only an endless deployment of given names in given contexts that keep the future open. That means that the value of the variable X must be incessantly reevaluated, endlessly transvalued, that X in itself, if there is such a thing, is invaluable.

Let X be, I will say, at the risk of shocking, God, for example.[109]

In the name of a theology to come, a spectral theology, in the name of a new species of theologians, haunto-theologians, let us assume the risk, let us take on the responsibility of letting the X of justice be God. Then the genealogy of the theology to come, the derivation of this haunto-theology, would be as follows:

(1) The *interval*:

Let the X be God, the one who calls for justice to flow like water across the land (Amos 5:24), justice for the least among us, for the widow, the orphan, and the stranger, for *ta me onta*, the nothings and nobodies of the world (1 Cor 1:28). That replacement, translation, or determination of X would require writing the biblical God *sous rature*, an iteration of the ancient name of the ancient of days; writing it by not writing it, YHWH, blessed be his name. It would be a repetition that produces a completely different story about God, here "reduced" in the phenomenological sense to the *event* that is

---

109 Derrida, "How to Avoid Speaking," 110.

harbored in the name of God, which releases what is going in the name of God.

Let the "force of law" be religion, the institutions, the books, the authorities, the historical communities, all of which exist and have *ousia*, real being, real power, real estate, while the X of justice, God, is without power, not present, not yet or never, and has no place to lay down its head.

(2) The *event*.

God does not exist. So what? There is God.

God does not exist. So what? God insists.

God does not exist. So what? There are God effects, God events, flashes of God happening here and there. Like quanta flashing in and out of existence, like quantum leaps, spanning the interval between the indeterminate undecidability of the name of God and determinate decisions producing God sparks. God happens in the interval between the undeconstructibility of the call that takes place in the name of God and the deconstructibility of the world, of the institutions, books, authorities that assume the responsibility for the name of God, for responding to it, for giving it a place, its "spacetimemattering."

(3) *Substitutability*.

It may be that the name of God is the best name we have for justice or for love; or it may be that justice or love are the best names we have for God. There is no resolving that undecidability. There is no transcendental signified, no name that gets a pass, no name above other names that arrests the play, that stills the flux, that brings final peace. The worst evils, the most terrible bloodshed, can be and are committed in the names of God, love, and justice. What would we not do for these things? Sometimes the very worst things. Any peaceful requiescence inoculated from evil is reserved for the grave, *requiescat in pace*. In time, in the meantime, and it is always the meantime, our hearts are restless. We will always need names, other names, names we have never heard, names that have not come yet, unimaginable values for the variable X. X marks the spot of the coming, of the to-come. In the expressions the coming God or the God to come, the "to-come" is more important than justice or God.[110]

---

110 Derrida, "Politics and Friendship," in *Negotiations: Interventions and Interviews: 1971–2001*, trans. Elizabeth Rottenberg (Stanford, Calif.: Stanford University Press, 2002), 182.

God is not an infinite being, but the name of God is the name of the infinitival, *à venir*. (If this really were a religion, God forbid, advent would be its only liturgical season; it would be a 24/7 adventism.) It calls us, and it, whatever it is, does not comply with what we call it, *Ça, das Ding, il y a, Deus absconditus, deus sive natura, es gibt,* being itself, and on and on, world without end, Amen.

One of the first fruits of haunt-ology is to provide us with a gloss on the biblical "reign of God" (*basileia theou*) that frees it from its imperialism. The rule of God is spectral, like the calling of a caller of unknown provenance and identity. The rule of God is not a strong force, like the force of law, but the weak force of a call, which does not belong to the realm of existence. Its rule is not that of a mundane power, like heavenly hosts of mighty angels descending upon the earth, bringing fire and destruction to the evil doers. Much less is the rule of God found in blood-spilling terrestrial armies bearing banners saying *in hoc signo vinces*. The reign of God is a rule without force, a realm without royal power. Nothing assures us of victory. The rule of God may very well be found among the defeated, like Jesus forgiving his executioners. It does not enjoy the splendor of being, but stirs among the nothings and nobodies, *ta me onta*, and the glory it delivers is difficult.[111] It is a strange kingdom, upside down, an inverted world, altogether a spooky and uncertain business. The reign of God is unconditional but without sovereignty. It insists, but it does not exist. God's coming kingdom is a weak force, always to-come, always calling and being recalled, appearing in evanescent, intermittent, episodic events, in transient happenings, in the interstices and intervals, in fragments, in (sacred) remnants and ruins, in divine debris.

There is God whenever a stranger is made welcome, a gift given, the hungry fed, the naked clothed, mercy and compassion shown.

There is God whenever two or three are gathered in and by the event that is harbored in the name of God.

There is God whenever the glory of the earth, the grandeur of the world is affirmed, whenever all things great or small are celebrated, *tout autre est tout autre*.

There is God. Like occasional shoots of green life springing up in the crevices of rocks, like sparks given off in the dark of night, like

---

111   That is the argument of Caputo, *Cross and Cosmos: A Theology of Difficult Glory.*

fleeting glimpses of something we are not sure is really there, like strange forms of life flourishing in the cold dark depths of still unexplored sea bottoms or on galaxies far, far away. Thus do God and the gods arrive. Glory be to the world, all the worlds, worlds without end, worlds without why, amen. Thus does deconstruction, if there is such a thing, proceed, thus does it abide by the strange logic, the odd irregular haunto-logic of the event.

"Ghost Dance," Cut Scene

"Do you believe in ghosts?" she asks.

"Yes, I do, yes," he replies, "I have always thought that something spooky is going on, *revenants* and *arrivants* everywhere I turn, memories of the immemorial, promises of the unforeseeable, something spectral and out of joint, something that I call, half in jest, hauntological."

"Only half?" she asks. "What is the other half?"

"If I knew that," he says, "I would know everything."

"Johannes Climacus, for whom Kierkegaard was a ghostwriter, said the comic is the incognito of the religious. Is that it? Do you believe that?"

At this suggestion, he simply smiles, the devil in his eye.[112]

---

112 This scene, of course, is a ghost. It does not exist. So what?

PART ONE

The Villanova Roundtable
A Conversation with
Jacques Derrida

The Villanova Roundtable
A Conversation with Jacques Derrida

EDITORIAL NOTE

On October 2, 1994, Jacques Derrida participated in a roundtable discussion that was the centerpiece of a day dedicated to the official inauguration of the new doctoral program in philosophy at Villanova University. Professor Derrida was speaking in English, extemporaneously and without a text, to questions put to him by Professors Walter Brogan, Thomas Busch, John D. Caputo, and Dennis Schmidt, all of Villanova's philosophy department. The question on Joyce was put afterward from the audience by Professor James Murphy, a Joyce specialist in Villanova's English department.

While this forum did not allow Derrida to develop the complexities of deconstruction, as he himself repeatedly protests, Derrida succeeded in putting things in a strikingly concise and illuminating way. His audience was mixed, composed of people from many different disciplines across the university, and Derrida held them spellbound for the better part of two hours. What follows is, I think, as eloquent and reliable an "introduction" to deconstruction as one is likely to find.

The reader should remember that Derrida is here improvising his answers and speaking in English, although his English is extremely good and much better than his modesty will allow him to admit. The first words he utters in the "Roundtable" are an apology for his English, and he asks us repeatedly throughout the discussion to have mercy on him. The "Roundtable" is not a carefully wrought manuscript that he has labored over at length but a faithful transcript of his extemporaneous remarks in the space of about an hour and a half one October afternoon in 1994.

I am grateful to Professor Derrida for kindly consenting to the publication of this conversation. I have annotated the text by supplying in

square brackets references to his published works and occasional footnotes that explain certain points. I have also made minor stylistic alter-
ations here and there to give the sentences a better flow. Professor
Derrida has graciously looked over the transcript and has himself made
only minor changes.

In the second half of the present volume, I have added the dangerous supplement of a commentary, in order to elaborate upon the necessarily abbreviated discussions imposed by the "Roundtable" format,
in which Derrida's suggestive but condensed observations are explored
in greater detail.

* * *

JOHN D. CAPUTO: Professor Derrida, I would like to begin today's discussion by raising the issue of what we are in fact doing here and
now, at this moment, which is inaugurating a doctoral program in
philosophy. This is a rich and suggestive "event," and it evokes many
themes that you have been addressing over the years in your work.

Many people, whose impression of deconstruction has been drawn
from the public media, might find this an odd thing for you to be
doing. They associate deconstruction with the "end of philosophy,"
while we are here beginning a new program in philosophy. They identify deconstruction with a destructive attitude toward texts and traditions and truth, toward the most honorable names in the philosophical
heritage. They think that deconstruction is the enemy of academic
programs and academic institutions, that it is anti-institutional and
cannot accommodate itself to institutional life.

Finally, you have often spoken about the very notion of "inauguration" as the irruption of something "absolutely new," and today we are
trying to inaugurate, to irrupt. We would be interested in knowing
what your reflections are on this inaugural moment.

JACQUES DERRIDA: First of all, I want to apologize for my English. I
must improvise here, and that will be a very difficult task for me. I
would like to thank the President and the Dean for their kind words
and for their hospitality, and to thank all of you for being present here.
It is an honor for me to be part of this exceptional moment in the
history of your university, and I am very proud of sharing this experi-

ence with you, especially because it is the inauguration of a philosophy program. I think that is very important and I will try to say something shortly about just what I think it is so important.

Before that, I would emphasize the fact that the institution of such a program is not only important for Villanova University; it is important for the community of philosophers both in this country and abroad. As you know, the space for philosophy has been more and more reduced in the industrialized societies. I myself, in my own country, try as far as I can to struggle in order to enlarge the space for philosophical teaching and philosophical research.[1] This program is important for your university, for the country, for other philosophical communities in the world. I say this, first of all, because the philosophers in this university who are conducting this program are already well known, both in this country and in Europe. I have some friends around me and I can assure you that they are very important philosophers for us, very precious thinkers. Their presence is a guarantee for the future of this program, and we know this in advance. A moment ago, I met for an hour with many of your graduate students, the students who will work in this program. I can tell you quite honestly that they are very bright. I was very happy to engage with them for an hour of intense philosophical debate; they are very well informed, very learned, and it makes me very optimistic about the future of this program. I want to congratulate you and everyone who participated in the creation of this program. I wish you the best, and in my modest way I will try to associate myself as far as possible with its life.

What is called "deconstruction"—and I will be very sketchy here, because time does not permit detailed analyses—has never, never opposed institutions as such, philosophy as such, discipline as such. Nevertheless, as you rightly said, it is another thing for me to be doing what I am doing here. Because, however affirmative deconstruction is, it is affirmative in a way that is not simply positive, not simply conservative, not simply a way of repeating the given institution. I

---

[1] For a commentary on Derrida's view of philosophy as an academic discipline and his "practical initiatives" in educational institutions, see below, Part Two, chap. 2, "The Right to Philosophy." See the writings collected in DD, PR, and, also, Jacques Derrida and Geoffrey Bennington, "On Colleges and Philosophy," ICA Documents, 4/5 (1986), 66–71; reprinted in Postmodernism: ICA Documents, ed. Lisa Appignanesi (London: Free Association Books, 1989), pp. 209–228; "Women in the Beehive: A Seminar with Jacques Derrida," in Men in Feminism, ed. Alice Jardine and Paul Smith (New York: Methuen, 1987), pp. 189–203.

think that the life of an institution implies that we are able to criticize, to transform, to open the institution to its own future. The paradox in the instituting moment of an institution is that, at the same time that it starts something new, it also continues something, is true to the memory of the past, to a heritage, to something we receive from the past, from our predecessors, from the culture. If an institution is to be an institution, it must to some extent break with the past, keep the memory of the past, while inaugurating something absolutely new [cf. PdS 139/*Points* 130–131]. So, I am convinced that today, although this program to some extent looks like other, similar programs, it does something absolutely new. The indication of this is found not simply in the structural organization of the program, but in the work, in the content of the work, of those who will run this program, the new themes. The fact, for instance, that the faculty includes such topics as Heidegger or deconstruction indicates that they are not simply reproducing, that they are trying to open something new and something original, something that hasn't been done in that way in other, similar universities or programs. So the paradox is that the instituting moment in an institution is violent in a way, violent because it has no guarantee. Although it follows the premises of the past, it starts something absolutely new, and this newness, this novelty, is a risk, is something that has to be risky, and it is violent because it is guaranteed by no previous rules. So, at the same time, you have to follow the rule and to invent a new rule, a new norm, a new criterion, a new law [cf. FL 50–52/DPJ 23]. That's why the moment of institution is so dangerous at the same time. One should not have an absolute guarantee, an absolute norm; we have to invent the rules. I am sure that the responsibility that is taken by my colleagues, and by the students, implies that they give themselves the new rule. There is no responsibility, no decision, without this inauguration, this absolute break. That is what deconstruction is made of: not the mixture but the tension between memory, fidelity, the preservation of something that has been given to us, and, at the same time, heterogeneity, something absolutely new, and a break. The condition of this performative success, which is never guaranteed, is the alliance of these to newness.

Let me now address the question of a program. In France, we have for a long time been confronted with similar issues. I have at the same time said two things which sound contradictory. On the one hand, I was fighting or opposing the rigid definition of programs, disciplines, the borders between disciplines, the fact that in my country philosophy was taught not only in the university but also in the last grade in the high school. So we founded another institution in 1975, a movement called the "Research Group for the Teaching of Philosophy,"[2] which opposed the dominant institution, which tried to convince our colleagues and French citizens that philosophy should be taught earlier than in this last grade of the high school, earlier than 16 or 17 years old. There should be philosophy across the borders, not only in philosophy proper, but in other fields, such as law, medicine, and so forth. To some extent these struggles were a failure; nevertheless, I am still convinced it was a good war. But at the same time I emphasized the necessity of discipline, of something specifically philosophical, that we should not dissolve philosophy into other disciplines, that we need at the same time interdisciplinarity, crossing the borders, establishing new themes, new problems, new ways, new approaches to new problems, all the while teaching the history of philosophy, the techniques, professional rigor, what one calls discipline. I do not think we need to chose between the two. We should have philosophers trained as philosophers, as rigorously as possible, and at the same time audacious philosophers who cross the borders and discover new connections, new fields, not only interdisciplinary researches but themes that are not even interdisciplinary.

Allow me to refer to another institution that I have been part of in France. I have already mentioned the "Research Group for the Teaching of Philosophy" in 1975. But in 1983, some friends and I founded a new institution called the "International College of Philosophy," in which we tried to teach philosophy as such, as a discipline, and at the same time, to discover new themes, new problems, which have no legitimacy, which were not recognized as such, in existing universities. That was not simply interdisciplinarity, because interdisciplinarity implies that you have given, identifiable competencies—say, a legal theorist, an architect, a philosopher, a literary critic—and that they work together on a specific, identifiable object. That's interdisciplinarity. But when you discover a new object, an object that up until now has not been identified as such, or has no legitimacy in terms of academic

---

[2] "Le Groupe de Recherches sur l'Enseignement Philosophique," founded in 1975 (DDP 146–153), along with the "Collège International de Philosophie," which Derrida mentions next, both of which I discuss below in Part II, chap. 2.

fields, then you have to invent a new competency, a new type of research, a new discipline. The International College of Philosophy granted a privilege to such new themes, new disciplines which were not, up to then, recognized and legitimized in other institutions.

So, you see, I am a very conservative person. I love institutions and I spent a lot of time participating in new institutions, which sometimes do not work. At the same time, I try to dismantle not institutions but some structures in given institutions which are too rigid or are dogmatic or which work as an obstacle to future research.

WALTER BROGAN: I would like to ask you a question that is very much related to the material that you have just been discussing, a question really also about beginnings and inauguration. Specifically, I want to ask about the relationship of your work to the Greeks as the inaugurators of the Western tradition. This semester we are reading your essay on Plato in our class in Greek philosophy.[3] As a matter of fact, this program in continental philosophy has very much at the forefront also a study of the history of philosophy. I wonder how you might characterize the connection of your own work and the work of deconstruction to the task of reading inherited texts from the tradition. You have already begun to address that question. Specifically, postmodernism is often situated at the end of tradition and is often characterized as having the task of dismantling the founding texts, such as those of Plato and Aristotle. Yet, in many ways, your reading of the *Phaedrus* is so attentive to the structural integrity and the composition of the dialogue. So I would like to ask you if this is a characteristic of your philosophy, this tension between disruption, on the one hand, and attentiveness, on the other. What would you suggest to us as people of this age, what strategies would you suggest we employ, in the reading of these texts?

JACQUES DERRIDA: First of all, I would say, yes, this tension is characteristic of everything I try to do. Now, at the risk of being a little oversimplifying, I would take this opportunity to reject a commonplace, a prejudice, that is widely circulated about deconstruction. That is, not only among bad journalists, and there are many of them, but among people in the academy who behave not like good journalists—I have

---

[3] "Plato's Pharmacy" (1968), in *Dissemination*, pp. 61–171.

the deepest respect for good journalists—but like bad journalists, repeating stereotypes without reading the text. Perhaps we will come back to this later on. This has been from the beginning a terrible problem for me, and not only for me, this caricature, this lack of respect for reading.[4] Because as soon as one examines my texts, and not only mine but the texts of many people close to me, one sees that respect for the great texts, for the texts of the Greeks and of others, too, is the condition of our work. I have constantly tried to read and to understand Plato and Aristotle and I have devoted a number of texts to them. If you will allow me to make a self-reference, my book on friendship [*Politiques de l'amitié*], which will appear the day after tomorrow in France [Paris: Galilée, 1994], is mainly a book on Plato and Aristotle on friendship. So I think we have to read them again and again and I feel that, however old I am, I am on the threshold of reading Plato and Aristotle. I love them and I feel I have to start again and again and again. It is a task which is in front of me, before me.

Now, nevertheless, the way I tried to read Plato, Aristotle, and others is not a way of commanding, repeating, or conserving this heritage. It is an analysis which tries to find out how their thinking works or does not work, to find the tensions, the contradictions, the heterogeneity within their own corpus [cf. *Khôra* 81–84/ON 119–121]. What is the law of this self-deconstruction, this "auto-deconstruction"? Deconstruction is not a method or some tool that you apply to something from the outside [cf. MpPdM 122–123/MfPdM 124]. Deconstruction is something which happens and which happens inside; there is a deconstruction at work within Plato's work, for instance. As my colleagues know, each time I study Plato I try to find some heterogeneity in his own corpus, and to see how, for instance, within the *Timaeus* the theme of the *khôra* is incompatible with this supposed system of Plato.[5] So, to be true to Plato, and this is a sign of love and respect for Plato, I have to analyze the functioning and disfunctioning of his work. I would say the same for the whole opening, a potential force which was ready to cross the borders of Greek language, Greek culture.

---

[4] One of Derrida's best articulations of his respect for reading is to be found in "Afterword: Toward An Ethic of Discussion," trans. Samuel Weber, in Jacques Derrida, *Limited Inc.* (Evanston, Ill.: Northwestern University Press, 1988). One of the principal aims of the commentary that follows in Part Two of this volume is to dispel this misrepresentation of deconstruction's approach to texts.

[5] See below, Part II, chap. 3, for a detailed discussion of Derrida's interpretation of Plato's *khôra*.

I would say the same for democracy, although the concept of democracy is a Greek heritage. This heritage is the heritage of a model, not simply a model, but of a model that self-deconstructs, that deconstructs itself, so as to uproot, to become independent of its own grounds, so to speak, so that, today, philosophy is Greek and it is not Greek [cf. ED 227–228/WD 153]. In my book on friendship, *Politiques de l'amitié*, I tried to analyze what happened to Greek thought with the advent of Christianity, especially with the concept of brotherhood.[6] The way the Christian concept of brotherhood transformed the Greek concept of brotherhood was at the same time something new, an inauguration, a mutation, a break, but this break, at the same time, was developing something which was potentially inscribed in the Greek tradition. So, we have to go back constantly to the Greek origin, not in order to cultivate the origin, or in order to protect the etymology, the *etymon*, the philological purity of the origin, but in order first of all to understand where we come from. Then we have to analyze the history and the historicity of the breaks which have produced our current world out of Greece, for instance, out of Christianity, out of this origin, and breaking or transforming this origin, at the same time. So there is this tension.

Going back to my own tendency or taste or idiosyncratic style: I love reading Greek; it is still a very difficult task, and when I read Plato I enjoy it. I think it is an infinite task. The problem is not behind me. Plato is in front of me. That's why today, in the midst of so many stereotypes and prejudices that are circulating about deconstruction, I find it painful to see that many people who address the question of the canon think they have to make a choice between reading Plato or other "great white males" and reading black women writers.[7] But why should we choose? Even before the question of the canon became so visible, no one in the university could be simultaneously a great specialist in Plato and in Aristotle and in Shakespeare. The choices had to be

---

[6] For an English text that adumbrates *Pol.*, see "The Politics of Friendship," trans. Gabriel Motzkin, *The Journal of Philosophy*, 85, No. 11 (1988), 632–644. For a discussion of the issues surrounding this book see below, Part II, chaps. 4 and 5.

[7] See Amy Gutman, "Relativism, Deconstruction, and the Curriculum," in *Campus Wars: Multi-Culturalism and the Politics of Difference*, ed. John Arthur and Amy Shapiro (Boulder: Westview Press, 1995), pp. 57–69, who accuses "deconstruction" (she never quite gets around actually to citing Jacques Derrida) of just such a view. This whole issue is discussed in more detail below, in Part Two, chap. 2, "The Right to Philosophy," and chap. 3, "A Hoax."

made, and that is the finitude of our condition. No one can at the same time be an expert in Plato and in Milton, for instance. We accepted this. It was common sense. Why today should we choose between the great canon—Plato, Shakespeare [see AL 414–433], Cervantes, and Hegel—and others on the other hand? The academic field is a differentiated field. Everyone can find his or her way and make choices. A program, of course, can become specialized, but this does not mean that there cannot be other programs with no exclusivity which would specialize in other fields. That is why I do not understand what is going on with this question of the canon. At least as regards deconstruction, it is interested in what is considered the great canon—the study of great Western works—and open at the same time to new works, new objects, new fields, new cultures, new languages, and I see no reason why we should choose between the two. That is the tension in deconstruction.

THOMAS W. BUSCH: If I might, I would like to follow up on a remark you made about internationalism in the sense of your founding of the International College of Philosophy and also what I take to be, in your book *Specters of Marx*, perhaps a call for a new form of internationalism. Recently a distinguished American historian said, apropos of the American motto *E pluribus unum*, that today, in the United States, we have too much *pluribus* and not enough *unum*.[8] Now, I have always considered deconstruction to be on the side of the *pluribus*, that is, as deconstructing totalities, identities, in favor of loosening them up in terms of diversity, disruptions, fissures. I think that is a lesson we have all learned from deconstruction. What I would like to ask regards any deconstructive salvaging of the *unum*. That is, can the *pluribus*, the diversity, itself become too dangerous? What does deconstruction say, if anything, in favor of the *unum*, of community? Is there a place for unity after deconstruction? What might it look like?

JACQUES DERRIDA: Thank you. Again a difficult question. Let me say a word first about the internationality that you refer to at the beginning. The internationality I referred to in this book, since Marx was

---

[8] Arthur Schlesinger, *The Disuniting of America: Reflections on a Multicultural Society* (New York: W. W. Norton Co., 1992); see the excerpt of this book in *Cultural Wars*, pp. 226–234.

the main reference of the book, was supposed to be different from what was called in the Marxist tradition the "International" [cf. SdM 139–142/SoM 84–86]. I think that, today, there are wars and a number of world crises in which international organizations such as the United Nations, for instance, have to intervene but cannot intervene the way they should. That is, international law, which is a good thing, nevertheless is still rooted in its mission, in its action, in its languages, in a Western concept of philosophy, a Western concept of the state and of sovereignty, and this is a limit. We have to deconstruct the foundations of this international law, but not in order to destroy the international organization. I think international organizations are something good, something perfectible, and something necessary, but we have to rethink the philosophical foundations of these international organizations.

That's one limit. The other limit, which is connected with the first one, has to do with the fact that these international organizations are, in fact, governed by a number of particular states which provide these international organizations with the means to intervene, with the military power, with the economic power, and, of course, the United States plays a major role in this. Sometimes it is a good thing, but it is at the same time a limit. So the universality of international law is in fact in the hands of a number of powerful, rich states and has to change, and it is in the process of changing, through a number of disasters, crises, economic inequalities, injustices, and so on. Hence, the international arm I think is looking for its own place, its own figure, something which would go beyond the current stage of internationality, perhaps beyond citizenship, beyond belonging to a state, to a given nation state. And I think that in the world today a number of human beings are secretly aligned in their suffering against the hegemonic powers which protect what is called the "new order." So that's what I mean by a "New International." Not a new way of associating citizens belonging to given nation-states, but a new concept of citizenship, of hospitality, a new concept of the state, of democracy. In fact, it is not a new concept of democracy, but a new determination of the given concept of democracy, in the tradition of the concept of democracy.[9]

---

[9] In addition to *Specters of Marx*, Derrida also discussed the problems of internationalism and the "new world order" in *The Other Heading*, both of which are discussed below in Part Two, chap. 4, which elaborates the question of deconstruction and the possibility of community.

Now, having said this—again very simply, in a way which is too simple—I think we do not have to choose between unity and multiplicity. Of course, deconstruction—that has been its strategy up to now—insisted not on multiplicity for itself but on the heterogeneity, the difference, the disassociation, which is absolutely necessary for the relation to the other. What disrupts the totality is the condition for the relation to the other. The privilege granted to unity, to totality, to organic ensembles, to community as a homogenized whole—this is a danger for responsibility, for decision, for ethics, for politics. That is why I insisted on what prevents unity from closing upon itself, from being closed up. This is not only a matter of description, of saying that this is the way it is. It is a matter of accounting for the possibility of responsibility, of a decision, of ethical commitments. To understand this, you have to pay attention to what I would call singularity. Singularity is not simply unity or multiplicity. Now, this does not mean that we have to destroy all forms of unity wherever they occur. I have never said anything like that. Of course, we need unity, some gathering, some configuration. You see, pure unity or pure multiplicity—when there is only totality or unity and when there is only multiplicity or disassociation—is a synonym of death. What interests me is the limit of every attempt to totalize, to gather, versammeln—and I will come to this German word in a moment, because it is important for me—the limit of this unifying, uniting movement, the limit that it had to encounter, because the relationship of the unity to itself implies some difference.

To be more concrete, take the example of a person or of a culture. We often insist nowadays on cultural identity—for instance, national identity, linguistic identity, and so on. Sometimes the struggles under the banner of cultural identity, national identity, linguistic identity, are noble fights. But at the same time the people who fight for their identity must pay attention to the fact that identity is not the self-identity of a thing, this glass, for instance, this microphone, but implies a difference within identity. That is, the identity of a culture is a way of being different from itself; a culture is different from itself; language is different from itself; the person is different from itself. Once you take into account this inner and other difference, then you pay attention to the other and you understand that fighting for your own identity is not exclusive of another identity, is open to another identity. And this prevents totalitarianism, nationalism, egocentrism, and so on. That is what I tried to demonstrate in the book called *The Other Heading*: in the case of culture, person, nation, language, identity is a self-differentiating identity, an identity different from itself, having an opening or gap within itself [AC 15–17/OH 9–11]. That totally affects a structure, but it is a duty, an ethical and political duty, to take into account this impossibility of being one with oneself. It is because I am not one with myself that I can speak with the other and address the other. That is not a way of avoiding responsibility. On the contrary, it is the only way for me to take responsibility and to make decisions.

That raises one of my questions regarding Heidegger. As you know, deconstruction owes a lot to Heidegger. That is a complex problem that I cannot take up now. Nevertheless, one of the recurrent critiques or deconstructive questions I pose to Heidegger has to do with the privilege Heidegger grants to what he calls *Versammlung*, gathering, which is always more powerful than dissociation. I would say exactly the opposite [cf. SdM 49–57/SoM 23–29].[10] Once you grant some privilege to gathering and not to dissociating, then you leave no room for the other, for the radical otherness of the other, for the radical singularity of the other. I think, from that point of view, separation, dissociation is not an obstacle to society, to community, but the condition. We addressed this a moment ago with the students.[11] Dissociation, separation, is the condition of my relation to the other. I can address the Other only to the extent that there is a separation, a dissociation, so that I cannot replace the other and vice versa. That is what some French-speaking philosophers such as Blanchot and Levinas call the *"rapport sans rapport,"* the relationless relation [cf. *Foi* 84–85].[12] The structure of my relation to the other is of a "relation without relation." It is a relation in which the other remains absolutely transcendent. I cannot reach the other. I cannot know the other from the inside and so on. That is not an obstacle but the condition of love, of friendship, and of war, too, a condition of the relation to the other.

---

[10] See below, Part Two, chap. 5, for a discussion of Derrida's notion of justice as a "dis-juncture" as opposed to Heidegger's interpretation of *dike* as *Versammlung*.

[11] In a private conversation (no faculty allowed!) with the graduate students.

[12] In *Totality and Infinity*, trans. Alphonso Lingis (Pittsburgh: Duquesne University Press, 1969), Emmanuel Levinas repeatedly speaks of a relationship from which the *relata* absolve themselves, that is, keep withdrawing themselves, "ab-lating" or "absolutizing" themselves, preserving and sheltering their singularity. See pp. 64, 102, 180, 195, 208, 220.

So, dissociation is the condition of community, the condition of any unity as such.

So, the state, to come back to the state: a state in which there would be only *unum* would be a terrible catastrophe. And we have had, unfortunately, a number of such experiences. A state without plurality and a respect for plurality would be, first, a totalitarian state, and not only is this a terrible thing, but it does not work. We know that it is terrible and that it does not work. Finally, it would not even be a state. It would be, I do not know what, a stone, a rock, or something like that. Thus, a state as such must be attentive as much as possible to plurality, to the plurality of peoples, of languages, cultures, ethnic groups, persons, and so on. That is the condition for a state.

DENNIS SCHMIDT: I have a very simple question. It follows some of the remarks you just made about the nature of community, about the impossibility of ethical life, the impossibility of justice, as being the condition of the appearance of justice. In some of your more recent work the topic of justice has surfaced far more explicitly and far more clearly, even though you might argue that it has been there all the time. I would like to ask you to elaborate a bit more on the nature of justice, how you understand justice. You speak, for instance in the Marx book, of the sense of justice that is so strong and so powerful that it shatters every calculus, every possible economy, that it can only be described in terms of the gift. In a number of little texts, such as *Passions, Sauf le nom,* and *Khôra* [Eng. trans., ON], which together form a sort of essay on the name, you say that this essay on the name needs to be understood, among its other dimensions, as political in its truth. Could you elaborate a bit more on the meaning of this justice that can only be described as a gift, that cannot be linked to any calculus, to any economy, to a dialectic, to a set of exchanges, to the possibility of vengeance or punishment? This might be an impossible question, but could you say a little bit more about that and say something about that in relation to the question of the name, and singularity, and some of the remarks you just made in response to Professor Busch?

JACQUES DERRIDA: Well, before I try to answer these questions, I would again say that, as you see, these questions cannot really be dealt with in such a forum, because they are difficult. Really to do justice to them you have to read texts, to revive a number of traditions, so it is very brutal to address these questions in such a way. If I were more responsible, I would simply say "No, I won't, I won't participate in this game." Nevertheless, sometimes it is not a bad thing, at least if you do not do it too often. It is not that bad that we try to encapsulate deconstruction in a nutshell. Let me offer you an anecdote. One day, two years ago, when I was in Cambridge—there was this terrible honorary degree crisis in Cambridge—and a journalist took the microphone and said, "Well, could you tell me, in a nutshell, what is deconstruction?" [*Points* 406]. Sometimes, of course, I confess, I am not able to do that. But sometimes it may be useful to try nutshells. So, what about this problem of justice in a nutshell?

It is true that, although the problem of justice has been on my mind in previous texts all the time, it is only in recent years that I have addressed this problem thematically. It was in the context of a conference at Cardozo Law school on "Deconstruction and the Possibility of Justice," where I had to address a text by Benjamin on violence [see FL 75ff./DPJ 29ff.]. I found it useful to make a distinction between law and justice, what one calls in French *le droit*, that is, right, or *Recht* in German. In English, when you say "law," you are say both right and law, *le droit et le loi*, at the same time, whereas in French, we distinguish between them. So I make a distinction between the law, that is the history of right, of legal systems, and justice. Following Benjamin, and at the same time trying to deconstruct Benjamin's text, or to show how Benjamin's text was deconstructing itself, I made this statement—in a nutshell—that the law could be deconstructed. There is a history of legal systems, of rights, of laws, of positive laws, and this history is a history of the transformation of laws. That why they are there. You can improve law, you can replace one law by another one. There are constitutions and institutions. This is a history, and a history, as such, can be deconstructed. Each time you replace one legal system by another one, one law by another one, or you improve the law, that is a kind of deconstruction, a critique and deconstruction. So, the law as such can be deconstructed and has to be deconstructed. That is the condition of historicity, revolution, morals, ethics, and progress. But justice is not the law. Justice is what gives us the impulse, the drive, or the movement to improve the law, that is, to deconstruct the law. Without a call for justice we would not have any interest in deconstructing the law. That is why I said that the condition of possibility of deconstruction is a call for justice. Justice is not reducible to the law, to a given system of legal structures. That means that justice is always unequal to itself. It is non-coincident with itself [cf. FL 34–36/DPJ 14–15].[13]

Then, in *Specters of Marx*, I went back again to the Greeks, to the word *dike*, to the interpretation of the Greek word translated by "justice." I contested the interpretation by Heidegger of *dike* and *adikia*, justice and injustice [see above, n.10]. I tried to show that justice again implied non-gathering, dissociation, heterogeneity, non-identity with itself, endless inadequation, infinite transcendence. That is why the call for justice is never, never fully answered. That is why no one can say "I am just" [cf. FL 52/DPJ 23]. If someone tells you "I am just," you can be sure that he or she is wrong, because being just is not a matter of theoretical determination. I cannot know that I am just. I can know that I am right. I can see that I act in agreement with norms, with the law. I stop at the red light. I am right. That is no problem. But that does not mean that I am just. To speak of justice is not a matter of knowledge, of theoretical judgment. That's why it's not a matter of calculation. You can calculate what is right. You can judge; you can say that, according to the code, such and such a misdeed deserves ten years of imprisonment. That may be a matter of calculation. But the fact that it is rightly calculated does not mean that it is just. A judge, if he wants to be just, cannot content himself with applying the law. He has to reinvent the law each time. If he wants to be responsible, to make a decision, he has not simply to apply the law, as a coded program, to a given case, but to reinvent in a singular situation a new just relationship; that means that justice cannot be reduced to a calculation of sanctions, punishments, or rewards. That may be right or in agreement with the law, but that is not justice. Justice, if it has to do with the other, with the infinite distance of the other, is always unequal to the other, is always incalculable. You cannot calculate justice. Levinas says somewhere that the definition of justice—which is very minimal but which I love, which I think is really rigorous—is that justice is the relation to the other.[14] That is all. Once you relate to the other as the other, then something incalculable comes on the scene, something which cannot be reduced to the law or to the history

---

[13] For a fuller discussion of Derrida's treatment of justice and the law, see below, Part II, chap. 5.

[14] See *Totality and Infinity*, p. 89 (FL 49/DPJ 22).

of legal structures. That is what gives deconstruction its movement, that is, constantly to suspect, to criticize the given determinations of culture, of institutions, of legal systems, not in order to destroy them or simply to cancel them, but to be just with justice, to respect this relation to the other as justice.

In the essays you mentioned [see ON] I tried to read a number of texts, mainly Plato's *Timaeus*, in terms of the question of the place, *khôra*, which disturbs and undermines the whole Platonic system, all the couples of opposition which constitute the Platonic system. This reflection on *khôra* is part of a political discussion. I tried to reconstitute this political scenario in order to suggest—and that is all that is possible here, without reopening Plato's text—that, if you take into account the strange structure of the *khôra*, of place, which is the opening for any inscription, for any happening or any event, then you have not only to deconstruct the traditional concept of politics, but to think of another way of interpreting politics, that is, the place for the place, the place for hospitality,[15] the place for the gift. You have to think politics otherwise. That is part of a number of gestures I have made in recent years to deconstruct the political tradition, not in order to depoliticize but in order to interpret differently the concept of the political, the concept of democracy, and to try to articulate these concepts of the political and of democracy with what I said about the gift and about singularity.

The only thing I would say about the gift—this is an enormous problem—is that the gift is precisely, and this is what it has in common with justice, something which cannot be reappropriated.[16] A gift is something which never appears as such and is never equal to gratitude, to commerce, to compensation, to reward. When a gift is given, first of all, no gratitude can be proportionate to it. A gift is something that you cannot be thankful for. As soon as I say "thank you" for a gift, I start canceling the gift, I start destroying the gift, by proposing an equivalence, that is, a circle which encircles the gift in a movement of reappropriation. So, a gift is something that is beyond the circle of

---

[15] Derrida's lectures on "hospitality" are as yet unpublished, but I have provided an overview of his argument below, Part Two, chap. 4, in connection with understanding his hesitations about the word "community."

[16] The most important discussions of the gift are in DT/GT and DM/GD, although the notion was already being analyzed in the texts of the 1970s, most notably *Glas*. I have treated this notion below, Part Two, chap. 5.

reappropriation, beyond the circle of gratitude. A gift should not even be acknowledged as such. As soon as I know that I give something, if I say "I am giving you something," I just canceled the gift. I congratulate myself or thank myself for giving something and then the circle has already started to cancel the gift. So, the gift should not be rewarded, should not be reappropriated, and should not even appear as such. As soon as the gift appears as such then the movement of gratitude, of acknowledgment, has started to destroy the gift, if there is such a thing—I am not sure, one is never sure that there is a gift, that the gift is given. If the gift is given, then it should not even appear to the one who gives it or to the one who receives it, not appear as such. That is paradoxical, but that is the condition for a gift to be given [DT 23–27/DT 11–14].

That is the condition the gift shares with justice. A justice that could appear as such, that could be calculated, a calculation of what is just and what is not just, saying what has to be given in order to be just—that is not justice. That is social security, economics. Justice and gift should go beyond calculation. This does not mean that we should not calculate. We have to calculate as rigorously as possible. But there is a point or limit beyond which calculation must fail, and we must recognize that. What I tried to think or suggest is a concept of the political and of democracy that would be compatible with, that could be articulated with, these impossible notions of the gift and justice. A democracy or a politics that we simply calculate, without justice and the gift, would be a terrible thing, and this is often the case.

JOHN D. CAPUTO: Can we talk a little bit about theology?

JACQUES DERRIDA: We have started already, but we could continue.

JOHN D. CAPUTO. You have written a book called *Circumfession* (*Circonfession*) which is constructed on an analogy with St. Augustine's *Confessions*. That is profoundly interesting to the members of the Villanova University community, which is an institution conducted by the Order of St. Augustine, a Catholic religious order. Like St. Augustine, you were born in what is today Algeria. You were even raised on a street called the *rue Saint-Augustin*.

JACQUES DERRIDA. Two months after I was born, I went back to the house, which was in Algiers, located on the *rue Saint-Augustin*.

JOHN D. CAPUTO: One of the most famous themes of the *Confessions* that you invoke is that, like St. Augustine, your mother was worried about you, that you too were a "son of these tears" (*filius istarum lacrimarum*). She was worried about whether you still believed in God, and she would not ask you about it [cf. *Circon.* 146/*Circum.* 154–155].

JACQUES DERRIDA. Never.

JOHN D. CAPUTO: She did not dare ask you, so she asked everyone else. You go on to say there that, while you "quite rightly pass for an atheist," still "the constancy of God in my life is called by other names [*Circon* 146/*Circum.* 154–155]." Now, I always been interested in the intersection of thinkers like Heidegger and the religious tradition; my earliest work was on the relationship between Heidegger and Meister Eckhart. One of the things that has fascinated me about your work, and of which I am reminded as I listen to you answering Professor Schmidt's question about justice, is how much what you say about justice resonates with the biblical notions of justice and care for singularity, as opposed to the philosophical notion, where justice is defined in terms of universality, of the blindness of justice. The question that I would pose to you today has to do with the messianic, something you address in *Specters of Marx*. In this book, the thematic of *à-venir* and *viens!*, of the impossible future, are framed in terms of what you call a "quasi-atheistic" messianic, which you distinguish from the historical "messianisms," those of the religions of the Book [SdM 265–268/SoM 167–169]. My question is, what do Judaism, the biblical tradition generally, and in particular the prophetic tradition of justice, mean for you and for your work? How can biblical religion and deconstruction communicate with each other? Can they do each other any good? Are they on talking terms with each other?

JACQUES DERRIDA: First of all, I am really intimidated here, not only by this audience, but by this reference to St. Augustine. The way I refer to St. Augustine is really not very orthodox; it is rather—a sin! I have to confess that my relation to St. Augustine's *Confessions* is a little strange. If I had to summarize what I am doing with St. Augustine in *Circumfession*, I would say this. On the one hand, I play with some analogies, that he came from Algeria, that his mother died in Europe, the way my mother was dying in Nice when I was writing this, and so on. I am constantly playing, seriously playing, with this, and quoting sentences from the *Confessions* in Latin,[17] all the while trying, through my love and admiration for St. Augustine—I have enormous and immense admiration for him—to ask questions about a number of axioms, not only in his *Confessions* but in his politics, too. So there is a love story and a deconstruction between us. But I won't insist on St. Augustine, here. It is too difficult, and the way the text is written cannot be taken into account in a forum like this.

To address, more directly, the question of religion—again, in an oversimplifying way—I would say this. First, I have no stable position on the texts you mentioned, the prophets and the Bible. For me, this is an open field, and I can receive the most necessary provocations from these texts as well as, at the same time, from Plato and others. In *Specters of Marx*, I try to reconstitute the link between Marx and some prophets through Shakespeare [cf. SdM 75–78/SoM 41–44]. This does not mean that I am simply a religious person or that I am simply a believer. For me, there is no such thing as "religion" [cf. *Foi*, 37 ff.]. Within what one calls religions—Judaism, Christianity, Islam, or other religions—there are again tensions, heterogeneity, disruptive volcanos, sometimes texts, especially those of the prophets, which cannot be reduced to an institution, to a corpus, to a system. I want to keep the right to read these texts in a way which has to be constantly reinvented. It is something which can be totally new at every moment.

Then I would distinguish between religion and faith. If by religion you mean a set of beliefs, dogmas, or institutions—the church, e.g.—then I would say that religion as such can be deconstructed, and not only can be but should be deconstructed, sometimes in the name of faith. For me, as for you, Kierkegaard is here a great example of some paradoxical way of contesting religious discourse in the name of

---

[17] Derrida uses Latin in *Circumfession* to emphasize the degree to which the Judaism in which he grew up had been assimilated into a Christian world—his family, for example, spoke of "baptism" and "communion" instead of circumcision and *bar mitzvah*. Lacking a language of his own, which should have been either Hebrew (as a Jew) or Arabic (as an Algerian), the French he speaks is a "foreign language," the language of the colonizers, "Christian Latin French," and not his own. See *Circon.* 264–268/*Circum.* 286–290. For a further discussion of Derrida's treatment of the *Confessions* in *Circumfession*, see John D. Caputo, *The Prayers and Tears of Jacques Derrida: Religion Without Religion* (Bloomington: Indiana University Press, 1997), §18. For more on the messianic, see below, Part Two, chap. 6, and *Prayers and Tears*, §§9–10.

a faith that cannot be simply mastered or domesticated or taught or logically understood, a faith that is paradoxical. Now, what I call faith in this case is like something that I said about justice and the gift, something that is presupposed by the most radical deconstructive gesture. You cannot address the other, speak to the other, without an act of faith, without testimony.[18] What are you doing when you attest to something? You address the other and ask, "believe me." Even if you are lying, even in a perjury, you are addressing the other and asking the other to trust you. This "trust me, I am speaking to you" is of the order of faith, a faith that cannot be reduced to a theoretical statement, to a determinative judgment; it is the opening of the address to the other. So this faith is not religious, strictly speaking; at least it cannot be totally determined by a given religion. That is why this faith is absolutely universal. This attention to the singularity is not opposed to universality. I would not oppose, as you did, universality and singularity.[19] I would try to keep the two together. The structure of this act of faith I was just referring to is not as such conditioned by any given religion. That is why it is universal. This does not mean that in any determinate religion you do not find a reference to this pure faith which is neither Christian nor Jewish nor Islamic nor Buddhist, etc.

Now, I would say the same thing about the messianic.[20] When I insisted in *Specters of Marx* on messianicity, which I distinguished from messianism, I wanted to show that the messianic structure is a universal structure. As soon as you address the other, as soon as you are open to the future, as soon as you have a temporal experience of waiting for the future, of waiting for someone to come: that is the opening of experience. Someone is to come, is *now* to come. Justice and peace will have to do with this coming of the other, with the promise. Each time I open my mouth, I am promising something.

---

[18] In his most recent discussion of religion, "Foi et Savoir: Les deux sources de la 'religion' aux limites de la simple raison," in *La Religion*, ed. Jacques Derrida and Gianni Vattimo (Paris: Seuil, 1996), pp. 9–86, Derrida explores the relationship between faith and religion, at the end of which he elaborates upon this question of faith and testimony. For a commentary on this text in particular, see Caputo, *Prayers and Tears*, §11. The question of testimony is of growing importance to him; all the additions he made in the 1993 Galilée edition of *Passions* (ON 3ff.) to the text that appeared in English in 1992 have to do with testimony.

[19] In *Foi* 28, Derrida speaks of messianic justice as a "universalizable culture of singularities," thus combining both the singular and the universal into one expression.

[20] I have discussed Derrida's treatment of the messianic below, Part Two, chap. 6.

When I speak to you, I am telling you that I promise to tell you something, to tell you the truth. Even if I lie, the condition of my lie is that I promise to tell you the truth. So the promise is not just one speech act among others; every speech act is fundamentally a promise. This universal structure of the promise, of the expectation for the future, for the coming, and the fact that this expectation of the coming has to do with justice—that is what I call the messianic structure. This messianic structure is not limited to what one calls messianisms, that is, Jewish, Christian, or Islamic messianism, to these determinate figures and forms of the Messiah. As soon as you reduce the messianic structure to messianism, then you are reducing the universality and this has important political consequences. Then you are accrediting one tradition among others and a notion of an elected people, of a given literal language, a given fundamentalism. That is why I think that the difference, however subtle it may appear, between the messianic and messianism is very important. On the side of messianicity there is faith, no doubt. There is no society without faith, without trust in the other. Even if I abuse this, if I lie or if I commit perjury, if I am violent because of this faith, even on the economic level, there is no society without this faith, this minimal act of faith. What one calls credit in capitalism, in economics, has to do with faith, and the economists know that. But this faith is not and should not be reduced or defined by religion as such.

Now, I will end this discussion with this point. The problem remains—and this is really a problem for me, an enigma—whether the religions, say, for instance, the religions of the Book, are but specific examples of this general structure, of messianicity. There is the general structure of messianicity, as the structure of experience, and on this groundless ground there have been revelations, a history which one calls Judaism or Christianity and so on. That is a possibility, and then you would have a Heideggerian gesture, in style. You would have to go back from these religions to the fundamental ontological conditions of possibilities of religions, to describe the structure of messianicity on the groundless ground on which religions have been made possible.

That is one hypothesis. The other hypothesis—and I confess that I hesitate between these two possibilities—is that the events of revelation, the biblical traditions, the Jewish, Christian, and Islamic traditions, have been absolute events, irreducible events which have unveiled this messianicity. We would not know what messianicity is without messianism, without these events which were Abraham, Moses, and Jesus Christ, and so on. In that case singular events would have unveiled or revealed these universal possibilities, and it is only on that condition that we can describe messianicity. Between the two possibilities I must confess I oscillate and I think some other scheme has to be constructed to understand the two at the same time, to do justice to the two possibilities. That is why—and perhaps this is not a good reason, perhaps one day I will give up this—for the time being I keep the word "messianic." Even if it is different from messianism, messianic refers to the word Messiah; it does not simply belong to a certain culture, a Jewish or Christian culture. I think that for the time being I need this word, not to teach, but to let people understand what I am trying to say when I speak of messianicity. But in doing so I still keep the singularity of a single revelation, that is Jewish, Christian revelation, with its reference to Messiah. It is a reinterpretation of this tradition of the Messiah [cf. SdM 265–268/SoM 167–169].

Let me tell you a story, something I reread recently, and which I quote in the book on friendship [*Politiques de l'amitié*, 55n1], which will be published in a few days. Maurice Blanchot tells this story.[21] The Messiah was at the gates of Rome unrecognized, dressed in rags. But one man who recognized that this was the Messiah went up to him and asked him, "When will you come?" I think this is very profound. It means that there is some inadequation between the now and now. He is coming now; the messianic does not wait. This is a way of waiting for the future, right now. The responsibilities that are assigned to us by this messianic structure are responsibilities for here and now. The Messiah is not some future present; it is imminent and it is this imminence that I am describing under the name of messianic structure.

Now, there is another possibility that I also mentioned in this book on friendship: that the Messiah is not simply the one, the other, that I am constantly waiting for. There would be no experience without the waiting on the coming of the other, the coming of the event, and justice. But the Messiah might also be the one I expect even while I do not want him to come. There is the possibility that my relation to the Messiah is this: I would like him to come, I hope that he will

---

[21] Maurice Blanchot, *The Writing of the Disaster*, trans. Ann Smock (Lincoln: University of Nebraska Press, 1986), pp. 141–142.

come, that the other will come, as other, for that would be justice, peace, and revolution—because in the concept of messianicity there is revolution—and, at the same time, I am scared. I do not want what I want and I would like the coming of the Messiah to be infinitely postponed, and there is this desire in me. That is why the man who addressed the Messiah said, "When will you come?" That is a way to say, well as long as I speak to you, as long as I ask you the question, "When will you come?", at least you are not coming. And that is the condition for me to go on asking questions and living. So there is some ambiguity in the messianic structure. We wait for something we would not like to wait for. That is another name for death.

JAMES MURPHY: I want to ask you about the influence of your work on literary texts and in reverse, in particular your works on James Joyce, where the influence seems to go from him to you, and then from you back again. So you are deconstructing Joyce while Joyce is deconstructing you. Could you expand upon this relationship?

JACQUES DERRIDA: It is already very difficult to write on Joyce, but to speak on Joyce is even more difficult. [22] Nevertheless, I will try to say something. A long time ago, in 1956–57, I spent a year at Harvard, and what I did there was to read Joyce in the Widener Library, which provided my encounter with *Ulysses*. Since then, Joyce has represented for me the most gigantic attempt to gather in a single work, that is, in the singularity of a work which is irreplaceable, in a singular event—I am referring here to *Ulysses* and to *Finnegan's Wake*—the presumed totality, not only of one culture but of a number of cultures, a number of languages, literatures, and religions. This impossible task of precisely gathering in a totality, in a potential totality, the potentially infinite memory of humanity is, at the same time and in an exemplary way, both new in its modern form and very classical in its philosophical form. That is why I often compare *Ulysses* to Hegel, for instance, to the *Encyclopedia* or the *Logic*, as an attempt to reach absolute knowledge through a single act of memory. This is made possible only by loading every sentence, every word, with a maximum of equivocalities, virtual associations, by making this organic linguistic totality as rich as possible. Of course, at the same time, this attempt reassembled

---

[22] See below, Part Two, chap. 7.

the history of literature and inaugurated and produced a break in the
history of literature. What I tried to show also in my work on Joyce is
that, at the same time, the writing of these works functions as an in-
junction to the academy, that is, to literary critics to come, to the
institution of Joycean scholarship, to build a sort of beehive, an infinite
institution of people working as interpreters and philologists, people
deciphering Joyce's signature as a singular signature. From that point
of view I think that Joyce is a great landmark in the history of deconstruction. That is why the reference to Joyce is important to me.

In my first book on Husserl [*Husserl's "Origin of Geometry": An
Introduction*, 1962] I tried to compare the way Joyce treats language
and the way a classical philosopher such as Husserl treats language.
Joyce wanted to make history, the resuming and the totalization of
history, possible through the accumulation of metaphoricities, equivocalities, and tropes. Husserl, on the other hand, thought that historicity was made possible by the transparent univocity of language, that is,
by a scientific, mathematical, pure language. There is no historicity
without the transparency of the tradition, Husserl says, while Joyce
says there is no historicity without this accumulation of equivocality
in language. It is from the tension between these two interpretations
of language that I tried to address the question of language [cf. HOdG
104–107/HOG 102–104]

I would mention only two other points in Joyce in reference to our
current discussion. One has to do with what Joyce calls at some point
the legal fiction of fatherhood [UG 135/AL 304]. This is a very Christian moment, when Stephen Daedalus says that paternity is a legal
fiction, and he refers to well-known Christian texts. Why is that so?
Because one is supposed to know who the mother is. There is the
possibility of bearing witness to who the mother is, whereas the father
is only reconstructed, inferred. The identification of the father is always resigning a judgment; you cannot see the father. Our experience
today is that it is not only the father who is a legal fiction, from which
it draws and has drawn its authority. Freud confirms this by saying that
patriarchy represents progress in the history of mankind, because to
determine who the father is, you need reason, whereas to determine
who the mother is, you need only sensible perception. I think he is
wrong, and he has always been wrong but we know this now better
than ever. For today the mother is also a legal fiction from that point
of view. Motherhood is something which is interpreted, the theme

of a reconstruction from experience. What one calls today surrogate mothers, for instance, and all the enormous problems that you are familiar with, attest to the fact that we do not know who the mother is. Who is the mother in the case of surrogate mothers? And when we realize that motherhood is not simply a matter of perception, we realize that it has never been so. The mother has always been a matter of interpretation, of social construction. This has enormous political consequences, which we do not have time to deal with now. But if we had time, I would try to show what the equivocal consequences would be of this fact that the situation of the mother is the same as that of the father. That is the first thing I insisted on in this text on Joyce.

The second thing I would select here has to do the question of the "yes." In my short essay on Joyce, I tried to deal only with the word "yes" as it was performed, so to speak, in *Ulysses*. I tried to show all the paradoxes that are linked to the question of the "yes," and this has to do with the fact that deconstruction is "yes," is linked to the "yes," is an affirmation. As you know, "yes" is the last word in *Ulysses*. When I say "yes" to the other, in the form of a promise or an agreement or an oath, the "yes" must be absolutely inaugural. Inauguration is the theme today. Inauguration is a "yes." I say "yes" as a starting point. Nothing precedes the "yes." The "yes" is the moment of institution, of the origin; it is absolutely originary. But when you say "yes," you imply that in the next moment you will have to confirm the "yes" by a second "yes." When I say "yes," I immediately say "yes, yes." I commit myself to confirm my commitment in the next second, and then tomorrow, and then the day after tomorrow. That means that a "yes" immediately duplicates itself, doubles itself. You cannot say "yes" without saying "yes, yes." That implies memory in that promise. I promise to keep the memory of the first "yes." In a wedding, for instance, or in a promise, when you say "yes, I agree," "I will," you imply "I will say 'I will' tomorrow," and "I will confirm my promise"; otherwise there is no promise. That means that the "yes" keeps in advance the memory of its own beginning, and that is the way traditions work. If, tomorrow, you do not confirm that today you have founded your program, there will not have been any inauguration. Tomorrow, perhaps next year, perhaps twenty years from now, you will know whether today there has been an inauguration. We do not know that yet. We pretend that today we are inaugurating something. But who knows? We will see. So "yes" has to be repeated and repeated immediately. That is what I call iterability. It implies repetition of itself, which is also threatening, because the second "yes" may be simply a parody, a record, or a mechanical repetition. You may say "yes, yes" like a parrot. The technical reproduction of the originary "yes" is from the beginning a threat to the living origin of the "yes." So the "yes" is haunted by its own ghost, its own mechanical ghost, from the beginning. The second "yes" will have to reinaugurate, to reinvent, the first one. If tomorrow you do not reinvent today's inauguration, you will be dead. So the inauguration has to be reinvented everyday.

JOHN D. CAPUTO: Professor Derrida, thank you very much.

PART TWO

A Commentary:
Deconstruction in a Nutshell

1

Deconstruction in a Nutshell: The Very Idea (!)

"One day, two years ago, when I was in Cambridge . . . a journalist took the microphone and said, 'Well, could you tell me, in a nutshell, what is deconstruction?' Sometimes, of course, I confess, I am not able to do that. But sometimes it may be useful to try nutshells."

—"Roundtable," 16

THE APORETICS OF THE NUTSHELL

Deconstruction in a nutshell? Why, the very idea!

The very idea of a nutshell is a mistake and a misunderstanding, an excess—or rather a defect—of journalistic haste and impatience, a ridiculous demand put by someone who has never read a word of Derrida's works (*Points* 406). Nutshells enclose and encapsulate, shelter and protect, reduce and simplify, while everything in deconstruction is turned toward opening, exposure, expansion, and complexification (*Points* 429), toward releasing unheard-of, undreamt-of possibilities *to come*, toward cracking nutshells wherever they appear.

The very meaning and mission of deconstruction is to show that things—texts, institutions, traditions, societies, beliefs, and practices of whatever size and sort you need—do not have definable meanings and determinable missions, that they are always more than any mission would impose, that they exceed the boundaries they currently occupy. What is really going on in things, what is really happening, is always to come. Every time you try to stabilize the meaning of a thing, to fix it in its missionary position, the thing itself, if there is anything at all to it, slips away (VP 117/SP 104). A "meaning" or a "mission" is a way to contain and compact things, like a nutshell, gathering them

into a unity, whereas deconstruction bends all its efforts to stretch beyond these boundaries, to transgress these confines, to interrupt and
disjoin all such gathering.

Whenever it runs up against a limit, deconstruction presses against
it. Whenever deconstruction finds a nutshell—a secure axiom or a
pithy maxim—the very idea is to crack it open and disturb this tran-
quillity. Indeed, that is a good rule of thumb in deconstruction. *That*
is what deconstruction is all about, its very meaning and mission, if it
has any. One might even say that cracking nutshells is what deconstruction *is*. In a nutshell.

But then have we not gone too far? Have we not run up against a
paradox and an aporia? To put in a nutshell what refuses to let itself
be so put, not just because, as a matter of fact, deconstruction is too
complicated to summarize, but because it is, in principle, opposed to
the very idea of a nutshell and bends all its efforts to *cracking* nutshells.
And then to see, having said this, that *that* is not a bad way of putting
what deconstruction *is*, if it is. Once we have dismissed the very idea
of a nutshell, indignantly slammed the door behind us, it swings backs
and slams us in return (you know where). Let us call this the aporetics
of the nutshell.

Still, this aporia is not the end of the road. For the paralysis and
impossibility of an aporia is just what impels deconstruction, what
rouses it out of bed in the morning, what drives it on and calls it into
action. Indeed, one might even say, maybe it has already been said,
that "the experience of the impossible" (FL 35/DPJ 15), being in an
impossible fix, is just what deconstruction is all about.[1] Indeed, even
when no one has stuck a microphone in his face, whenever he simply
feels the need to summarize and briefly characterize deconstruction,
Derrida often has recourse to this expression: "experience of the impossible." He even says it is the "least bad" way to define deconstruction,
that is, the least bad nutshell.

Deconstruction is the relentless pursuit of *the* impossible, which
means, of things whose possibility is sustained by their impossibility,
of things which, instead of being wiped out by their impossibility, are
actually nourished and fed by it. Derrida says he likes the old word

---

[1] I have documented at some length the pervasiveness of this expression in Derrida's works in *Prayers and Tears of Jacques Derrida*. A recent issue of *The Oxford Literary Review*, 15, Nos. 1–2 (1993), ed. Timothy Clark and Nicholas Royle, was very
nicely entitled "Experiencing the Impossible."

"experience," taken not in the traditional, dusty phenomenological sense, which means to perceive what presents itself, but rather when it is "dusted off" a little so that it can take on a deconstructive sense. Then "experience" means running up against the limits of what can *never* be present, passing to the limits of the unpresentable and unrepresentable, which is what we most desire, namely, the impossible (PdS 221, 387/*Points* 207, 373). The impossible is more interesting than the possible and provokes more interesting results, provided that anything at all results. Therefore, it is "not that bad that we try to encapsulate deconstruction in a nutshell," to give it its least bad definition, provided we do not try it too often and provided we admit, nay, love, the impossible situation in which it is ensnared, by which it is impassioned.

That is the foolhardy, impossible task we set ourselves here. To follow Derrida around the "Roundtable" as he lays out, expounds, "exposes" certain basic gestures in a deconstructive approach to things, just enough to encapsulate it, to mark off its style and what he himself will call its "signature," to catch the spirit, some of the several and uncontainable spirits, of a certain way to read and write, to think and act called deconstruction—all along appreciating the aporia in which this implicates us. For the aporia of the nutshell is not without merit: to see that in deconstruction wherever we find a nutshell, the idea is to crack it, *and*—this is *the* impossible—to see that that is what deconstruction is, that that is a certain way, *per impossibile*, to condense it. In a nutshell, a certain auto-deconstructing nutshell.

We may read the "Roundtable" as offering several such nutshells, several succinct encapsulations of deconstruction in terms of justice, the gift, the messianic, the institution, traditions, hospitality, faith, the affirmation of the other, the *viens*, the *oui, oui*, the impossible, etc. Indeed, I will go so far as to say that, once you "try nutshells," as Derrida puts it, the precise problem will be *not* that deconstruction cannot be concisely condensed into a nutshell—I have found many a nutshell strewn around Derrida's texts—but, if anything, that there are too many nutshells scattered hither and yon. That is a result at which we ought not to express too much surprise or dismay, for in a philosophy where "dissemination" plays a major role, we should expect rather more disseminative strewing than Heideggerian gathering. But it is a well-known philosophical axiom, handed down to us by the ancients—I am sure it is to be found somewhere in Diogenes Laertius—

that too many nutshells make for no nutshell at all, as when a man swears up and down that he is making now a deep and lifelong vow, that this the defining moment in his life, that his whole life is condensed into this single moment, but does this regularly, on the hour, each time revising his resolution.

So, then, we will need a way to think about the nutshell, an abstract, theoretical model of the nutshell, a paradigm (or two) powerful enough to help us "think"—in the transitive mode—the nutshell in its very being and essence, its very coming-into-being and emerging into unconcealment as a nutshell, its very *Wesen* (understood verbally, to be sure), if it has one. Several such complex and advanced models leap to mind:

• Think of the nutshell on this disseminative model I just mentioned, as a seed to plant, to be squirreled away here and there, like an acorn or a chestnut, within the nurturing soil. By planting nuts that they sometimes forget, which then grow into mature trees, squirrels serve an important ecological and disseminative function (provided that their memories are weak enough). So, with enough nuts and squirrels, you could have a full-grown forest, a whole field of deconstructive works and practices.

• But if it troubles you to think of Derrida and deconstruction as a bunch of nuts and squirrels, something we are trying in fact in the present work devoutly to avoid, think of these little nutshells, these little capsules, "pyrotechnically"—*feu la cendre*—which, alas, must eventually turn to ash.[2] Think of them as compact little fireworks devices that, when set off—the trick being how to release their energy and power without getting burnt—fill the sky with the most magnificent display of color and form, not to mention a terrific, explosive boom. Deconstruction then would be a way to light the night air with awe-inspiring color, with a magnificent pyrotechnic plumage, beginning with a simple little saying or phrase.

• Or you may, in a related way, think of these nutshells as six missiles fired into the establishment's camp, so that if the powers that be saw one of them heading at their head they would, after shouting

---

[2] As a trace and a figure of the trace, as a quasi-being neither quite present nor absent, the image of the "cinder" runs throughout Derrida's work. See *Cinders*, trans. Ned Lukacher (Lincoln: University of Nebraska Press, 1991), a bilingual edition containing the text of *Feu la cendre* (Paris: Des femmes, 1987).

"incoming," quickly scatter.[3] The limitations of this and the previous model are twofold. On the one hand they invite his critics to think of Derrida as simply shooting off his mouth, which again is a confusion we aim to quell. On the other hand, they give an unduly negative idea of deconstruction, as if the aim of deconstruction is simply to take aim on our most cherished institutions and blow them out of the water, as if deconstruction is not to be distinguished from a simple destruction.[4] That again is something of which we mean to disabuse our readers, if there are any.

• So, then, in a final gesture, think of these nutshells, still one more time, as samplers to be tasted, like those selections of four or five of the best products of the local microbrewery served on an inviting tray, and think of the present volume as a "Derrida Sampler" and just such a tray. The result of reading this little book, then, will have been to savor some of the several flavors of deconstruction, the idea being not to slake one's thirst but to stir one's desire, to whet one's appetite to drink more deeply of the deconstructive well.

But I must add a word of caution about the advanced, abstract, and highly theoretical character of the models here proposed, a word to the wary about what I do *not* mean by a nutshell, and this is important in order to protect Derrida and deconstruction whenever it tries nutshells. Although I vow and promise, and concentrate my entire life into this resolution, that I will speak American English and not bury the reader alive in jargon, I am not saying that what follows is really simple and easy to understand, that deconstruction can be treated in a facile way. Although nutshells are made for cracking, they can still be hard to crack, and I do not mean to engage in false advertising, to trick the unwary, into thinking that I am going to simplify and summarize to an extreme. I am taking up certain themes, certain motifs, without pretending to take up everything, and exhibiting how deconstructive approaches work (since there is not only one and there are many deconstructions). I want to show what sorts of moves deconstruction makes in given situations, what sorts of results it produces under cer-

---

[3] I borrow this model from a piece by Derrida on the arms race, "No Apocalypse, Not Now (full speed ahead, seven missiles, seven missives)," trans. Catherine Porter and Philip Lewis, *Diacritics*, 14 (Summer 1984), 20–31.

[4] For example, in *Foi* 62ff., Derrida worries about grenades or shells in connection with Islamic fundamentalism.

tain circumstances, what are some of its characteristic gestures, strategies, styles, twists and turns. I am doing so within a limited amount of
space, with the hope that, later on, readers, having been disabused of
the abuse heaped on deconstruction, will be motivated to look into
these matters further, to try to crack these nuts on their own, which
will involve buying a certain amount of difficulty for themselves. Like
Johannes Climacus,[5] whose methodological difficulty is also drama-
tized near the end of The Life of Brian, I am trying by these nutshells
to get the reader, to get you, to do something on your own without its
being said that Derrida or I got you to do it and thereby made it easy
for you. Neither Derrida nor I am trying to rob you of your anxiety.

The Axiomatics of Indignation: The Very Idea!

The idea will be to give the reader an idea of what deconstruction is
up to or about, just enough, without burying you in every microdebate
into which Derrida and deconstruction has been drawn,[6] without
drawing you down every complex corridor of a formidably subtle
thinker. The questions put to Derrida by his interlocutors in the
"Roundtable" aim, on the whole, at dispelling the idea that Derrida is
a nut. It is not uncommon to portray Derrida as the devil himself, a
street-corner anarchist, a relativist, or subjectivist, or nihilist, out to
destroy our traditions and institutions, our beliefs and values, to mock
philosophy and truth itself, to undo everything the Enlightenment has
done—and to replace all this with wild nonsense and irresponsible
play. That, alas, is how he is portrayed by his—often very irresponsible—critics who speak in the name of academic responsibility. Elaborating and documenting the way the "Roundtable" puts the torch to
this stupefying misrepresentation of deconstruction is a principal goal,
nay, the most solemn duty, of the present volume.
    The thrust of each of the questions put to Derrida in the "Roundta-
ble" was to press him about the relevance of deconstruction to the
most traditional values of institution, tradition, community, justice,

---

[5] Kierkegaard's Works. XII.1. Concerning Unscientific Postscript to the "Philosophical Fragments," trans. Howard Hong and Edna Hong (Princeton: Princeton University Press, 1992), pp. 72–80.
    [6] For an account of the various debates into which Derrida has entered, see Niall
Lucy, Debating Derrida (Melbourne: Melbourne University Press, 1995).

and religion. The occasion was a solemn moment in the life of Villa-nova University, a well-established university in the middle of its second century of life, which was inaugurating a new doctoral program in a department that is one of the departments that define—what else can I say?—the "mission" of this university. So, all were on their best behavior, trying to make deconstruction (look) respectable, and Derrida was eloquent about the place of deconstruction at the heart of our most time-honored and hoary institutions.

Derrida was trying to persuade us that deconstruction is on our side, that it means to be good news, and that it does not leave behind a path of destruction and smoldering embers. Of course, he was not saying, God forbid, that deconstruction is—and he is *also* accused of this—a form of conservativism. He has always done everything he can to resist conservativism, has always tried to be productive not reproductive, to reread and revise the oldest of the old, to unfold what has been folded over by and in the tradition, to show the pliant multiplicity of the innumerable traditions that are sheltered within "tradition." The very idea that the tradition is one—"*the one* history itself . . . *the one* tradition"—is what needs to be "contested at its root," he says (*Sauf* 85/ON 71). A tradition is not a hammer with which to slam dissent and knock dissenters senseless, but a responsibility to read, to interpret, to sift and select responsibly among many competing strands of tradition and interpretations of tradition. If you have a tradition, you have to take *responsibility* for it and for its multiplicity (SdM 40/SoM 160). But that, of course, is the only way to conserve a tradition. That is why Derrida says in the "Roundtable," to the surprise no doubt of many, "So, you see, I am a very conservative person." For he sees deconstruction as a way to keep the *event* of tradition going, to keep it on the move, so that it can be continually translated into new events, continually exposed to a certain revolution in a self-perpetuating auto-revolution. That is an aporia that conservativism can never swallow. That is why conservativism is such a limp and mummifying theory of a "tradition," which is a bigger, wider, more diffuse and mobile, more self-revising and "auto-deconstructing" idea than "conservativism."

Let me risk, with fear and trembling, the following axiom which governs what I call a certain "axiomatics of indignation" that Derrida seems to provoke: the most fundamental misunderstanding to beset Derrida and deconstruction is the mistaken impression that is given of a kind of anarchistic relativism in which "anything goes." On this view, texts mean anything the reader wants them to mean; traditions are just monsters to be slain or escaped from; the great masters of the Western tradition are dead white male tyrants whose power must be broken and whose name defamed; institutions are just power-plays oppressing everyone; and language is a prison, just a game of signifiers signifying nothing, a play of differences without reference to the real world. Thus the dominant reaction that Derrida provokes among his critics, who do not content themselves with simply disagreeing with him, is indignation. His critics seem immediately to shift into high dudgeon, cloaking themselves in a self-righteous "moral" or "ethical" mantle—where ethics has the look of a self-approving good conscience—appointing themselves Defenders of the Good and the True. Critics of deconstruction feel obliged to rush to their closets, dust off and don their academic suits of armor, and then collectively charge this enemy of the common good, their lances pointed at his heart. For if Derrida's shenanigans arouse their ire when deconstruction is confined to reading Joyce or Mallarmé, you can imagine how the tempers of these Knights of the Good and True flare when deconstruction threatens to spill over into the streets, when it gets translated into politics and ethics. Then the influence of this dreadful nihilism is intolerable, for it poses a threat to the common good. *Ergo*, we, the Good and the Just (self-authorized and self-knighted, to be sure)—that is what "we" almost always means—must stamp it out.

Just in case you think I am exaggerating or making this up, let us revisit the occasion to which Derrida briefly refers when in the "Roundtable" he adverts to "this terrible honorary degree crisis in Cambridge." In the spring of 1992 Derrida was nominated to receive an honorary degree from Cambridge University. On May 9, 1992, a letter was published in the London *Times* urging the faculty of Cambridge to vote against awarding this degree to Derrida (see *Points* 419–421). To begin with, we may ask, who had appointed the signatories protectors of Cambridge University? Does the University not have its own board of protectors? Has it not been able to get along for centuries without such help? Are the dons not adult enough to be able to make up their own minds? Be that as it may, the alleged grounds for this extraordinary intervention of outsiders—this was the first time in thirty years that such a vote was required[7]—were, among other things, that

---

[7] See N. Rothwell, "Those Dons and the Derrida To-Do," *Australian Higher Education Supplement*, 626 (May 13, 1992), 13; "Honour Served in Derrida Affair," ibid., 627 (May 20, 1992), 13, 20; Bennington and Derrida, *Jacques Derrida*, p. 331.

Derrida's "style defies comprehension" and that "where coherent assertions are being made at all, these are either false or trivial." The
final blast in this letter runs like this:

> Academic status based on what seems to us little more than semi-intelli-
> gible attacks upon the values of reason, truth, and scholarship is not,
> we submit, sufficient grounds for the awarding of an honorary degree
> in a distinguished university [Points 420–421].

The signatories, who say they are signing "sincerely"—including
Ruth Barcan Marcus and Wilfred Van Orman Quine (some gratitude![8]) in the United States—constitute a kind of international association of "officials of anti-deconstruction" (Pass. 41/ON 17) who, while
trying very hard to make themselves look international (Barry Smith
gets to sign his name twice, once as the *agent provocateur* and once as
"International Academy of Philosophy" at Liechtenstein!) are in fact
for the most part intensely narrow "analytic" philosophers. Of Marcus,
in particular, one might say that she has made a career out of—her
"academic status seems to us based upon"—attacking "continental"
and more generally non-analytic philosophers wherever she finds
them, and maintaining the dominance of a narrow and culturally irrel-
evant style of philosophizing in the American Philosophical Association and Ivy Leagues departments of philosophy, resistant to its own
history, to history itself, and to the socio-political matrix of philosophizing in every age.

In this, alas, she and her friends have largely succeeded, with the
result that philosophy today tends to be of almost no importance whatsoever in the United States and in most of its major universities.
Indeed, the only places one can read Hegel—not to mention Derrida—in these institutions are the comparative literature and modern
language departments, something that has served greatly to promote
the growth of departments other than philosophy. In a fascinating and
provocative study, John McCumber has suggested recently that this
cultural and political isolation, this "bleak house" of analytic philosophy, was a state of affairs actively embraced by analytic philosophy in

---

[8] One of Derrida's earliest publications was a translation into French of an article
by Quine, "Les frontières de la théorie logique," trans. J. Derrida and R. Martin,
Études Philosophiques, 2 (1964), 191–208. Also, in his autobiography, Quine reports
borrowing the office of Derrida while in Paris for a visit. See W. V. O. Quine, The
Time of My Life: An Autobiography (Cambridge: The MIT Press, 1985), p. 355.

the era of McCarthyism, a way of protecting itself from attack by the House Un-American Activities Committee in the 1950s, that has persisted, anachronistically, into our own day.[9] Richard Rorty, the one American philosopher to break loose from that church of latter-day analytic *Aufklärers* and to make himself, in the spirit of William James or John Dewey, into a public intellectual, has been excommunicated from their club, no doubt by the Unanalytic Activities Committee— after having excused or excommunicated himself from their ranks.

It is inconceivable to me that the signatories of this letter, despite their "yours *sincerely*," have read Derrida with care, if they have read him at all. What they know of Derrida, I would bet the farm, if I had one, has been gathered by hearsay and the public press, from secondary, not to say second-rate sources, from dinner-hour gossip at annual meetings of groups like the A.P.A., from at most a casual scanning of a famous text or other. Their condemnation of Derrida is not a carefully reasoned and researched judgment, but an allergic reaction to something different, an expression of contempt for a different philosophical style by which they are shocked and scandalized; but it is impossible to believe they have carefully studied what they have denounced. In other words, their condemnation of Derrida violates on its face the very "values of reason, truth, and scholarship" with which they so self-righteously cloak themselves, in the name of disinterestedly "protecting" Cambridge University from itself. As if anyone asked them! As if, and "this is *also* extremely funny" (*Points* 404) even as it is extremely serious, the faculty of Cambridge University needed to be protected from itself by the International Academy of Philosophy of Liechtenstein![10]

The very idea!

The very idea that anything as irresponsible as this letter could be signed in the name of responsible scholarship, that the people who signed such a thing can sleep at night, gives one an idea of the axiomatics of indignation, of the reaction that the name "Derrida" provokes. So the reader will trust me when I say that Derrida is a bit of

---

[9] See John McCumber, "Time in the Ditch: American Philosophy and the McCarthy Era," *Diacritics*, 26, No. 1 (Spring 1996), 33–49. McCumber also suggests that the record of the American Philosophical Association in defending its own members from attacks by the HUAC was singularly "unpleasant."

[10] He won the vote, the first necessary in thirty years, 336 to 204; see Bennington and Derrida, *Jacques Derrida*, p. 331.

a *bête noire* in certain bastions of the academic establishment, both American and French. Alas, the meanness of spirit and intellectual shortsightedness of it all! For Derrida's analyses often converge with, and have even taken their point of departure from, "analytic" philosophers. Derrida patiently explores the meanings and use of words with a sensitivity—at certain moments even matching the same level of tediousness of analytic philosophy—that would be the envy of any Ivy league dissertation director.[11]

You will believe me, then, although I will also document it, that Derrida and "deconstruction," as we will see, have been blamed for almost everything. For ruining American departments of philosophy, English, French, and comparative literature, for ruining the university itself (provided that they are ruined), for dimming the lights of the Enlightenment, for undermining the law of gravity, for destroying all standards of reading, writing, reason—(and 'rithmetic, too)—and also for Mormon polygamy. Derrida even gets a finger (pointed at him) for the nationalist wars in Central Europe and for Holocaust revisionism, even as he has been accused, if it is possible to be guilty of all these things at once, of an apolitical aestheticism, for being a flower child of the 1960s still being read in the 1990s, a quasi-academic Timothy Leary inviting us to tune into textuality and drop out of reality. The list goes on.

(For Mormon polygamy?)

The way out of these misunderstandings of Derrida—which incidentally also accuse him of undermining the very idea of misunderstanding anything, since "anything goes" (*Points* 401)—is to see that, far from being nihilistic, deconstruction is deeply and profoundly "affirmative." *Oui, oui.* To be sure, deconstruction does not affirm what *is*, does not fall down adoringly before what is *present*, for the present is precisely what demands endless analysis, criticism, and deconstruction. (An old and hoary tradition—*n'est-ce pas?*—that goes back to Socrates, with whom philosophy, on some accounting, opened its doors.) On the contrary, deconstruction affirms what is to come, *à*

---

[11] This is not to say that red faces are found lacking among Continentalist critics. J. Claude Evans, *Strategies of Deconstruction: Derrida and the Myth of the Voice* (Minneapolis: University of Minnesota Press, 1991) seems to me also to punctuate his arguments against Derrida with a flow of insults, debating at length whether Derrida's reading of Husserl is a joke or whether we are supposed to take it seriously.

venir, which is what its deconstruction of the present, and of the values of presence, is all about. So radical is this deconstructive impulse that the *à venir* itself is not to be construed in terms of presence, viz., as the "future present," as something that will eventually roll around if we are patient, but rather as something that is structurally and necessarily to come, always still outstanding, never present. Deconstructive analysis deprives the present of its prestige and exposes it to something *tout autre*, "wholly other," beyond what is foreseeable from the present, beyond the horizon of the "same." Deconstruction, I will argue here, is the endless, bottomless affirmation of the absolutely undeconstructible.

But let us keep the metaphorics of the nutshell straight: the "undeconstructible" does not mean the "uncrackable" but, rather, that in virtue of which nutshells can be cracked, in order to make an opening for the coming of the other. The undeconstructible, if such a thing exists, is that in virtue of which whatever exists, whatever poses as assured and secure, whole and meaningful, ensconced, encircled, and encapsulated is pried open—cracked open and deconstructed.

Accordingly, everything in deconstruction—here comes a nutshell (heads up!)—is organized around what Derrida calls *l'invention de l'autre*, the in-coming of the other, the promise of an event to come, the event of the promise of something coming. Indeed, I will argue below, deconstruction is best thought of as a certain *inventionalism*. For if Derrida is anything but an essentialist, someone who hangs everything on the hook of unchanging essences, that does not mean he is a conventionalist, which is but an alternative way to hang things up (or tie them down), this time by way of a certain settled but contingent way things have tended historically to have fallen out. Both essentialism and conventionalism are too binding for him, too much inclined to hang things up or tie them down, whereas the business of deconstruction is to open and loosen things up. Deconstruction means to be essentially anti-essential and highly unconventional, not to let its eyes wax over at the thought of either unchanging essences or ageless traditions, but rather to advocate an in-ventionalistic incoming, to stay constantly on the lookout for something unforeseeable, something new. Deconstruction is a way of giving things a new twist; it is bent on giving things a new bent, which is what sets the nerves of both essentialists and conventionalists on edge.

For example, and this is not just an example but the very idea of deconstruction, everything in deconstruction is turned toward a "democracy to come." For even if the existing democracies are the best we can do at present, the least bad way to organize ourselves, still the present democratic structures are deeply undemocratic. They are corrupted, among other things, by the money that blatantly buys votes, by corporate contributions to politicians and political parties that frees their corporate hand to fill the air and water with carcinogens, to encourage smoking by the youngest and poorest people in our society; by cowardly politicians who believe in nothing, who change their views with each new poll, who perpetuate themselves with demagogic promises, who appeal to the worst and lowest instincts of the populace; by media that corrupt national discourse, that fuel the fires of nationalist resentment and racism and stampede voters. (Rather the way the letter in the *London Times* tried, unsuccessfully, I am happy to report, to stampede the Cambridge dons.)

American politicians regularly predicate their careers on promises to lower taxes, exclude immigrants, throw the weakest and most defenseless people in our society—usually black and Hispanic women and children—on their own under the cloak of "reform" and "freedom," thereby filling the pockets of the richest members of society. In the highest hypocrisy of all, they try to ram down every one's throat a right wing, xenophobic, reactionary Christianity that has nothing to do with, which flies in the face of, Jesus's prophetic fervor and his stand with the weakest and most outcast among people. They claim that the United States was founded on Christian principles while dismissing the mass genocide of native Americans by the colonizing, Christianizing, missionary Europeans. Their "Christian" message of hatred for the other and self-aggrandizement, their skill at turning the crucifixion into a profitable business, has more to do with the self-righteous hypocrisy of what Kierkegaard called "Christendom" than with Jesus's prophetic denunciation of the powers that be.[12]

Democracy does not exist, and the corruption of existing democracies must become the subject of endless analysis, critique, and decon-

---

[12] For a way to read Kierkegaard—something that I am always interested in—that shows his convergence with "post-modernism," whatever that means, let us say with recent Continental thought, including Derrida, which takes Kierkegaard, and not just Nietzsche, as an antecedent of recent Continental thought, see *Kierkegaard and Post-Modernity*, ed. Martin Matustik and Merold Westphal (Bloomington: Indiana University Press, 1995).

struction, for these democracies are hardly democratic. The idea of such analyses is not to level democratic institutions to the ground but to open them up to a democracy to come, to turn them around from what they are at present, which is the pre-vention of the other, forces that forestall in advance anything different or radically new. The very idea, the very in-ventionalist idea, of deconstruction is to open democracy to its own promise, to what it promises to become: to provide a chance or an opening for the invention, the in-coming, of the other (which is not a bad way to define immigration). Preparing for the in-coming of the other, which is what constitutes a radical democracy — that is what deconstruction *is* (*Psy.* 59–60/RDR 60), something that would also be, on my accounting, a little more biblical and a lot less hypocritical.

(In a nutshell).

That is why the "Roundtable" took the form it did, to provide Derrida with the opportunity to address a more or less traditional audience on issues on which he has provoked a more or less (mostly more) indignant reaction. Issues such as these — tradition, community, justice, democracy, religion, and institutional life — are close to the hearts of everyone, if they have a heart. Remember, this very discussion was an important moment in the life of a traditional institution that invited Jacques Derrida to be the man of the moment, the man who was asked to illuminate this inaugural moment. Derrida was trying to look respectable, which is not hard, because he and deconstruction are worthy of the highest respect. Indeed, and here comes another nutshell, one might go so far as to say deconstruction is respect, respect for the other, a respectful, responsible affirmation of the other, a way if not to efface at least to delimit the narcissism of the self (which is, quite literally, a tautology) and to make some space to let the other be. That is a good way to start out thinking about institutions, traditions, communities, justice, and religion.

APOLOGIA: AN EXCUSE FOR VIOLENCE

I should say a word or two about the present format, about the multiple violence of forcing Derrida to speak in English (when he complains that the whole world is gradually being forced to speak English), to make himself understood by a mixed audience composed of people from across all the colleges and departments in the University, but, above all, to give relatively compacted answers within the confines of about an hour and a half. To begin with, I openly confess to a proper and proportionate amount of guilt for perpetrating such violence, about which Derrida quite rightly complains throughout the "Roundtable." *Cur confitemur deo scienti* (*Circum.* 19/*Circum.* 18)? Derrida says at one point in the "Roundtable," just after another impossible question had been put to him, "If I were more responsible, I would simply say 'No, I won't, I won't participate in this game.' " After which, he proceeds to say something very interesting in response to the question. (The aporetics of the nutshell.) But I would also propose, in my own defense, that there is something very fitting about putting Derrida on the spot like this and hence I offer the following "apology" for all this violence.

Derrida is very much a public philosopher, an urban, cosmopolitan intellectual—contrary to Heidegger, say, who beat a hasty retreat to his *Hütte* in the Schwarzwald whenever the opportunity presented itself. By this I mean that he is someone whose work, whose productivity, has never been insulated from the international reaction it provokes, whose work has flourished in an ongoing interaction with an international readership. His published writings, by and large, are collections of papers given at conferences and lectureships around the world to which he has been invited by people who have been reading his work at the time and who have reason to believe that he would have something to say on a given topic. His writing always arises, he says, "from some *external* provocation," "some request, invitation, or commission" (PdS 363/*Points* 352; cf. 128/119). His hosts think they can predict what Derrida will say on this or that issue, so they invite him, and his job is to surprise them without disappointing them, to live up to the invitation and a very considerable reputation while starting out from scratch, *de novo*.

That, of course, is partly a reflection of the jet age, which makes international philosophizing and conferencing possible. (It is interesting to ponder how the ease of international travel would have affected Kant, who never left Königsberg. Would Kant, like Heidegger, have been content to stay at home and watch these big birds fly overhead?) But I think this international colloquializing has, in addition, a lot to do with Derrida's own philosophical style or signature. His works do not reflect a long-range plan or private program staked out in advance years ago that he has been relentlessly and single-mindedly carrying out. He has not been grimly stalking some philosophical prey. Each time he takes up a topic, he says, it is as if he has never written anything before, as if he is starting all over again in the face of an overwhelming novelty and strangeness (PdS 363/*Points* 352).

So, if Derrida has a style, a signature, a dominant tone, a unity of purpose, if his works weave a certain fabric, it is up to someone else to trace that signature out later on, to counter-sign it for him. It is not his business and it would be stultifying for him to have to obey any such internal imperative, to censor himself, to pursue such an image, to abide by a contract that has been signed for him without his consent.

"I have never had a 'fundamental project,' " he says in an interview (PdS 367/*Points* 356).[13] He has not projected to write three great critiques, as Kant did; nor do hundreds of assistant professors, in heat over promotion and tenure, pour over his works and fill the journals with articles speculating on the likely contents of the missing part of a great treatise that he left unfinished, in which he would finally announce the meaning of Being. Even *Of Grammatology*, the closest thing to a comprehensive treatise in his writings, started out as a discussion article on three books published in the early 1960s.[14] His texts thus embody the very occasionalism, chance, and openness to the coming of something unforeseeable that he loves so much as a theorist. Each work wrestles anew, *de novo*, with the idiosyncrasies of ever shifting singularities. His works reflect the ability, to be described below, to keep his head without having a heading (*cap*), to forge ahead in another way than with a heading, to move ahead without having a plan that programs things in advance, which is part of the twist he gives to the title of a little book of his called *The Other Heading*. (That is also not a bad way, incidentally, to condense deconstruction into a nutshell.)

Derrida has done a great deal of his work in public, or at least not far from the public: writing on airplanes, trying to finish papers in time

---

[13] To the extent there is such a project, it is one that is not to be carried out: "As for a book project, I have only one, the one I will not write, but that guides, attracts, seduces everything I read. Everything I read is either forgotten or else stored up in view of this book" (PdS 151/*Points* 142).

[14] "De la grammatologie," *Critique*, No. 223 (December 1965), 16–42; No. 224 (January, 1966): 23–53. See DLG 7n1/OG 323n1 ("Preface").

for conferences he is to address, formulating titles over the telephone, in more or less continual conversation with others, on both sides of the Atlantic, a lot of trans-Atlantic phone calls, sleeping in more hotel rooms than he cares to remember, responding to questions and worrying over his response, taking advantage of the several graces of the moment that get him through the day, especially if is it a day on which he is asked to put deconstruction in a nutshell. For a while he was wary about being photographed and giving personal interviews, but since he has given in, his interviews have proven to be immensely illuminating and have provided one of the most helpful entrées to his work, as any reader of *Points . . .* can testify.

So, while we confess, in public, and beg both his and his readers' forgiveness, to doing him violence, to forcing compacted answers out of him on the spot, in front of a large audience, with a microphone in his face, it is at least a violence to which he has become accustomed and with which he has learned to cope with an amicable grace and felicity, with a charm and clarity that surprises only those who do not know him. There is no pure non-violence, but only degrees and economies of violence, some of which are more fruitful than others. (That is a Derridean way of saying that nobody ever said life is easy.)

Nutshells, Six of Them

I have tried in the present commentary to present Derrida as straight-forwardly as the twists and turns of deconstruction permit. In another work, *The Prayers and Tears of Jacques Derrida: Religion Without Religion*, to which I commend the reader as a follow-up to the present "introduction," I have raised the stakes of my interpretation and put a faster spin on my reading. While I would bet the farm, again, that I am right about Derrida's "prayers and tears," that this represents the way Derrida loves to be read, I will admit that *Prayers and Tears* is a high-risk reading in which I have ventured to speak of what Derrida himself has called "my religion," or at least his religion "without" religion, "without" (*sans*) being for him a technical term. I think that this religio-messianic twist gives deconstruction the right bent, that it well describes its proclivity and propensity, its tendency toward what is to come. That messianic tendency is discussed in Chapter 7 of the present work, and it is developed further in *Prayers and Tears*, which the present readers are cordially invited to visit. The present work means to be more straightforward and to pay attention to the way that deconstruction is distorted by its critics. For it is one thing to give deconstruction the right twist and quite another to bend it out of shape.

The present "Commentary" simply follows Derrida around the "Roundtable" as he, prompted by his interlocutors, and full of fear and trembling, serves up a number of nutshells in the course of responding to six questions about his work. Like a dutiful *Extraskriver*, serving as a supplementary clerk to the quasi-philosophy of the supplement,[15] I take up each question in the order in which it is asked and, as best I can, try to fill in his extemporaneous remarks by elaborating upon the more careful explorations of these themes in his published writings.

Remember, too, both the spirit and the letter of the occasion, that Derrida has been invited as the guest of honor on a day set aside to inaugurate a new doctoral program in philosophy. Indulge yourself in the fiction that, like James Joyce's *Ulysses* (or "Hill Street Blues," if you haven't read *Ulysses*), this all takes place on a single day, and that the question of inaugurations is on everybody's mind, so that the discussion begins and ends with the question of the day, with the question of beginnings, of how something gets started.

The six themes raised by the interlocutors do excellent service for getting us under way toward deconstruction, serving up, let us say, six nutshells, all of which have something to do with the connection of deconstruction with the most honorable elements of "our" "traditions." Allowing myself to be led by the various knights of this Derridean "Roundtable" (who look like tax collectors to me), I will argue that deconstruction is, in turn: the right to philosophy; the love of the Greeks; a community without community; justice; the messianic (a certain religion); and finally, yes, affirmation, yes.

In a nutshell. Six of them.

Maybe more.

---

[15] For more on being an "*Extraskriver*," see *Kierkegaard's Works. VI. Fear and Trembling and Repetition*, trans. Howard Hong and Edna Hong (Princeton: Princeton University Press, 1983), p. 7. For a Derridean staging of the scene created by an *Extraskriver*, see my *Against Ethics: Contributions to a Poetics of Obligation with Constant Reference to Deconstruction* (Bloomington: Indiana University Press, 1993).

2

The Right to Philosophy

"I bring good news."

—OCP 209

"So, you see, I am a very conservative person. I love institutions and I spent a lot of time participating in new institutions, which sometimes do not work."

—"Roundtable," 8

OF RIGHTS, RESPONSIBILITY AND A NEW ENLIGHTENMENT

Though it obviously raises an eyebrow or two in many quarters, nothing is more fitting than to invite Derrida to speak at the inauguration of a new program in philosophy—"new," "program," and "philosophy" all being words that Derrida has thought about at great length. Despite the popular image of deconstruction as some sort of intellectual "computer virus" (*Points* 406) that destroys academic programs, disciplinary specializations, institutional structures, indeed the university and—where will it end?—reason itself,[1] deconstruction is in fact a philosophy—and practice—of institutions, and Derrida is a lover of

---

[1] See Amy Gutmann, "Relativism, Deconstruction, and the Curriculum," in *Campus Wars*, pp. 57–69. Gutmann *never once* cites Jacques Derrida but simply uses the word "deconstruction" to stand for the view that intellectual standards are nothing more than masks for the will to power (pp. 60–61), that is, more generally, for everything bad, arguing among other things that deconstruction leaves us defenseless against Mormon polygamy (pp. 64–68)! See also John Searle, "Postmodernism and the Western Rationalist Tradition," in ibid., pp. 28–48; "The Storm Over the University," *The New York Review of Books*, 27, No. 19 (December 6, 1990), 34–42; and "Is There a Crisis in American Higher Education?" *The Bulletin of the American Academy of Arts and Sciences*, 46, No. 4 (January 1993), 24–47. The Searle-Derrida debate goes all the way back to "Signature Event Context" (1971) (MdP 365ff./MoP 307ff.). Then, of course, there is always the unforgettable Allan Bloom, *The Closing of the American Mind* (New York: Simon & Schuster, 1987).

institutions (especially ones that honor him—there being, after all, only degrees of narcissism!). If we repeat with a difference an old joke about marriage—the university is a great institution, but who wants to live in an institution?—we get an idea of what deconstruction is up to. As a philosophy of institutions, deconstruction is, while suspicious of institutional power, intent on making institutions livable—open-ended, porous, and on the *qui vive*—and structured around programs that do not try to program everything (DDP 593/Sendoffs 19). Its aim, Derrida says in the "Roundtable," is "to open the institution to its own future" (RT 6), and even, whenever possible, to open new institutions. Deconstruction loves to attend openings, if not to preside over at least to assist in openings. Far from being an academic renegade and antagonist of philosophy and philosophy programs, one more undertaker in the long "history of the deaths of philosophy," one more apocalyptic proclaiming still again "the end of philosophy," Derrida is one of philosophy's staunchest advocates, an activist strongly committed to the idea that philosophy is today all the more necessary (PdS 118/*Points* 110). It will surprise only those who know little about Derrida[2] that, over the course of an active life, he has consistently rallied to the defense of philosophy and undertaken various practical initiatives aimed at promoting the teaching of philosophy.

Let the word go forth and let there be no mistake: philosophy for Derrida is one of our most fundamental rights. But let the word also go forth that "rights" is not the *first* word in deconstruction, which is the central point to be considered in figuring the difference between a "new" Enlightenment he has called for (DDP 496/PR 19) and the old one defended by Searle and Gutmann. For rights come after responsibility, which is the first word, if there is one. If Derrida is a renegade, a word he would not utterly renounce, he is a highly responsible one. The work of deconstruction is set in motion, engaged (*engagé*) only by

---

[2] For example, neoconservative apologist Gertrude Himmelfarb includes Derrida in her tirade against the influence of "post-modernists" in American universities in her *On Looking into the Abyss: Untimely Thoughts on Culture and Society* (New York: Knopf, 1994). In a review of Himmelfarb, Michael Howard, a former Regius Professor of History at Oxford, says that "Derrida has tried to evade the problem [of the Holocaust] by emitting a dense cloud of unintelligible verbiage" and goes on to call him one of a group of "frivolous game-players who make a virtue of their moral irresponsibility" who undermine the standards of scholarship and the university. *The New York Times Book Review*, March 6, 1994, pp. 11–12. This, of course, is all said in the name of careful reading!

a pledge (*gage*) of responsibility, indeed of unlimited responsibility, because a "limited responsibility" (drawing oneself into a "corporate" circle) is just an excuse to credit oneself with a good conscience (DDP 108). For Derrida, deconstruction is set in motion by something that calls upon and addresses us, overtakes (sur-prises) and even overwhelms us, to which we must respond, and so be responsive and responsible. Endlessly.

Whenever anything very hallowed and revered comes into *question* in deconstruction, as sometimes happens—be it religion or law, science or democracy, even knowledge or philosophy itself—such questioning, be assured, arises from the height—or depths—of responsibility (whichever image gives you more comfort or warmer assurance). Whatever trouble Derrida manages to make, whatever seams he manages to expose in our most venerable garments, whatever disturbance can be traced back to him—that is all rooted in the deepest sense of responsiveness to something that is silently astir in these hoary and prestigious structures. Deconstruction is not irresponsible. How could it be—if deconstruction *is* responsibility itself, if there is such a thing? Whenever something is deconstructed, or, better, whenever something is allowed to auto-deconstruct itself right before our eyes, as sometimes happens, that is to say, whenever deconstruction gets under way, that always happens in the name of an "undeconstructible responsibility" (DDP 35), which is what sets the heart of Derrida aflame, and of deconstruction, too (if it has a heart).

This sense of responsibility being well understood, we may say that deconstruction reserves the *right* (*droit*) to ask any question, to think any thought, to wonder aloud about any improbability, to impugn the veracity of any of the most venerable verities. But do not be misled: that seemingly self-righteous, even legalistic characterization does not mean that deconstruction takes itself to be the master and judge of all it surveys. Indeed the very idea that philosophy is some sort of supreme tribunal sitting in judgment on all that passes in review before its judicial eye is the very sort of thing Derrida would unseat. (Derrida does not like courts and lawyers any more than the rest of us.) He does not want philosophy to be a sitting judge but rather a wanderer and nomad, on the move, on call, without the wherewithal to lay down its head, hastening hither and yon whenever the call of the "other" summons it into action. This seemingly impudent and self-assertive sense of the rights of philosophy springs from a boundless, maybe even vaguely biblical, sense of responsibility for the neighbor and the stranger.

For deconstructive thinking is acutely sensitive to the contingency of our constructions, to the deeply historical, social, and linguistic "constructedness" of our beliefs and practices. But that is not because it has appointed itself the supreme arbiter of what is true and false. On the contrary, it is because it confesses that it does not "know" the "secret" that sits in the middle and smiles at our ignorance. In other words, deconstructive thinking is a way of affirming the irreducible alterity of the world we are trying to construe—as opposed to the stupefying nonsense that deconstruction reduces the world to words without reference. So the philosopher on Derrida's telling is not an *Aufklärer* who sits in judgment over all our judgments, a meta-judge or hyperjudge presiding over our judgments as a court of last appeal (DDP 89ff.), picking things to pieces. That is the seat the old Enlightenment seeks to fill. But in the new Enlightenment, quite the opposite is the case. For Derrida, the philosopher is a bit of a "rag picker" himself,[3] looking for the bits and pieces that tend to drop from sight in the prevailing view of things, listening with cocked ear for the still small voices of what he, following Levinas, calls the "other" or even the "wholly other" (*tout autre*). A deconstructive "thinking," even before it becomes philosophy, "finds itself *engaged*, inscribed in the space opened and closed by this pledge (*gage*)—given to the other, received from the other" (DDP 28). The image of the rag picker takes on added impact when it is connected with Blanchot's use of the story of the Messiah dressed in rags that Derrida discusses in the "Roundtable." This figure, which Cornell borrows from Benjamin, is also a highly biblical image, and constitutes a much more humble form of "gathering" that stands in delicious contrast to Heideggerian gathering, which gathers the glories of *phainesthai* into a Greco-German glow.

That is why, like a bit of a rag picker (Walter Benjamin), like a collector of "fragments" (Johannes Climacus), this new Enlightenment puts responsibility (to the other) before rights (of the self), why it puts heteronomy before autonomy, *pace* Kant, who is something of a

---

[3] See Drucilla Cornell's wonderful depiction of Derrida, borrowing from Walter Benjamin, as a rag picker (chiffonnier) in her *The Philosophy of the Limit* (New York: Routledge, 1992), chap. 3.

father of the modern university.[4] We may think of it this way: decon-struction reserves the right to ask any question but it is not the right to question that comes first. Rather, the first question, if there were such a thing, would itself have already come as an answer, a response to the address of the other, whose advance, whose coming or incoming—*l'invention de l'autre*, the incoming of the other—deconstruction all along affirms. To put it in a nutshell: deconstruction is the affirmation of the coming of the other (*Psy.* 59-60/RDR 60), to which coming it is all along responding, about which it is being very responsible. Prior to any question, preceding, passing through, and surpassing question-ing, is a more original affirmation, a "yes" to the other, to the neighbor and the stranger, a "yes" that comes before the question, before science and critique and research, even before philosophy, an affirmation of something to come.[5] Any question that is put in deconstruction always comes as a *question en retour*, a question put in return or response to a previous solicitation, a way of answering back by questioning back, as a question put in response to a prior question, a second question that comes after one has already been put in question. So what sounds like a sassy and legalistic "right" to ask any question is something that has surrendered all its rights in order first to say *yes* to something that comes first. Questions are not the first word but the second, the second yes (*oui, oui*).

So, remember, and this is one of the axioms in this axiomatics of the nutshell, whenever deconstruction seems to cause or get itself into trouble, or even to look a little negative and destructive and likely to raise the wrath of the Good and the Just, remember that deconstruc-tion is being very responsible and affirmative, indeed that deconstruc-tion *is* affirmation, responsibility, *engagement*, which are the touchstones of a new Enlightenment.

The idea of our "right" to this or that, which nowadays has been extended to animals and trees, not without reason, is one of the most

---

[4] Derrida's reading of Kant on university studies may be found in "*Mochlos*, or, The Conflict of the Faculties," trans. Richard Rand and Amy Wygant, in *Logo-machia: The Conflict of Faculties* (Lincoln: University of Nebraska Press, 1992). The other studies in this valuable volume are an effective antidote to the nonsense perpe-trated in the work of Bloom, Searle, Gutmann, and Himmelfarb (see above, nn. 1–2).
[5] *Criticism in Society*, Interviews by Imre Salusinszky (New York and London: Methuen, 1987), p. 20.

honorable legacies of the Enlightenment. While Derrida is often made out to be the sworn enemy of the Enlightenment, he would contend, and we with him, that in fact the deconstruction he advocates is a continuation of what is best about the Enlightenment, but by another means. His idea of the right that deconstruction reserves to ask any question illustrates very nicely Derrida's relationship to the Enlightenment, which is not uncomplicated. As he often says, his interests lie in provoking not an anti-Enlightenment but a new Enlightenment, in questioning the "axioms and certainties of Enlightenment," but to do so precisely in order to effect "what should be the Enlightenment of our time" (*Points* 428). True, he is a critic of the Enlightenment, but critique is the most honorable of Enlightenment works, even when it is directed at the Enlightenment, which must be thick-skinned enough to undergo self-critique. For it may be that what the Enlightenment seeks cannot be found on the basis that the Enlightenment lays. That is precisely what Derrida thinks about rights. For his idea of a right is not a right rooted in an autonomous rational subject, the seated right of an (old) *Aufklärer* who is the sitting judge and master of all it surveys. It is a mobile right to respond to a call by which one has been visited—"before any contract" (FL 55/DPJ, 25)—a right that one has to answer whenever one has been addressed. Nor is his right a right inscribed in nature itself, a natural right, a universal essence, since it preserves the right to question the very idea of nature and essence. So, if deconstruction were to have a constitution, the "bill of rights" would come second, after the "bill" or, better, the "confession of responsibilities," and its declaration of independence would come right after its declaration of *dependence*, for rights are rooted in responsibility.

The talk about rag picking helps us see that part of the difference between the old and the new Enlightenment is a question of style. Derrida's more *avant-garde* style makes the old *Aufklärers* nervous, even when their aims are often the same as his. Gutmann and Derrida, for example, are both seriously interested in democracy and "democratic education," and they share more in common than her loose talk about deconstruction suggests.[6] Derrida's doubts about the absolute judicial authority claimed by and for Enlightenment Reason, by and for "pure Reason" (capitalized), do not constitute an outright attack

---

[6] See Amy Gutmann, *Democratic Education* (Princeton: Princeton University Press, 1987).

upon reason, upon giving good reasons, the best you can under the circumstances. If the old Enlightenment makes everything turn on "Reason," the New Enlightenment wants to know the reason for reason, wants to take responsibility *for* what at a specific point in history calls itself reason and the age of reason, and to consider carefully what is being declared "irrational" in the name of reason, instead of simply marching to its tune (DDP 473-474/PR 9). Nor does Derrida desire to break with the old Enlightenment's desire for "emancipation" (DPJ 28) Rather, deconstruction means to continue the struggle for emancipation but by another means and in another key, by taking a second look at the very things the old Enlightenment tended to devalue— literature, faith, and the messianic, for example—just in order to look for the sorts of things that tend to drop through the grids of the old Enlightenment. Like one who picks among the rags, Derrida "consorts" with suspicious characters, like all the strange figures in Genet's novels who appear in the right-hand column of *Glas* to the great scandal of Hegel's "absolute knowledge." But the effect of this new Enlightenment would be not to jettison reason but to redefine and redescribe it, for example, by steering clear of the simple opposition of reason and faith and seeing the extent to which reason is deeply saturated by faith; not to jettison emancipation but to continue to seek it in places that are overlooked by the old Enlightenment. In the new Enlightenment, things are always more unlikely and complicated than the simple oppositions favored by the old *Aufklärers*—like Kant and Marx—might suggest.

Philosophy is the right to ask any question about all that we hold sacred, even and especially about reason and philosophy itself. Does that mean that philosophy itself comes into question in deconstruction? To be sure, but always from a love of philosophy, or from a love of what philosophy loves—knowledge and truth (no capitals, please) and ethics and every other honorable and prestigious name in philosophy's intimidating repertoire. But in deconstruction this love demands that we admit that philosophy does not have the last word on the things that we love.

The "right to philosophy" (*le droit à la philosophie*), both to study and to teach it, to read and write, discuss and publish it, is everyone's. It is in particular not the private property of a self-validating academic establishment comfortably housed in prestigious academic institutions, of professors whose works circulate within a closed circle of institutions, journals, publishers, and associations (DDP 13). It is precisely the threat posed by deconstruction to their closed circle that arouses the wrath of analytic philosophers like Barry Smith[7] and Ruth Marcus. But this does not mean that Derrida denies that philosophy is a technical, disciplinary specialty. He has always insisted, as he repeats in the "Roundtable," on the need for specialized, disciplinary training in a "philosophy department," much like his own very technical training in Husserl's transcendental phenomenology. His misinformed critics notwithstanding, he has always battled against dissolving philosophy into literature or the humanities. The right to philosophy does not mean you can go "right to—straightaway to—philosophy" (*droit à philosophie*)—without careful preparation and disciplined work (DDP 14-15).

But this specialization, he says, is "paradoxical" and should not be made to serve conservative ends. For over and beyond this technical specialty, philosophy is not just one discipline among many, the one housed in the "philosophy department." Philosophy must be ex-posed, dis-located, ex-propriated and ex-patriated, made to understand that it cannot be wholly confined within the limits of a disciplinary specialization (DDP 22-23). Philosophy must be audacious and made to "cross the borders" (RT 7) of the disciplines. Philosophy cannot contain what it contains. Unlike other specialized disciplines philosophy should have not be finally contained by disciplinary horizons, and what horizons philosophy has it should press to the limits, so that it constantly pushes beyond its familiar objects, themes, and certitudes (DDP 32-33).

For Derrida, philosophical questioning, proceeding from the basis of a technical specialty, tends to shade off into the larger space of a general deconstructive thinking (*une pensée déconstructice*, DDP 28) which, taken in its broadest sense, means the unfettered freedom to think, the right to ask any question. As he says in a 1989 interview:

> The only attitude (the only politics—judicial, medical, pedagogical and so forth) I would *absolutely* condemn is one which, directly or indirectly, cuts off the possibility of an essentially interminable questioning, that is, an effective and thus transforming questioning [PdS, 252/ Points 239].

---

[7] See *European Philosophy and the American Academy*, ed. Barry Smith (LaSalle, Ill.: Open Court, Hegeler Institute, 1994).

To be sure, some of the most powerful examples of such questioning, of "thinking," are to be found in the canonical "history of philosophy"—from the Greeks to Augustine, Neoplatonism, and the high middle ages, from Descartes, Kant, and Hegel up to Husserl and Heidegger. About the uncircumventable necessity to study closely and faithfully these great dead white European males (although St. Augustine may have been a slightly swarthy North African), to read them with disciplinary rigor and interdisciplinary inventiveness, Derrida does not entertain the slightest doubt. These are writers upon whom he himself has extensively and lovingly commented, and that work he regards as "an infinite task." (RT 10) "[E]ach time that I read Kant," he says, "it is always the first time" (DDP 81). In the "Roundtable," he says, "[H]owever old I am, I am on the threshold of reading Plato and Aristotle. I love them and I feel I have to start again and again and again. It is a task which is in front of me, before me." Let that word go forth as well, clearly and unambiguously!

Still, it is important to preserve the "tension" in Derrida's attitude to "philosophy." The light that shines in the new Enlightenment constantly illuminates a scene that is more complicated than we first thought. For it is from the same sense of "responsibility" that Derrida is engaged in the battle for philosophy, to extend the right to teach and study the great dead white masters of philosophy as far as possible, to follow with painstaking detail the elaborate and well-formed system of distinctions and oppositions that mark the work of Plato, Kant, or Husserl *and yet also* to undertake the most vigilant deconstruction of these oppositions, to learn to read the masters "otherwise" (*autrement*), to hear within them the stirring of other possibilities, the in-coming of other events. Philosophy *and* its deconstruction, the deconstruction of philosophy, philosophy as deconstruction—all belong to a single operation, and if one does not understand how these two go together, then one does not understand either separately. For deconstruction is not—we will repeat this again and again—a destruction or demolition, but a way of releasing and responding, of listening and opening up, of being responsible not only to the dominant voices of the great masters, but also to other voices that speak more gently, more discreetly, more mildly in the texts of dead white European males and in quite a few other texts, too (DDP 88-89).

The thinking that takes place in philosophy, thus, cannot in the end be confined to technical philosophy, or to the canonical history of philosophy, even if that is the place one starts; it is also to be sought and found in many other places, in law, linguistics, and psychoanalysis. Above all, the thinking that occurs in philosophy communicates in a very special way for Derrida himself with literature. If philosophy is a questioning that pushes against the limits of language and knowledge, that is no less true of literature and of its experience of language; both philosophy and literature push against the impossible (PdS 387/ *Points* 372-374). Hence, like philosophy, "literature" too fluctuates between a narrow, disciplinary sense and a more general sense where it tends to shade off into a general deconstructive thinking. It is this more general sense that he has in mind when he says that "literature" is "the right to say everything," "a certain noncensure," "the space of a certain democratic freedom." "No democracy without literature; no literature without democracy" (*Pass.* 65/ON 28). Of philosophy, the right to think, and of literature, the right to write, we can say the same thing: they represent "the unlimited right to ask any question, to suspect all dogmatism, to analyze every presupposition, even those of ethics or the politics of responsibility" (*Pass.* 65-66/ON 28).

Jacques Derrida himself has never, personally, been able to decide between philosophy and literature or to leave one behind for the other (AL 34).[8] As the "Protean" right to say anything and everything, the unlimited right of writing and reading, the right to defy laws of prohibition, to engender fictions against the prevailing sense of reality, literature is an "institution which tends to overflow the institution," which even destabilizes the distinction between nature and institution. Contrary to his critics, Derrida is not arguing that "anything goes" nor is he turning truth over to caprice, but he is arguing strongly for a democratic open-endedness that makes those who have appointed themselves the Guardians of Truth nervous.

---

[8] One effect of this fluctuation on Derrida's part is that there has tended to be something of a war between his more philosophical and his more literary readers. For a sarcastic review of this battle, see Geoffrey Bennington's "Deconstruction and the Philosophers (The Very Idea)," in his *Legislations: The Politics of Deconstruction* (London: Verso, 1994). Bennington is discussing, among other things, Rodolphe Gasché, *The Tain of the Mirror* (Cambridge, Mass.: Harvard University Press, 1986) and Irene Harvey, *The Economy of Différance* (Bloomington: Indiana University Press, 1986), both of which appeared in the same year and wagged their fingers at the literary theorists for missing the hard, straight, serious philosophical side of Derrida, thereby contributing mightily to the popular image of him as a relativist and subjectivist. I have also reviewed these pieces in "Derrida: A Kind of Philosopher," *Research in Phenomenology*, 17 (1987), 245–259.

On a practical and political level, he is talking about censorship—of which Khomeini's "contract" on Salmon Rushdie is perhaps the paradigmatic case, the *ne plus ultra* of censorship (AL 37). He is resolute about preserving the right to say things that are not allowed, to analyze and criticize what the powers that be consider a closed question. Conceptually, he is arguing that the very idea of *littera*, of "letters," of writing, philosophical or literary, scientific or political, is resistant to the possibility of closing a question down. For the letter, by its very structure, is repeatable, disseminative, public, uncontainable, unfettered to any *fixed* meaning, definition, destination, or context. He is arguing not that our discourse has *no* meaning or that *anything* goes but, on the contrary, that it has too many meanings so that we can fix meaning only tentatively and only so far. And that does not spell anarchism; it is not bad news. The letter not only permits but requires and releases endless reading and responding, re-reading and repeating, commentary and counter-signing. Indeed, if we did not know better, if we were less vigilant *Aufklärers*, we might be tempted to say that releasing these readings represents the defining mission of deconstruction around which the totality of its work is centered! So let us say instead that such release, such cracking open, belongs to the aporetic axiomatics of the nutshell.

Literature and philosophy are not ingredient elements *in* a democracy for Derrida, but defining and creative forces that open up the space *of* democracy, that constitute democracy, constituting Derrida's declaration of independence. The right to philosophy is not one more element in a homogeneous field of rights, like the right to work, because philosophy is presupposed *a priori* in every "right to" this or that (DDP 64-65). Democracy survives and flourishes just to the extent that it preserves the right of all to philosophy and literature, which is the right of a democracy to criticize and correct itself, to ask any question about itself, which is why philosophy and literature and right go to the heart of what Derrida calls a "democracy to come." The very idea of a right is a philosophical one—deriving from the philosophy of the Enlightenment. Therefore, the state must preserve the right to philosophize, even if, paradoxically, the right to philosophize, to ask any question, would lead philosophers beyond the Enlightenment, or beyond a *certain* Enlightenment and its tradition of "natural rights" (DP 68-69), since deconstruction is the continuation of the Enlightenment by another means, a way of thinking rights otherwise, and hence the invention of an other Enlightenment.

For rights in deconstruction, as we have seen, derive not from nature or from the essence of autonomous rational agents—as in the Enlightenment—but rather, in something of a post-Enlightenment or post-critical way, from very heteronomic and responsible patients, from the depths of responsibility, which is undeconstructible. So, if it is true enough that democracies provide the surest element within which the right to philosophy can be exercised—as Richard Rorty likes to remind us—it is no less true that the rightful exercise of philosophy entails the right to analyze and criticize, to deconstruct, both the Enlightenment and all existing democracies, in their present and actual determinations, including even in their very foundations in the Enlightenment. For all this is undertaken in deconstruction in the name of democracy, of an undeconstructible democracy to come, which is the "promise of an event and the event of a promise. An event and a promise which constitute the democratic" (DDP 70-71).

That is why Derrida is glad to be on hand, is honored to be invited, if someone wants to start a new program in philosophy.

INSTITUTIONAL INITIATIVES

Over the years, Derrida has been personally active on a number of political fronts. Early on, an opponent of the French war in Algeria and the American war in Vietnam (MdP 131-135/MoP 111-114), he has been active on behalf of Nelson Mandela,[9] was one of the founders of the Jan Hus Association, a society formed to express solidarity with persecuted Czech intellectuals (which earned him a night in jail), supports the rights of Palestinians, and participates in international associations aimed at protecting the rights of writers everywhere.[10] Recently, Derrida has taken an active part in calling for a new trial for Mumia

---

[9] See Derrida, "The Laws of Reflection: Nelson Mandela, In Admiration," trans. Mary Ann Caws and Isabelle Lorenz, in For Nelson Mandela, ed. Jacques Derrida and Mutapha Tlili (New York: Henry Holt, 1987), pp. 13–42; and, for a commentary, see Robert Bernasconi, "Politics Beyond Humanism: Mandela and the Struggle Against Apartheid," in Working Through Derrida, ed. Gary Madison (Evanston, Ill.: Northwestern University Press, 1993), pp. 94–119.

[10] See the biographical sketch by Bennington in Jacques Derrida, pp. 325–336.

Abu-Jamal, a broadcast journalist and African-American, who was convicted of killing a Philadelphia policeman in a trial that has been widely criticized by legal scholars. Having lived on death row since his 1982 conviction, Abu-Jamal has been frustrated in his attempts to win a new trial, despite the unearthing of a considerable body of new evidence, in no small part because he is dealing with a Pennsylvania governor who campaigned on the death penalty. Abu-Jamal drew international attention to his plight when he published *Live from Death Row*, a searing indictment of American criminal justice, and Derrida has contributed a preface to the French translation, which has just appeared.[11]

That is why the "death of philosophy" would be, as a practical, political, and institutional matter, nothing short of a disaster for Derrida. It would spell the end of democracy, of the promise of democracy, dimming the very idea, if it is an idea, of what is to come. Far from being a matter for rejoicing or a result at which deconstruction aims, as his critics charge, the end of philosophy would spell terror, the suppression of dissent and questioning, the end of reading, an enclosing totalization, a totalizing closure. On a practical level, this is translated into Derrida's deep alarm at any attempt to curb or constrain philosophical instruction in the schools, even as he is alarmed by efforts to suppress or limit the rights of writers.

Furthermore, Derrida has, over the years, undertaken a series of " 'institutional' initiatives" (DDP 96), as he mentions in the "Roundtable," including his efforts in 1975 to expand the teaching of philosophy in the French high school (*lycée*) beyond the final year (*Terminale*), his central role in the creation of the "Collège International de Philosophie" in 1983, and the 1990 "Report of the Commission on Philosophy and Epistemology," the relevant documents of which are collected in *Du droit à philosophie*, filling over six hundred pages.[12]

Deconstruction is an analytic operation aimed at keeping thinking

---

[11] See Mumia Abu-Jamal, *En direct du couloir de la mort* (Paris: La Decouverte, 1996), the French translation of *Live from Death Row* (New York: Avon Books, 1996). Attorney Leonard Weinglass presents Abu-Jamal's case in the "Afterword," pp. 167–185.

[12] A translation of the most important of these documents has been projected for some time now by Harvard University Press under the title *Institutions of Philosophy*, ed. Deborah Esch and Thomas Keenan. See William R. Schultz and Lewis L. B. Fried, *Jacques Derrida: An Annotated Primary and Secondary Bibliography* (New York: Garland, 1992), p. 48 (A19).

and writing alive, keeping them open to surprise, by keeping on the alert to the institutions in which they are housed. If language is the house of being, institutions are the house of language. That is why Derrida describes deconstruction as "an institutional practice for which the concept of institution remains a problem" (DP 88). Indeed, we are apt to be misled by speaking of "housing" as if the institution were merely external. Deconstruction is integrally, and not merely passingly or incidentally, devoted to an analysis of the way philosophy functions in an institutional setting, of philosophy and literature *in* the "institution," *as* an institution or "establishment," as a socio-politico-juridico-institutional structure. For institutional structures tend to harden over and to protect philosophy from the restlessness and anarchic freedom of writing in which philosophy is inscribed. Instead of protecting philosophy, institutions can easily end up protecting us *from* philosophy. It has never been true that deconstruction consisted in some merely "internal" and "apolitical" analysis of texts, isolated and insulated from the institutions in which these texts are read and by which these readings are monitored. For the institutional "context" belongs integrally to the "general" text, the archi-textuality of which deconstruction is the analysis. Institutions reach all the way down into the so-called internal structure of the text, making the very distinction between internal and external questionable, turning the inside out and letting the outside in. The classical idea that institutions are merely external structures having nothing to do with philosophy itself, in its internal essence, is a conservative illusion. Deconstruction has always been a political and institutional analysis.[13]

So, when it comes to the right to philosophy, Derrida has been all along advancing on two fronts. In the course of a very considerable amount of practical activity he has also steadily accumulated an extensive body of theoretical reflection on educational institutions. *Du droit à la philosophie*, in which these writings are collected, is not only a call to action but the name of a very large book aimed at transforming philosophy from an "establishment" into a "provocation" (PPR 561). Let us look briefly at two of his most well-known practical interventions, the two Derrida singles out in the "Roundtable": the first under a conservative government, the next under its socialist successor.

---

[13] See the first two interviews in *Points* for an illuminating discussion by Derrida of the sensitivity of deconstruction to its institutional and political matrix (PdS 130–181/*Points* 5–77). *Points* is a particularly valuable introduction to deconstruction.

* * *

(1) Derrida was the central figure in the foundation in 1975 of GREPH (*Le Groupe de Recherches sur l'Enseignement Philosophique*), Research Group on Philosophical Teaching (see DDP 146–153). GREPH was formed in order to offer resistance to an attempt on the part of a post-1968 conservative French government that was bent on diminishing the role of philosophy in French culture. In this connection, GREPH made contact with public media and sponsored a number of conferences, the best known of which was the "Estates General of Philosophy" in 1979, all in an effort to "enlarge the space for philosophical teaching and philosophical research," as he says in the "Roundtable." GREPH mobilized in particular against the government's program of curtailing the teaching of philosophy in the Lycée (PdS 93–94/*Points* 88). Such a curtailment would have weakened the "critical" component in *lycée* education, and, needless to say, would have been felt in the universities, too, where the need to train such teachers would have been correspondingly eliminated. To limit the teaching of philosophy, even and especially on the high school level, is to limit the unlimited right to question, to nip thinking in the bud. Calling into question the nest of assumptions—about philosophy, society, and the educational process—which lead to the conclusion that philosophy could not be studied at an early age, GREPH advocated the expansion of philosophical education and even experimented with teaching philosophy to children aged 10 or 11.[14] Beyond pursuing these practical measures, GREPH was interested in the very concept of teaching philosophy: in the ways in which philosophy is affected by its being taught, the ways in which teaching is affected when it is philosophy that is to be taught, in the history and evolution of the "philosophy professor," the modes of recruiting philosophy teachers, and the character and make-up of the institutions in which it is taught, the social and historical context in which philosophy is taught, the political stakes of teaching philosophy.

(2) In 1982, shortly after the election of François Mitterand and of a socialist majority, the new Minister of Research and Industry, Jean-Pierre Chevènement, reversing the "reforms" of the previous administration, commissioned a study to be headed up by Derrida that led directly to establishing the *Collège International de Philosophie* (DDP

---

[14] *Criticism in Society*, ed. Salusinszky, pp. 13–14.

577 ff./Sendoffs 7–8).[15] The Collège, which opened its doors on October 10, 1983, with Derrida serving a one-year term as its first elected Director (he was succeeded by Lyotard), illustrates quite nicely what the right to philosophy ought to look like in the concrete for Derrida, and it repays a closer look. This can be conveniently organized around the name of the institution.

Collège. Inasmuch as the Collège is itself an institution, it finds itself in an impossible situation: for while it means to be suspicious of all institutional power and hierarchy, programs and programming, missions and destinations, the Collège needs to have some sort of institutional structure and direction. To be sure, a paralyzing impossibility is not an objection for Derrida, but rather an impulse and an indicator that things are really getting interesting. Accordingly, the Collège must not exempt itself from its own analyses; its founders must recognize that the Collège itself, and the topics it pursues, will—if its founders are successful—tend to acquire "legitimacy" and become "established" (DDP 594/Sendoffs 20). So, the Collège must make every effort to be vigilant about its *collegiality* (DDP 574-576) It must be so structured as to bring together scholars and researchers in such an open-ended way as precisely to resist any "stable hierarchy," to provide for a free and autonomous association that preserves maximum mobility as regards both the themes that are studied there and the scholars and researchers who teach there (DDP 574). The mission—its mission without mission, without narrowing and confining definition—of the College will be:

> [T]o organize research on objects—themes, which are not sufficiently represented in existing institutions in France or outside France. Objects and themes which are marginalized or repressed or not sufficiently studied in other institutions; philosophical or not philosophical institutions [OCP 210].

---

[15] For the relevant documents see "Titres," DDP 551–576; "Coups d'envoi," DDP 577–618/Sendoffs 7–43. For further information, see the interview with Imre Salusinszky, in *Criticism in Society*, ed. Salusinszky, pp. 9–24; Vincent Leitch, "Research and Education at the Crossroads: A Report on the Collège International de Philosophie," *Substance*, No. 50 (1986), 101–114. Leitch's piece is informative but one-sidedly "po-mo": while the word "responsibility" never appears, "rhizomatic" is spread all over its surface; again, Leitch concludes, quite amazingly, by saying that "postmodern" movements like deconstruction display "less concern" with "justice" than with "novelty" (p. 113), whereas Derrida says that deconstruction *is* justice. See above, "Roundtable," n. 1.

This is not to say that what is studied in existing institutions, basic courses in Plato and Aristotle, for example, is not important, or that deconstruction is conducting a war on the canon or standard curricula or the technical training of philosophers. It is never a question of choosing between proving oneself according to the most traditional disciplinary standards *and* putting those standards to the test (DDP 491/PR 17). But the specific mission of the Collège itself is to thematize what is *not* studied or legitimized in these established institutions, what is excluded by their missionary zeal, what tends to drop through the grids of existing institutions—and this on the bet or the risk that something is always being lost when things operate in regularized and routinized ways. But as he says in the "Roundtable," it is never necessary to chose *between* the canon and "new works, new objects, new fields, new cultures, new languages." (RT 11) ("It is never a question of choosing between . . ." is another nutshell.)

The Collège will thus have no tenure or chairs, no academic "ranks," no fixed or core curriculum, no grades or standard degrees. It will especially *not* be an "aristocratic and closed 'center for advanced studies' " (PdS 119/*Points* 111), at the very sound of which name knees everywhere turn to water. The sole criterion for teaching or doing research there is whether one can propose an object for research that has been "marginalized or excluded or disqualified in other institutions" (OCP 211), "insufficiently 'legitimated' " (PdS 119/*Points* 110)—*and* that promises to repay study, since not every bizarre, unusual, or illegitimate idea is a good one.

Philosophy. Furthermore, it must be understood that the Collège is to be a college of philosophy because philosophy is not dead and over with:

> As soon as you give up philosophy, or the word philosophy, what happens is not something new or beyond philosophy, what happens is that some old hidden philosophy under other name—for instance the name of literary theory or psychology or anthropology and so on—go on dominating the research in a dogmatic or implicit way. And when you want to make this implicit philosophy as clear and as explicit as possible, you have to go on philosophizing. . . . That's why I am true to philosophy [OCP 218].

To dance over the death of philosophy is to end up dancing to some old and now forgotten philosophical tune, which is why it is necessary to keep philosophy as open-ended and unlimited questioning alive. The continual effort to worry over presuppositions, to keep on questioning and talking, is what is called philosophy, and that must be kept going.

The idea behind the Collège is to disturb the reigning and conjoined ideas of philosophy and the university that go back to the founding of the University of Berlin in 1810 which have "defined the role of philosophy in the university" ever since (OCP 210). On this "paradoxical" model the philosopher is both everything and nothing. As a kind of Neo-Kantian overseer and surveyor of the whole of academic space, philosophy stands atop an academic pyramid staking out the domain of the various disciplines that are localized in the different "departments" down below. Thus far, the philosopher is taken to be a certain omnipotent philosopher-king. But, at the same time, the "department of philosophy" is itself localized in one of these particular compartments, and hence becomes a "subject" of the king, enlisted thus in the service of the whole. A "department of philosophy" is thus both impotent and omnipotent (DDP 572-573). The ultimate effect of this paradoxical model is more and more to "reduce the space of philosophical teaching and philosophical research" (OCP 211) to a small department in a large university or multi-versity, which is why we today are worried about the end or death of philosophy.

This model of philosophy, which holds sway from Kant to *Being and Time*, goes back to Kant's idea of philosophy as a critical tribunal, as a judge who marks off the limits of possible experience and the boundaries of the various domains of knowledge, morals, art, and religion. For Kant the first question of philosophy is the question *quid juris*, with what *right* do we claim to know or be obliged to do this or that. The Kantian schema of philosophy takes the form of what Derrida calls a "hyperjudicialism," where the philosopher is not merely a judge but a hyper-judge, a judge of the judges, who surveys and legitimatizes the rules of judgment for the several regions of human judgment. The philosopher not only gives the law (*droit*) of a subject matter, but also the truth of the law and of its judgments, for the exercise of which Kant says the philosophical faculty needs the absolute right to speak the truth. Philosophy is not just one particular domain of legitimate judgment, but the absolute source of all legitimation, "the law of the law, the justice of justice," *le droit du droit, la justice de la justice* (DDP 96-97), as such.

Kant's "critical philosophy," which elevates the philosopher to a supreme tribunal, transcending the particular disciplines, thus forms a modern, critical—"transcendental"—counterpart to the pre-critical aspiration of classical "metaphysics" for "transcendence" (*epekeina tes ousias*). Kant gives the philosopher a symbolic mastery of the world, before which everything must pass in review—even if in fact (*quid facti*) the philosopher is a professor (and not a king) with little or no real power. The world is a system, philosophy is its encyclopedia, and the university is a metonym for the universe and society as a whole. Even if the Enlightenment denounces totalitarianism, this is a very totalizing ideal (DDP 98-99).

It should also not go unnoticed that, in this hyper-judicial scheme, the philosopher himself reserves the right to be ignorant of the specific contents of the particular domains of the encyclopedia, even while claiming the right to speak of the essence of knowledge in general and of the meaning of each region of being or objectivity. Even if philosophers in fact do know about other things (in France they tend to know the humanities and social sciences, in Anglo-America they tend to know mathematics and the physical sciences), philosophy, as the science of science, is "structurally" ignorant; such knowledge is taken to be unnecessary and exterior to the philosophical act. This supreme philosopher-judge, resting atop his tribunal, serenely asking *quid juris* of everything passing in review before him, has an "impotent power" (DDP 100-101). The neo-Kantian philosopher/judge, on Derrida's telling, is like a sidewalk beggar hallucinating that everyone passing before him needs his permission to pass.

To resist that idea of philosophy and that institutional framing of philosophy is the reason deconstruction has come into the world. Such resistance would be its mission, if deconstruction did not also resist the idea of having a mission. The Collège set out to disturb the pyramid and to effect a more horizontal—and hospitable—arrangement. This it does not by way of "interdisciplinary" work (DDP 569ff.; PdS 118/ *Points* 110), which is an essential but already well-legitimated practice within existing institutions, something that has already become a "classical" concept (ICA 213). Interdisciplinarity confirms (rather than deconstructing) disciplinarity by establishing lines of communication among already constituted disciplines, collaborative work among people with different competencies—as when students of history, literature, philosophy, and theology come together in a "medieval studies" program. The Collège, on the other hand, is in search of *new* objects for which there are no existing competencies, objects for which no one has had "training," topics about which no team of specialists can be assembled. That itself requires that there be no expectation of the immediate applicability of this work, no demand that it serve an immediate and evidently useful purpose. Such objects are studied in what is called at the Collège six different "intersections," viz., philosophy in intersection *with* science, art and literature, politics, psychoanalysis, internationalities—and with philosophy itself. All this is aimed at provoking philosophy into "new moves" in a "new space" in which it does not "recognize itself," exposed to an other which is not *its* other—that negation of itself by which it mediates itself into a higher form of itself—which moves philosophy into an exposure with "others" it cannot reappropriate.

In the report to M. Chevènement, Derrida illustrates the general categories of "themes" or "objects" he would propose investigating, among which I would mention his interest in the problems of the technology of telecommunications (DDP 608-610/Sendoffs 32–33), and the philosophical implications of the life sciences, problems issuing from the new medical technologies, like questions surrounding organ transplants, genetic engineering, new techniques of torture, the new ways we have found to occupy outer space, information technologies, "smart" weapons and the new modes of warfare (DDP 600–605/Sendoffs 25–29). In the first year, for example, there was a seminar on philosophical problems surrounding hospital autopsies.[16]

International. Finally, while the Collège is not the first institution to regard itself as international, international here is intended to mean something different (OCP 215-217). The Collège wishes not only to invite foreign visitors but also to include them in the Collège as decision-making "organic members," with the effect even of delimiting the authority of the French language within the Collège. Not only does the Collège pursue the familiar international links, French and German, for example, or French and American, or even the much more difficult French and British, but it also seeks to cross barriers with non-European languages, cultures, and philosophy that are hardly known

---

[16] Leitch, "Research and Education at the Crossroads," 102.

in France, like Asian and African philosophy (OCP 225), of which the debate over Placide Tempel's *Bantu Philosophy* serves as an example.[17]

This internationalism is no Enlightenment universalism that would mean to spread a monochromatic European universal over the globe, to paint the whole world European, and to treat what is not European as "pre-European," which means pre-rational, but a kind of linking or networking that breaks open what would otherwise be self-enclosed nationalisms and lets otherwise silenced voices be heard. It does not seek to dissolve the national identities into a universal medium. Its idea of translation is to cope with the different and idiomatic national differences—translation is both necessary and impossible—and to keep them exposed to one another to prevent self-enclosure. Indeed, one of the problems that interests Derrida is the growing and increasingly hegemonic universality of the English language around the world which tends to wipe out difference. If by Enlightenment one means a uniform universalism, then that is something to deconstruct. But, by the same token, insofar as the Enlightenment dissolves obscurantism, authoritarianism, and fanaticism, nothing is more *aufklärisch* than deconstruction (OCP 220-221).

BETWEEN THE "DEPARTMENT OF PHILOSOPHY" AND
A PHILOSOPHY TO COME

If one asks where, in the university, one finds deconstruction, in what department, one would have to say that it inhabits the distance between the departmentalized academic specialties of philosophy or literature or law, or architecture, or religious studies, etc., and something absolutely new, absolutely singular, and unprecedented:

> I dream of a writing that would be neither philosophy nor literature, nor even contaminated by one or the other, while still keeping—I have no desire to abandon this—the memory of literature and philosophy [AL 73].

---

[17] See Paulin J. Hountondji, *African Philosophy: Myth and Reality*, 2nd ed. (Bloomington: Indiana University Press, 1996) for a critique of Placide Tempels's view that there is an indigenous, distinctly non-Western "African philosophy" as an ethnocentric myth.

Deconstruction is nourished by a dream of the invention of the other, of something to come, something absolutely unique and idiomatic, the invention, the in-coming, of an absolute surprise. Such a work would likewise involve the invention of its readers, the forming or constituting of a new community of readers around it, a community which does not exist—how could it? Such readers would get on-the-job training, on the spot, when it comes (AL 72) Indeed, this is a general rule, a nutshell, of deconstruction: it always inhabits the distance between something impossible, justice or the gift, say, of which we dream, and all the existing actualities and foreseeable possibilities, with which we are more or less discontent.

But how are such thinkers to be trained in the meantime? For it is *always* the meantime, the in-between time, just because what is coming is always to come, *à venir*. In the meantime, it would be necessary to undergo the most rigorous and classical training in departments of philosophy and literature, of religion and law, etc. Where else? That is why Derrida is happy to be on hand when a new program in philosophy is being instituted, why he is the perfect guest for such an occasion. But these programs must always be open-ended, porous, experimental, nonprogrammable, vigilant, self-questioning, self-revising, exposed to their other, inventive of the other.

In a nutshell, deconstructive.

3

Khôra: Being Serious with Plato

> "I am on the threshold of reading Plato and Aristotle. I love
> them and I feel I have to start again and again and again. It
> is a task which is in front of me, before me."
>
> —"Roundtable," 9

> "We have gotten more than we think we know from 'tradi-
> tion,' but the scene of the gift also obligates us to a kind of
> filial lack of piety, at once serious and not so serious, as
> regards the thinking to which we have the greatest debt."
>
> —PdS 139/Points 130

A Hoax

On May 18, 1996, *The New York Times* reported on its front page a story of a hoax that was played on *Social Text*, the chief outlet of the "cultural studies" movement; the headline of the story ran "Postmodern Gravity Deconstructed, Slyly." The *Times* reported a story that had just appeared in *Lingua Franca* and subsequently created quite a controversy, in which a physicist named Alan Sokal revealed that he had submitted a satire entitled "Transgressing the Boundaries: Toward a Transformative Hermeneutic of Quantum Gravity" aimed at making what postmodernist sociologists of science say about "gravity" look silly, which is what the *Times* meant by "deconstructed." The editors of *Social Text* took it quite seriously and had just published it, which led to Sokal's "gotch'ya." Taking on a look of perfect gravity, Sokal took on what he took to be the relativism of the cultural studies movement, particularly as regards "hard science"—the gravely serious issue of the principle of gravity in mathematical physics.[1] Sokal, for whom "gravity" is not a suggestion, but the law, said that he defended the truth of "the silliest quotes about mathematics and physics from the most prominent academics. . . . I invented an argument praising them and linking them together. All this was very easy to carry off because my argument wasn't obliged to respect any standards of evidence or logic."

Sokal feels obliged to rise to the defense of "science" against its "bashers," which is obviously what he thinks "deconstruction" means. Sokal's rakish claim was that in a postmodern perspective "the space-time manifold ceases to exist as an objective physical reality; geometry becomes relational and contextual; and the foundational conceptual categories of prior science—among them, existence itself—become problematized and relativized." Defending himself to the *Times* reporter, Stanley Aronowitz, co-founder of the journal and City University of New York professor, said Sokal is "ill-read and half-educated" and "got it wrong." That does not seem like much of a defense, as it leaves the reader to wonder what "standards of evidence or logic" editor Aronowitz uses when he accepts articles for publication in his journal. Stanley Fish, among other things Executive Director of Duke University Press, which publishes *Social Text*, was incensed that anyone should disturb, disrupt, transgress, mime, satirize, or subvert postmodernists (who spend their time, of course, doing just that to everybody else). Fish said he was not amused, that this was a bad joke, not funny at all, and then, like an aging Shakespeare scholar, invoked the most classical and straight standards of academic propriety against Sokal. Questioning the very ethics of Alan Sokal, Fish took all this very seriously and indignantly argued that the sociology of science is in the serious business of delimiting science, not of bashing it, of showing the extent to which scientific claims are embedded in social, political, and even sexual systems possessed of serious political implications.[2]

---

[1] See Alan D. Sokal, "Transgressing the Boundaries: Toward a Transformative Hermeneutics of Quantum Gravity," *Social Text* (Spring/Summer 1996), 217–252; and "A Physicist Experiments with Social Studies," *Lingua Franca* (May/June 1996), 62–64. *Science Wars*, ed. Andrew Ross (Durham, N.C.: Duke University Press, 1996) is a separate printing of this issue of *Social Text*, whose contributors are responding to a wave of criticism headed by Paul Gross and Norman Levitt's *Higher Superstition* (Baltimore: The Johns Hopkins University Press, 1994), which presents the cultural studies critique of "value-free science" as "science-bashing."

[2] Stanley Fish, "Professor Sokal's Bad Joke," *The New York Times*, May 21, 1996, p. 23, "Op-ed" page. The disanalogy, if I may weigh in on this dispute, between the

In a letter sent out over the Internet which he had withdrawn from publication because the *Times* would not publish it in full, Sokal says that he knows all that and that he is interested only in exposing the excesses of the sociology of science!

Sokal's satire, the *Times* reporter comments, is an "impenetrable hodgepodge" bolstered with lengthy footnotes and citations of the work of Aronowitz and "the likes of Jacques Derrida." The likes of Jacques Derrida! Alas, that Derrida should live to hear his name used as a sign of non-sense and resistance to gravity! Alas, that something as serious as "deconstruction" would come to do service for such silliness! Restoring the gravity of deconstruction, showing that deconstruction is serious business, clearing the name of a very responsible man, seeing the serious side of what Derrida and others call "transgression," which tickles Sokal's funny bone—that is serious business.

The last thing Derrida is interested in doing is undermining the natural sciences or scientific knowledge generally. A "deconstruction" of natural science, were it undertaken seriously and with a sufficient sense of gravity, would be good news. Its effect would be to keep the laws of science in a self-revising, self-questioning mode of openness to the "other," which here would mean the scientific "anomaly," the thing that defies or transgresses the law (*nomos*). A deconstructive approach to science would keep the scientific community open to the upstarts, the new ideas, the audacious young graduate students who come up with unexpected hypotheses that at first look a little funny and then a little brilliant. A deconstructive approach to natural science would maintain that the "laws" of science are always deconstructible (revisable) just in virtue of an science to come, one that is presently unforeseeable. A deconstructive approach to science would be good news and hard science. The sneaking suspicions that something may be wrong with what we currently believe, while keeping a watchful eye that current paradigms not be taken dogmatically, that something else, something other, still to come, is being missed—that deeply decon-

---

rules of baseball and the law of gravity seems to me to outweigh the analogy. For a twit of Fish's indignation, see also Tom Frank, "Textual Reckoning," in *These Times* (May 27, 1996), 22–24. *The New York Review of Books* used this opportunity to take a shot at Derrida in Steven Weinberg, "Sokal's Hoax," *The New York Review of Books* (August 8, 1996), 11–15; Weinberg, a Nobel laureate in physics, says we need "to protect ourselves from the irrational tendencies that still beset humanity," implying that if Derrida and deconstruction get hold of our children's minds, it will not be long until "burning witches" makes a come-back (p. 15).

structive frame of mind goes to the heart of hardball science, if it has
a heart!

So, if deconstruction would have interesting and constructive things
to say about science, very much in the spirit of the most responsible
and serious Kuhnian and post-Kuhnian philosophers of science,
Anglo-Americans philosophers all, I might add;[3] if deconstruction is
gravity itself; if, more generally, a "deconstruction" of science or theology, of literature or law, of whatever, is always an attempt to open it
up, not bash it or knock it senseless, then how did Derrida's good name
get dragged into this hoax? How, to put it in a nutshell, do "Derrida"
or "deconstruction" eventually come to mean the devil himself?

In the "Roundtable," the case in point is not physics but Greek
philosophy. But the serious study of Greek philosophy, of Plato and
Aristotle, for example, will serve very well to stake out Derrida's views
about doing serious work, about standards and criteria in any academic
discipline—from investigating the laws of gravity to the study of Original Sin—and, hence, to dissociate him from the silliness, the stupidity, the stupefying nonsense, that he thinks that anything goes.

Deconstruction Is Serious Business

"Doing deconstruction," if deconstruction is something to do, is not
a matter of the very latest, up-to-date, ahead-of-itself, *avant-garde,*
postmodern one-upmanship. Deconstruction has to do with the oldest
of the old as well as with what is coming. If there is anything at all to
deconstruction, then what it describes, namely, a certain auto-deconstructing tendency built right into things, is as old as the hills, as ancient as Plato, as medieval as Thomas Aquinas, as modern and
enlightened as Descartes, Kant, and Hegel—and Newton. In the
"Roundtable," Derrida reaffirms his love of the great tradition of Greek
philosophy and of Plato and Aristotle in particular. He tells us that as
regards the Greeks he is a perpetual beginner, that they are always
ahead of him, that reading them is an infinite task that is always "be-

---

[3] I have made a halting, imperfect beginning for myself in this direction in my
Radical Hermeneutics: Repetition, Deconstruction, and the Hermeneutic Project
(Bloomington: Indiana University Press, 1987), chap. 8. The work of Robert Crease
is among the most interesting in this field of a "hermeneutics" of the natural sciences,
which is, I think, importantly consonant with a deconstructive approach to science.

fore" him. Derrida is perfectly serious. Contrary to the popular misrepresentations of deconstruction as some sort of enemy of the tradition, something that ignores or distorts the great "canon," Derrida treats great dead white European males like Plato with scrupulous and loving care. So, to "do deconstruction"—and do it we must lest it be done unto us—we must take the Greeks seriously, and especially Plato, whose discussion of the khôra in Timaeus 48–52 draws Derrida's particular interest.[4] Deconstruction, after all, is serious business! It is gravity itself, if it has an itself.

In the current chapter, in order to get some idea of the seriousness of Derrida's approach to the tradition, I will begin by setting forth what he called early on his "exorbitant method"; then I will take up the "example" he proposes to us of a deconstructive analysis: his treatment of Plato's khôra. Finally, I will offer an opinion about why it is that Derrida's interest is drawn to the khôra. I will show how Plato's treatment of the khôra serves Derrida as a "sur-name" for différance, that is, a kind of "allegory" of différance. For khôra exposes a certain "impurity" (Khôra 94/ON 126) and intractability at the very core of philosophical concepts, a certain retreat and recession from philosophy's grasp, right there in Plato, who is the very paradigm of what we mean by philosophy, the horse's mouth of philosophy, thus leading us up to the very limits of philosophy—and to the heart of deconstruction, if it has a heart.

Plato and Aristotle, Derrida says, are always ahead of him. Reading them is always a matter of starting over again, always an infinite task. "We"—always an immensely problematic term for Derrida—are all

---

[4] Actually, Plato drew Derrida's interest early on, as well, in an extremely famous article entitled "Plato's Pharmacy" (1968), the first part of Dissemination, a well-known piece that has been extensively commented on, which is mentioned in the question put to him by Professor Brogan in the "Roundtable." For this reason, I have chosen to gloss, instead, Derrida's later interest in Plato, which is also the one that is on his mind in the "Roundtable," which he worked out in two essays written some twenty years later, "How Not to Speak: Denials" (1985) and "Khôra" (1987). For help with "Plato's Pharmacy," see Walter Brogan, "Plato's Pharmakon: Between Two Repetitions," in Derrida and Deconstruction, ed. Hugh Silverman (New York: Routledge, 1989), pp. 7–23. For a very helpful commentary on Derrida's Plato, early and late, see Catherine H. Zuckert, Postmodern Platos (Chicago: The University of Chicago Press, 1996), chaps. 7–8. For criticisms of "Plato's Pharmacy," see Stanley Rosen, Hermeneutics as Politics (New York: Oxford University Press, 1987); and, more recently, Yoaf Rinon, "The Rhetoric of Jacques Derrida. I. 'Plato's Pharmacy,' " Review of Metaphysics, 46 (1992), 369–386; "The Rhetoric of Jacques Derrida. II. 'Phaedrus,' " Review of Metaphysics, 46 (1993), 537–558.

children of the Greeks. At least the Greeks form a considerable *part* of "our" grandparentage, of at least some of "us," since those of "us" who hail from Asia or were hauled unwillingly from sub-Saharan Africa have different genealogies and usually do not feel all that Greek. While Derrida's admiration for Heidegger should not be underestimated, he wants no part of Heidegger's "Greco-" and "Euro-centrism," which goes hand in hand with Heidegger's concomitant mythologizing and theologizing of the "homeland" of Being, of Being's mother tongue, and of the Germans-as-Heirs-of-the-Hellenes, the master myth (and myth of the masters) that steered much of Heidegger's thought and abominable politics. That is both wildly funny, Derrida says, and extremely dangerous (DLE 109–110/OS 68–69). Still, despite Heidegger's excesses, if "we" means both the NATO-ese world of Euro-Americans and the colonizing reach that world has made into the rest of the world, then we are always bound to study the Greeks if we want to understand who we are and what we can become and what is going on around the globe.

But this reading of the Greeks is not to be "conservative" or reproductive, not because Derrida rejects the very idea of such a reading, but because such a reading is always a first reading, preparatory, preliminary, ground-laying, contextualizing. This first reading is to be followed by a more "productive," fine-grained, distinctly deconstructive reading, which explores the tensions, the loose threads, the little "openings" in the text which the classical reading tends to close over or put off as a problem for another day, which is really just a way to forget them. But that means that the very idea of a deconstructive reading *presupposes* this more reproductive and classical reading that stays on all the expressways and does not pursue the little sideroads or venture into unmarked areas. The classical reading follows what we might call the dominant tendencies of the text, the smooth superhighways with numbered exits. Only after that reading, or through it, or best of all along with it, does a deconstructive reading settle in to point out the dead-ends and aporias and to make things more difficult. As Heidegger said, authenticity is a modification of inauthenticity; being different is always a modification that gives a new bent and twist to the same. But always, please remember, all this is in order to open things up, to find a way to read "otherwise" (*autrement*), in the name of the incoming of the other (*l'invention de l'autre*).

The relationship between the first and the second readings, between the dominant and the deconstructive readings, may be seen to mirror the relationship between the mainstream institutions and the Collège. The idea is not to jettison the classical discipline, but to disturb it by way of exploring what systematically drops through its grid and, by so disturbing it, to open it up. There is a fair amount of confusion about this, I think, in the popular representations of Derrida. Alan Sokal, *The New York Times*, and *The New York Review of Books* certainly got themselves confused about it. Such critics tend to see deconstruction and whatever is meant by "transgression" as an "anything goes" hermeneutics given over to arbitrary and, despite its critique of subjectivity, highly subjectivist readings that are of not much help to serious students—of Greek philosophy or the law of gravity or anything else, not all that far removed from witch-burning! Thus, the distinction between first and second readings, between classical and deconstructive readings, tends to be construed popularly as the distinction between gravity (literally!) and levity, between serious (scholarly, "responsible") readings on the one hand and silly (unscholarly, irresponsible, even dangerous) readings on the other. But, for Derrida, a deconstructive reading is exceedingly close, fine-grained, meticulous, scholarly, serious, and, above all, "responsible," both in the sense of being able to give an account of itself in scholarly terms and in the sense of "responding" to something in the text that tends to drop out of view. Indeed, Derrida has little patience with the nonsense that is often imported under the label of the "play of signifiers." "The inferences," he says, "to which these games of association and society pastimes have for a long time been giving rise are facile, tedious, and naively jubilatory" (UG 111/AL 289).

AN EXORBITANT METHOD

Because of the confusion over this issue, and the importance of getting Derrida right on this point, let us follow a passage that is often overlooked in *Of Grammatology*, even though it appears in the famous discussion of deconstruction as an "exorbitant method," exorbitance of course presupposing an orbit to displace. Derrida is about to scandalize the Good and the Just, the Knights of Good Conscience, by saying "there is nothing outside the text" (DLG 226–227/OG 157–158), which he calls "the axial proposition of this essay" (DLG 233/

OG 163). That is the famous, scandalous part, and one of the most thoroughly misrepresented utterances in contemporary philosophy. A deconstructive reading, Derrida says, always settles into the distance between what the author consciously intends or means to say (*vouloir-dire*), that is, what she "commands" in her text, and what she does not command, what is going on in the text, as it were, behind her back and so "sur-prises," over-takes, the author herself. That distance, or gap, is something the deconstructive reading must "*produce*." Clearly, such a structure, or relationship, cannot be produced by a respectful, reproductive, doubling, self-effacing commentary that follows the conscious choices the author is making, since that, to the extent that it is possible, will pick up only one end, the conscious intentionality, of the relationship.

But at this point Derrida says, and this is the part that is overlooked by his critics (and too often by his admirers):

> This moment of doubling commentary should no doubt have its place in a critical reading. To recognize and respect all its classical exigencies is not easy and requires all the instruments of traditional criticism [DLG 227/OG 158].

To read Plato and Aristotle well, one must learn Greek, learn as much as possible about their predecessors, contemporaries, and successors, about their religious, social, political, and historical presuppositions, understand the complex history of subsequent interpretations of their works, etc. This is "not easy"; indeed, it is an infinite task, and deconstruction is not a license to circumvent it. For otherwise, if this reading does not take place, then "anything goes," and readers may say of a text whatever comes into their heads:

> Without this recognition and this respect, critical production would risk developing in any direction at all and authorize itself to say almost anything [DLG 227/OG 158].

Yet this respectful commentary is necessary but not sufficient:

> But this indispensable guardrail has always only *protected*, it has never opened a reading [DLG 227/OG 158].

We cannot establish the relationship between what the author commands and does not command if we do not first get a command of what of the author says or, better, what is being said in the text. Such a classical exigency, Derrida says, provides guardrails, parameters, horizons within which interpretation takes its first steps. Now, if such guardrails are enforced absolutely, they will grind the "tradition" to a halt, "mummify" it, as Nietzsche would say, so that the tradition of reading Plato and Aristotle will become a matter of handing on readymade results, passing along finished formulas for mechanical repetition and recitation. Then the traditional criticism will not protect at all, unless you regard embalming as a form of protection. So, the only way to be really loyal to a tradition, that is, to keep it alive, is not to be too loyal, too reproductive; the only way to conserve a tradition is not to be a conservative.

That is why the possibility must be kept alive of reading otherwise, which means always passing *through* the classical discipline, and never having abandoned or jettisoned it, to explore what it omits, forgets, excludes, expels, marginalizes, dismisses, ignores, scorns, slights, takes too lightly, waves off, is just not serious enough about! About all these omitted—"de-legitimated"—elements, the deconstructive reading is scrupulous, gravely in earnest, deadly serious. A deconstructor is like an inspector who is gravely concerned with a little crack he observes in an airplane's fuselage (given the laws of gravity), while everyone else on the inspection team is eager to break for lunch—thus reversing the popular stereotype that the deconstructive reading is silly and sloppy.

The deconstructive reading is "transgressive" of the protection that the traditional reading affords. In what sense? That, Derrida says, can be answered negatively. It does not mean: (1) saying whatever comes into your head about the text, however absurd and ridiculous—although that is evidently what Amy Gutmann, Alan Sokal, Gertrude Himmelfarb, William Bennett (DDP 488n1/PR 15n8), and *The New York Times* think "deconstruction" is—which is why Gutmann thinks it gives aid and comfort to Mormon polygamy while Steven Weinberg is worried about witch burning!

(2) Nor does this trans-gression consist in an act of absolute transcendence by means of which one lifts oneself out of one's textual boots or peeks around behind the text to some sort of naked, prelinguistic, *hors*-textual, ahistorical, uninterpreted fact of the matter called the thing-in-itself, or Real Being, or the "transcendental signified," or whatever sets your heart aflame. We are all always and already, on Derrida's telling, embedded in various *networks*—social, historical, linguistic, political, sexual networks (the list goes on nowadays to in-

clude electronic networks, worldwide webs)—various horizons or pre-suppositions, which is what Derrida means by the "general text" or "archi-text" or "textuality" or, here, just "text." And it is in this context that he formulates the memorable text, "There is nothing outside of the text" ("*il n'y a pas de hors-text*") (DLG 227/OG 158). For, on Derrida's view, if ever we try to lay aside the enframing texts of Plato and Aristotle and look "directly" at the things themselves of which they spoke, we will do so only through *other* frames, other horizons, other socio-historico-linguistico-political presuppositions, other "differential" relationships or networks, which in Derrida's language are de-scribed as the "differential play" of the "trace" or of *écriture* (about which more shortly). Derrida is not trying to bury the idea of "objectiv-ity" but, a little like Kant, to force us to formulate a more sensible version of it than of some ahistorical *Ding-an-sich*.

Of this "textual" point, literature is an *exemplary* example. There *really is* no Jane Eyre (alas, I love her madly) outside the text of *Jane Eyre* whom we may consult, say, to find out if she *really did* hear Mr. Rochester call her name, "Jane," from across the moors; and, having published her book, Charlotte Brontë has lost all right authoritatively to settle these matters for us. But what literature exhibits "purely," exemplarily, as it were, is true in varying ways and degrees of every other discourse. No one ever gets privileged access to the Secret that sits smiling behind all language and interpretation waiting for us but to knock; we are all in the same textual boat together, forced to do the best we can with such signs and traces as we can piece together, work-ing out of one worldwide-web site or another. It is not that texts and languages have no "referents" or "objectivity" but that the referent and objectivity are not what they pass themselves off to be, a pure transcendental signified. Derrida is not trying to destroy texts or the ability to read texts or to turn everything—the great Greeks, Plato and Aristotle, mathematical physics and the law of gravity included—into fiction, or to deny the distinction between reality and fiction; he is trying, rather, to disrupt "the tranquil assurance that leaps over the text toward its presumed content, in the direction of the pure signified" (DLG 228/OG 159). "*Il n'y a pas de hors-text*" means: there is no reference without difference, that is, without recourse to the differen-tial systems—be they literary or mathematical—we have at our dis-posal.

Well, then, what *does* Derrida mean by "transgression"?

A transgression requires something to transgress, a border that prohibits passage, a limit that forbids trespass, a forbidden apple to invite the bite. We must, accordingly, learn to read Plato and Aristotle, study hard and pass our exams in our legitimated "Intermediate Greek" and "History of Ancient Philosophy" courses, submit ourselves to the most classical exigencies of "professional rigor and competence," pass through the asceticism of the most traditional "discipline," legitimate ourselves according to the most classical norms (DDP 491/PR 17)—in short, take whatever the masters of legitimation can hand out. But this must not become an excuse for conservatism, for a conservative, reproductive traditionalism that does not "produce" anything, or allow an opening for the other, for the invention of the other. The invention of the other requires first the conventions of the same in reference to which one sets out to find something contravening and counterconventional, something transgressive of the horizon of legitimation. Transgression is a controlled contravention or invention, requiring the discipline of an already standing frame or horizon to transgress, which is why it is described as a "double gesture." Transgression thus is a passage to the limit *(passage à limites, à frontières)*, the crossing of a well-drawn border that we all share, giving something straight a new bent or inclination or twist. One can imagine that Derrida has in mind an impudent doctoral student in physics giving the standard paradigm, not to mention the full professors, a certain amount of hell, which is quite different from uninformed criticism!

Derrida's idea is not to let the first reading become the last word and not to break the "tension" between the dominant, classical readings and the transgressive readings, between the much revered standing paradigms and the anomalies that circulate within and eventually open up the system. Conservatism breaks the tension in one way, by taking its stand within the standing horizons and present paradigms, shooting out of the skies everything transgressive, while the silliness descried by Alan Sokal or Amy Gutmann—and Jacques Derrida!—breaks it in the opposite way, by not passing through the classical discipline and so removing any borders to trespass.

Without an example, all of this might sound like so much smoke and mirrors, a bit of intellectual razzle-dazzle. Derrida's example in the "Roundtable" is Plato. Even and especially in a philosopher as "canonical" as Plato, who in a certain sense sets the scene for and defines the terms of the canon, who is the canon for the canon, even here "the possibilities of rupture are always waiting to be effected" and "the most radically deconstructive motifs are at work" (AL 53). An important metaphysical text like Plato's is never "homogeneous," never self-identical, "never totally governed by 'metaphysical assumptions' " (AL 53). Radical motifs can always be detected and released:

> It can always be shown (I have tried to do so, for example, in relation to the *khôra* of the *Timaeus*) that the most radically deconstructive motifs are at work "in" what is called the Platonic, Cartesian, Kantian text [AL 53].

Derrida uses the same example of the *khôra* in the "Roundtable" (RT 9), so his analysis of Plato's *khôra* will repay our study, to "illustrate" how to "do" deconstructive readings of the great canon, how they "work." For Plato, it will turn out, is not just another, not even the first, "example" of what is called "philosophy" and the philosophical canon. Plato is a beginning we can never get past or behind; we are always beginners beginning with Plato.

KHÔRA

In the essay entitled *"Khôra,"* Derrida draws a distinction between the "philosophy" of Plato and the "text," a distinction that, we will see, parallels the distinction between dominant-reproductive and transgressive-productive readings of Plato. "The philosophy of Plato," Derrida says, is an abstraction and a simplification, while the *text* from which it has been excised is complex and heterogeneous, a multiplex of innumerable threads and layers. The text, he says, produces numerous "effects"—semantic and syntactical, constative and performative, stylistic and rhetorical, etc.—only *one* of which is its "philosophical content." "Platonism" is an artifice—but not an arbitrary one—constructed by cutting and pasting, trimming Plato's text neatly around the borders, combing out all the knots and conundrums, the involutions and convolutions, creating the safe, sanitized, distilled "effect" called Plato's "philosophy":

> This will be called Platonism or the philosophy of Plato, which is neither arbitrary nor illegitimate, since a certain force of thetic abstraction at work in the heterogeneous text of Plato can recommend one to do so. . . . "Platonism" is thus certainly one of the effects of the text signed

by Plato, for a long time, and for necessary reasons, the dominant effect, but this effect is always turned back against the text [*Khôra* 81–82/ON 120].

The "philosophy" of Plato, which is an ensemble of "theses," of "philosophemes," of thematic philosophical "claims," which corresponds then to the "dominant," reproductive reading, can be turned against the "text" of Plato, which is an ensemble of textual events—"this ensemble without limit which we here call *the text*" (*Khôra* 83/ON 120)—in which are embedded any number of other, "transgressive" tendencies. The philosophy can then be made to monitor or police the text, "dominating, according to a mode which is precisely all of philosophy, other motifs of thought which are also at work in the text" (*Khôra* 82/ON 120). A homogeneous and dominant, thetic and philosophic effect of the text is made to bend back on the text as a whole, made to govern it rigorously, made to keep watch over its inexhaustible heterogeneity for deviations and transgressions.

Privileging the philosophy of Plato is what Derrida means by "logocentrism," making the logic of the argument, the demonstrably true or false claims, the center, while sending everything else off to the periphery as mere rhetoric or ornamentation, letting the logic lead the letter. The result of this logocentric hegemony of the "philosophy," this concentration of "theses," is that the text is "neutralized," "numbed," "inhibited," even though these heterogeneous forces continue to stir in their inhibited form. Platonism is not only the first "example" in the West of the construction of such a "philosophy," but also the paradigm that "commands this *whole* history," since "philosophy" will always be in one way or another "Platonic."

> Hence the necessity to continue to try to think what takes place in Plato, with Plato, what is shown there, what is hidden, so as to win there or to lose there [*Khôra* 84/ON 121].

"Deconstruction" will consist in a fine-grained reading of the text, of the literality and textuality of the text, slowly, scrupulously, seriously, in releasing the still-stirring forces that "philosophy" and logocentrism strive to contain.

By taking up the *khôra*, Derrida turns—predictably—to an unpredictable, dark, and remote spot in the vast and gleaming architecture of Platonism. When we think of Plato, we think of the *two* worlds or regions allegorized in the cave: the upper world of the intelligible

paradigms, the sphere of invisible and unchanging being in the sun of
the Good that shines over all, as opposed to the sensible likenesses of
the forms in the changing, visible world of becoming, to which the
distinction in the faculties between sure *logos* and merely probable
doxa corresponds. When presented with a neat distinction or opposition of this sort—and this distinction inaugurates philosophy, carves
out the very space of "meta-physics"—Derrida will not, in the manner
of Hegel, look for some uplifting, dialectical reconciliation of the two
in a higher third thing, a concrete universal, which contains the
"truth" of the first two. Instead, he will look around—in the text itself—for some third thing which the distinction omits, some untruth,
or barely true remnant, which falls outside the famous distinction,
which the truth of either separately or both together fails to capture,
which is neither and both of the two.

In the *Timaeus*, the missing third thing, a third nature or type (*triton genos*, 52B)—*khôra*—is supplied by Plato himself. *Khôra* is the
immense and indeterminate spatial receptacle (*dekhomenon, hypo-
dokhe*) *in which* the sensible likenesses of the eternal paradigms are
"engendered," in which they are "inscribed" by the Demiurge, thereby
providing a "home" for all things. *Khôra* is neither an intelligible form
nor one more sensible thing, but, rather, that *in which (in quo)* sensible things are inscribed, a *tabula rasa* on which the Demiurge writes.
This receptacle is like the forms inasmuch as it has a kind of eternity:
it neither is born nor dies, it is always already there, and hence is
beyond temporal coming-to-be and passing away; yet, it does not have
the eternity of the intelligible paradigms but a certain a-chronistic a-
temporality. Because it belongs neither to the intelligible nor to the
sensible world, Plato says it is "hardly real." Moreover, while it cannot
be perceived by the senses but only by the mind, still it is not an
intelligible object of the mind, like the forms. Hence, Plato says it is
not a legitimate son of reason but is apprehended by a spurious or
corrupted *logos*, a hybrid or bastard reasoning. *Khôra* is neither intelligible being nor sensible becoming, but a little like both, the subject
matter of neither a true *logos* nor a good *mythos*.

So, what *khôra* is, is difficult to say. It is just this aporetic, enigmatic, tongue-tying third thing that draws Derrida's attention. For
here he comes upon something that tends to drift to the edge of philosophy's screen, beyond or *beneath (en decà)* philosophy's grasp (*Khôra*
93/ON 125), situated too low for philosophy's conceptual radar to pick

up, thereby eluding the order of categories that Plato has installed. Perhaps, Derrida says, this enigmatic structure, which fits into neither genre, is too neutral and indeterminate to have any "generic" determination at all, or to have anything at all to do with "generation," so that perhaps khôra "signal[s] toward a genre beyond genre," perhaps "beyond categorial oppositions, which in the first place allow it to be approached or said" (Khôra 17/ON 90). Like pure being, or pure nothingness; both and neither. This third thing, introduced not by some wild-eyed, disheveled deconstructor, his pants torn and his pupils dilated, but by the cold eye of sober old three-piece-suited Plato himself—it is mentioned in all the canonical commentaries—is just the sort of thing, or non-thing, to attract the interest of Derrida's "exorbitant method." This method, we now see, consists in closely, seriously, minutely following the text until we see that the orthodox, received, dominant interpretation has been produced by a wave of the hand that brushes aside the deviations and transgressive moments. (So now who is being serious and who is being silly?)

The word khôra is the common Greek noun for a concrete area or place; a khorion, for example, is a district or an estate, and khorismos is a separation in the sense of a gap or space between. Khôra is translated into Latin as locus and into French as lieu. For Derrida, who chooses to leave the word untranslated, although he plays with lieu throughout the piece, the khôra can be understood as a great abyss (abîme) or void which is "filled" by sensible things. Now, the discussion of the khôra, Derrida points out, is "located" in the middle, in the mid-place (milieu), of the text of the Timaeus. Inasmuch as the Timaeus is intended to survey the whole of the kosmos, like a "cosmo-ontologic encyclopedia" (Khôra 67/ON 113), this discussion occurs like a great chasm or abyss in the middle of the book. That is a "textual" feature of the Timaeus, the sort of thing logo-centric philosophers brush aside because of its seeming irrelevance to the "argument."

Now, for Derrida, the order of composition of the Timaeus, the quasi-law of its textuality, governing all the substitutions and permutations that go on in the text, is fixed by an elaborate mise en abîme. A mise en abîme is a vertiginous play of reflections, as when an image is infinitely reflected in a mirror held up against a mirror. For example, physicist Alan Sokal's satiric deconstruction of the principle of "gravity" was a mise en abîme that mocked the "gravity" of postmodernism, suggesting that the feet of postmodern thinking, not quite reaching the ground, lack traction. So, Derrida sets out to show that the staging (*mise en scène*) of the discussion of the *khôra* in the text of the *Timaeus* is a mirror-play of "*khôral*" images. Whence the rhetorical trope, *mise en abîme*—letting the same notion or image be reflected across several structures within the work, as in a play within a play—functions in the text of the *Timaeus* to "enact" or "perform" the meaning of the *khôra*. For the *khôra* is an "abyss," a void of empty space; it is also an infinite play of reflections in which the paradigms produce their images, simply "reflecting" sensible things like a mirror that is not altered by the images it reflects (*Khôra* 46–47/ON 104) The discussion in the *Timaeus* of the bottomless abyss of the *khôra* is staged in the text by a reflection without limit, without bottom or ground, of "khôral" images, by a play of reflections that induces in us, the readers of Plato, a sense of dizziness and vertigo as before an abyss. Whence Derrida's scrupulously close reading of the text—here turned to the opening "preface" to the *Timaeus* (17A–27B)—consists in exhibiting the several *mises en abîme* to be found in the text, and this by way of leading us into the indeterminate abyss toward which Plato's own categorial determinations advance.

Socrates opens the *Timaeus* by making a reference back (by "reflecting" back) to the *Republic*—"the chief theme of yesterday's discourse was the state" (*Timaeus* 17C). The *politeia*, Derrida points out, is structured around a certain "politics of sites" or places (*Khôra* 49/ON 104) in which each man, woman, and child is assigned his proper place (*khôran*). Justice is a certain just distribution of places, of the rulers, the military, and the craftsmen, each in their proper place. That political distribution goes hand in hand with the distribution of beings and cognitive faculties along a divided line, assigning each their measure of truth and reality according to the place each takes on the line, forming thus a kind of onto-theo-logic of place. (But where, then, is *khôra* on the line? What place is occupied by place "itself," if it has an itself? Where to locate on or in the divided line that which is neither sensible nor supersensible, although it is in a certain way both? By what faculty is it apprehended? On what place in the line is *khôra* to be found—or is the line in the *khôra*? What place does the philosopher himself, whose office it is to order by assigning place, occupy when he assigns these places?)

Socrates is a "khôral" figure in the dialogue, because Socrates "operates from a sort of non-place" (*Khôra* 55/ON 107), as a man who does not have a proper place. He is neither a poet, that race—or genos—of imitators, nor one of the sophists, those who wander from place to place full of empty words, neither of whom can speak well of the state and extend "yesterday's" conversation. In reference to those who can speak well, the genos of philosophers and leaders of the polis, he says to Timaeus, Critias, and Hermocrates, "you," "the people of your class," you people who have a place, a settled site in the city (the agora), from which to speak the truth of the politeia. Socrates himself feigns not to belong to this class, to have no place, to be at best like them, an imitation of them, and in so doing feigns to look like the feigners, the poets or the sophists, although he seeks to escape mere imitation (Timaeus 19Bff.). Hence, Socrates is a third thing, a certain "third kind" (triton genos), neither a true philosopher who knows the truth nor a mere dissembler, but a little like both. Socrates effaces himself and says he will let the true philosophers, Timaeus and his friends, do the talking, reserving for himself the role of an open receptacle for what his friends will offer him (20c), to be "informed" by them, to receive their gift. So, then, does Socrates not look like khôra (Khôra 59/ON 109)?

But let's be serious with Plato (Khôra 41–43/ON 101–102)! This is only the preamble to the Timaeus, a bit of theatrical staging, and Plato has not yet got down to business, to stating his claims, to laying out his logoi. But can we—and this is what Derrida is asking—speak seriously, properly, of the khôra, as if it were an eternal being about which we could give a stable logos? Or may we relax and enjoy ourselves, telling a likely story (ton eikoton mython) about it, which is all that the probable world of sensible appearances permits? Both and neither—since khôra is a third thing, neither intelligible nor sensible, the discourse on which can be properly situated neither as logos nor mythos, certain or probable.

Next, Derrida identifies the text of the Timaeus as itself having a "khôral" structure. For the Timaeus is structured like a vast receptacle, as a series of mythic or "narrative receptacles of receptacles" (Khôra 75/ON 116–17), a string of myths containing myths—the very structure of which (containing receptacles) mirrors khôra itself, which contains all. Critias tells a story (20Dff.) that bears all the marks of what Derrida likes to call a "postal" network, a message that passes through several postal "relays," which is in fact for Derrida a feature of every text, not just the Timaeus. The story Critias tells he remembers having been told as a child of ten by his ninety-year-old grandfather, Critias the elder. The latter had himself been told the story by the great Solon, who was a friend of Dropides, the father of the elder Critias. Solon was himself given the story by an Egyptian priest, who had learned it himself from ancient Egyptian writings that record the foundation of Athens. The story then told to Socrates by the younger Critias is thus embedded in layers upon layers of "textuality," multiple stratifications, boxes inside boxes, which helps gives us some idea of what a "text" is, namely, from *texere*, weaving together; any discourse, whether oral or written down, is a "text" and passes through these textual layers. In another place, Derrida points out a similar thing about the construction of the Book of Revelation in the New Testament, which does emblematic service as an indicator of the heavily textualized nature of what we call the "sacred scriptures." That raises various problems for a theory of "revelation," and not only for fundamentalists, which cannot be a matter of taking dictation from a divine speaker. The same thing is true of any text, ancient or modern, sacred or profane, which would always be structured, "constructed" of layer upon layer, fold upon fold, ply upon ply, so that to read a "text" is always to un-fold, de-construct, what is going on.

The story Critias tells concerns the most noble deed in the history of the Greeks, although it is unknown to the Athenians of the fifth century. In the Egyptian region called Sais on the Delta, the citizens have a deity called Neith, who they assert is the same as the one the Greeks call Athena;[5] hence, they regard themselves as brothers to the Athenians, having a common mother and goddess-foundress. This amazing thing Solon learned from an old Egyptian priest whom he met when he visited Sais. The old priest chides Solon and the Greeks

[5] Is Plato suggesting that Athena was black, "out of Africa," as suggested by Martin Bernal in his *Black Athena: The Afroasiatic Roots of Classical Civilization*. I. *The Fabrication of Ancient Greece, 1785–1985* (New Brunswick, N.J.: Rutgers University Press, 1987), pp. 51–52? Keeping the attention alive between the reproductive and productive readings is crucial. Nothing guarantees that an argument that appeals to us in no small part because it is impudent, unorthodox, and de-centering will not come undone from the sheer pressure of traditional scholarship. From what I can judge, the jury appears to be in and the verdict is bad for Bernal's delicious suggestion (it would have driven Heidegger over the edge!). Indeed, had Athena/Neith hailed from Egypt at all, as the myth at the beginning of the *Timaeus* suggests—which not a lot of scholars believe—she would be at best a little on the swarthy side, like St. Augustine, not a sub-Saharan Nubian. See Jasper Griffin, "Anxieties of Influence," *The New York Review of Books*, 43, No. 8 (June 20, 1996), 67–73.

for being perpetual children because they are unable to preserve written records of the most ancient times, both their own and that of others. For while the Nile protects the citizens of Sais from the excesses of nature, great cataclysms among the Greeks have periodically wiped out their historical archives. Thrown back on memory alone, Greek genealogies and stories are the tales of children. The priest proceeds to tell the astonished Solon, who was all ears, that Athens was nine thousand years old, a thousand years older even than Sais, and flourished as the greatest city of those ancient times. He describes the constitution that Athena gave them, which "by some mysterious coincidence" (25E) resembles the *politeia* about which Socrates had spoken "yesterday," so that what Socrates took to be but a painting of an ideal vision is in fact a portrait of a forgotten historical fact. Then the priest tells Solon of the unparalleled valor and skill of Athens in turning back an invasion by the formidable army launched from the island of Atlantis that saved the whole Mediterranean world from conquest. Afterward, a great earthquake destroyed ancient Athens and swallowed the island of Atlantis into the sea.

This whole story—about the value of preserving written records—is recalled with much effort overnight by the younger Critias (to whom it was recalled by the elder Critias, who remembered hearing it as a child from Solon, who recalled being told it by the priest), having been reminded of it by Socrates's discourse yesterday. How indeed could he forget a story that was burned into his mind at such an early age! Having said all this by way of "preface" (26C), Critias volunteers to Socrates to tell him the whole story in detail, for the story of Athenian victory over Atlantis will satisfy Socrates's demand to see the still life painted in the *Republic* put in motion, to see the *polis* at work, that is, at war. Critias divides the task between himself and Timaeus, who is the astronomer among them. To all this Socrates responds that he can think of nothing better than to receive this feast of reason. The remainder of the *Timaeus* is devoted to Timaeus's discourse on the creation of the *kosmos*, while what has been preserved of Critias's speech—concerning the battle with Atlantis—appears in the dialogue of that name.

So much "khôral" play, so many "khôral"-ographies, so many stagings, enactments, imagings, and reflections of *khôra* in the text before it becomes a philosopheme: "[A] chain of oral traditions," "[s]o many Greek children," reflections reflecting themselves—all of which is told

Socrates, who receives all (*Khôra* 72–73/ON 115), who reflects every image, and is remembered by Critias because it was told him as a child, at an "impressionable" age, when the story made a lasting imprint upon him, "as if painted with wax in indelible letters" (26c). In childhood, the mind is like a pure receptacle.

An enframing *mise en abîme* of fictions stages the scene the *Timaeus*: F1: the *Timaeus* is a fictitious dialogue which contains another fiction: it opens by "reflecting" (on) the conversation of "yesterday." F2: that second fiction, the *Republic*, constructs the fictive model of an ideal city. F3: the brief résumé of the *politeia* by Socrates at the beginning of the *Timaeus*. Socrates then says that he would like to see this ideal figure of the *politeia* put in motion, like a man looking at a painting of a beautiful animal who would like to see the animal given life, so that "today's" conversation would add a second, more living *graphe* to the first. For this Socrates says he himself would be all ears, or all eyes, a ready receptacle, but he is not capable of generating it himself. Critias accepts the challenge, volunteering to tell Socrates a story he rehearsed the night before to Timaeus and Hermocrates (= F4), which is the tale he learned from his grandfather (= F5), who in turn was told it by Solon (= F6), who was told it from a priest who read it in the old Egyptian writings (F7).

Of this multi-plex textualized surface—which we are otherwise inclined to treat as a kind of literary preamble to the serious philosophy to come—Derrida asks:

> In this theater of irony, where the scenes interlock in a series of receptacles without end and without bottom, how can one isolate a thesis or a theme that could be attributed calmly to the "philosophy-of-Plato," indeed to *philosophy* as the Platonic thing [*Khôra* 80/ON 119]?

To do so is to flatten out and smooth over all the folds and plies of the text, to "violently deny the structure of the textual scene," to brush off this play of reflections as incidental, marginal, accidental asides and indulge in still another fiction called "the philosophy of Plato."[6] The analysis serves to:

---

[6] The text is laced with ironies. The Athenians, the addressees to whom this tale is being told, are also the source, model, and inspiration of the tale. All this talk about tales being told is, of course, all written down by Plato, even as all these stories (fictions) are about the greatest deed or work (*ergon*) of the Greeks. Of Solon himself, a man of deeds, we are told that he would have been a great poet had he not been interrupted by the demands of actuality.

accentuate the dynamic tension between the thetic effect and the textual fiction, between on the one hand the "philosophy" or the "politics" which is here associated with him [Socrates]—contents of identifiable and transmissible meanings like the identity of a knowledge—and on the other hand a textual drift which takes the form of a myth, in any event of a "saying," whose origin appears always undefined, pulled back, entrusted to a responsibility that is forever adjourned, without a fixed and determinable subject. From one telling to the next, the author gets further and further away [*Khôra* 90/ON 123–24].

The origin of the text is more and more withdrawn, the author more and more ancient ("dead"), the text more deeply interwoven in other texts, so that there is no easily identified and assured origin in this genealogy, no clearly identified father of the text, which ends up being a bit of a bastard or an orphan. This in contrast to what is said in the *Phaedrus:* that while written texts are orphans, the living word always has its father/author on hand to defend it lest it be misunderstood.

Derrida's point here, as in "Plato's Pharmacy," his first and quite famous essay on Plato, is that every text, written or oral, is a bastard or an orphan, its father/author having departed, and that this is a *structural* feature of discourse, which is always already interwoven with and *contained by* other texts, whose roots sink into a dense context which we have only limited success in unraveling. Even a book of genesis is caught up in a genealogy and family history we cannot make out or remember. The text is always a bastard. This system or boxes inside boxes, containers containing containers—this *"khôral"* quality—is a feature of textuality itself. We are all like the Greeks whom the Egyptian priest scolds, children whose fathers have fled the family scene.

So, when Timaeus gets around to discussing *khôra* in the middle, in the mid-place (*mi-lieu*), of the *Timaeus* he invokes this "familial schema." *Khôra* is called a nurse who receives and nurtures sensible things into maturity, or a mother in whom the *eidos* fathers its offspring, sensible things. Of course, *khôra* is not really a wife or a nurse but *sui generis*, a third thing (*triton genos*), an individual (a "this") and not even a genus. She/it is too passive and indeterminate even to engender anything, and we cannot assimilate her/it into any anthropological or theological schemas. She/it is not an origin at all but, if anything, the "relation of the interval of the spacing to what is lodged in it to be received in it" (*Khôra* 92/ON 125). *Khôra* is not a normal origin or mother—she and the *eidos* do not make up a familiar family, a happy couple. But that is not bad news. The *khôra* is not the product of sloppy thinking, but a case where Plato has pressed the fabric of philosophy hard, where Plato finds himself up against something that slips free of philosophy, that eludes and is exterior to philosophy, older than philosophy, pre-philosophical, of which philosophy knows how to speak neither truly nor probably. That is why philosophy tends to stick to the father (*eidos*) and its legitimate son (*cosmos*), as if the father begets the son without the help of a woman—a bad biology to which the whole history of philosophy and theology gives ample witness.

To think out the origin of the *kosmos* one must go back to something outside thought, out of mind—like the antique Athens recalled by the Egyptian priest but wiped out without a trace and utterly forgotten by the Athenians of Socrates's day. By the same token, philosophy must invoke a forgotten preorigin which is structurally lost to philosophy's memory.

TWO TROPICS OF NEGATIVITY

It might appear at times that *khôra* looks a little like the unknown God, the *deus absconditus*, the mysterious origin beyond origin, about whom we cannot say a thing. This confusion or convergence of deconstruction and negative theology was something for which Derrida was criticized—why not congratulated?—right out of the gate, back in 1967, at the first presentation of the essay on *"différance,"* to which he has replied on several occasions, including a 1986 essay entitled "How Not to Speak: Denials" (*Psy.* 535ff./DNT 73ff.), which includes an interesting discussion of *"khôra."* While the essay *"Khôra"* is a preface—on the preface to the *Timaeus*—to a work that is still unpublished, "How Not to Speak" explores the analogy and, more important, the disanalogy of *khôra* with the God of negative theology. This essay provides us with an opportunity to learn a little something about *différance* and to understand something, albeit something negative, about the relationship between deconstruction and theology.[7]

---

[7] I have explored this question in some detail in my *Prayers and Tears of Jacques Derrida*, Part I; and in "The Good News About Alterity: Derrida and Theology," *Faith and Philosophy*, 10 (1993), 453–470; "Mysticism and Transgression: Derrida and Meister Eckhart," *Continental Philosophy*, 2 (1989), 24–39. See also Rodolphe Gasché, "God, For Example" in *Inventions of Difference* (Cambridge, Mass.: Harvard

In this essay Derrida draws our attention to the tension between what he calls two "tropics of negativity," that is, two opposing ways in which philosophical thought finds itself up against its limits, against something that resists being said, two things equally unsayable but for quite opposite reasons. The first is the most familiar and prestigious text in all of Plato's work—the one that makes all the standard anthologies used in "Introduction to Philosophy" courses—the famous and sublime passage from the *Republic*, 509Bff. in which Plato describes the idea of the Good as "beyond being" (*epekeina tes ousias*). Here the movement (the "tropic") of negativity, of not-saying or unsayability, is upward, hyperbolic, "obeying a logic of the *sur*, of the *hyper*, over and beyond, which heralds all the hyper-essentialisms" of Christian Neoplatonism. For the tradition of negative theology, stretching from pseudo-Dionysius the Areopagite to Meister Eckhart, turned on a view of the Christian God that had been basically cast in the terms of Plato's theory of the Good beyond Being. In this first movement, thinking has run up against an excess of transcendence, a being of such supereminent sur-reality that, while giving birth to being, movement, and knowledge, it is itself beyond them all. Still, as the offspring of its father and cause, the sensible world is "like" the Good, and, so, the excess of the Good is situated within an "analogical community" in virtue of which the sensible world is said to be "like" the intelligible world. Hence, the Good can be sensibly compared to the "sun" of the sensible world; for, like the sun, the Good is neither seeing nor visible, neither knowing nor intelligible, but a third thing, viz., their light, cause, and medium (*Psy.* 563–566).

But the *khora* constitutes another way to be otherwise than Being, another kind of third thing, one moving in a fully opposite direction and submitting to different tropes. Rather than "hyperexistence" or supereminent being, *khôra* seems to drop below being, barely to be at all, to be if at all next to nothing. Derrida maintains that Plato has adopted two very heterogeneous ways of speaking about this quasi-being or shadowy realm called *khôra*, about which it is admittedly very hard to speak, but for reasons that are opposite to the "Good." In the first strategy, the resistance of *khôra* to philosophical discourse is bro-

University Press, 1994), pp. 150–170; Kevin Hart, *The Trespass of the Sign: Deconstruction, Theology, and Philosophy* (Cambridge: Cambridge University Press, 1985); and the essays collected in *Derrida and Negative Theology* (DNT).

ken down and *khôra* is assimilated into philosophy, assigned a place interior to philosophy—and this by way of being treated according to the classical mode of analogy which governs the allegory of the cave. *Khôra* itself is neither intelligible nor sensible, but "participates" in predicates of *both*; hence, it can be analogically said to be "mother, nurse, sieve, receptacle, impression." That allows us to sketch a kind of Platonic "holy family": the father (= form) generates his offspring (= sensible thing) in the mother (= receptacle). Or we may say that the receptacle holds and embraces the sensible thing like a nurse (50D). That takes the foundling *khôra* off the streets and provides it with a home in the holy family of philosophy, in the interior of the canonical history of philosophy, as a predecessor of Aristotelian *hyle*, Cartesian *extensio*, and the pure form of space in Kant (*Psy.* 566–567/DNT 104–105).

But it is the second way that Plato *also* describes *khôra* that is of more interest to Derrida, for here *khôra* tends to slip outside philosophy, to resist any analogizing or participatory schema, to remain adrift and lost. Now, Plato says *khôra* is "amorphous," and even though things come to be and pass away in it, *khôra* itself does not become (or "participate" in) any of these things (50B–C). Although *khôra* takes on the look of the things with which it is filled, that is true only for the while that they persist and these things do not in any way stain or mark it in their brief station. Hence, *khôra* can be likened *neither* to its sensible imprints, which vanish from it without a trace, nor to intelligible paradigms, which are still more removed from it (*Khôra* 15–16/ON 89). It is, therefore, not a receptacle, because it is "older" than any receptacle, which is something later on inscribed in it. As something absolutely indifferent to anything sensible or intelligible, it cannot be treated metaphorically, which always amounts to providing a sensible likeness for something intelligible (*Khôra* 21–22/ON 92). It is not so much a third kind as no kind, without generic determination. *Khôra* is just there; "there is" (*il y a*) *khôra*, and this meant in the most minimalist sense. This "there is" must not be confused with any generosity; it is not to be taken to mean that it "gives" anything, as in the German "there is/*es gibt*." It is nothing kindly and generous, and does not "give" or provide a place, which is the trap that Heidegger falls into when he finds a "giving" in this *es gibt* which puts thinking-as-thanking in its debt. Nor is it properly receiving, since it is unaffected by that by which it is filled. It is not even absolutely passive inasmuch as both active and passive operations take place in it. It resists every theomorphic or anthropomorphic analogy. It is not any kind of "it" (*il*, *id*, *quod*) that is or does or gives anything.

Hence, *khôra*, which can be spoken of neither properly nor metaphorically, pushes up against the very limits of naming (*Khôra*, 15/ ON, 89). The point of his analysis, Derrida says, is to show that this impossibility of finding a proper name for *khôra*, the *mot juste* over and outside of some rhetorical trope or other, is not some sort of failing on Plato's part, or the bad luck this passage in the *Timaeus* has had in the history of interpretation, but a *structural* feature of Plato's thought. Plato has been forced by the things themselves to include *khôra* within his account—he cannot "not speak" of it—yet he does not know to "not speak" of it, that is, to respect its negativity. For the task of discussing the *khôra* is that of determining something indeterminable, something that cannot *in principle* take on any determination, neither that of the paradigm nor that of the copy. Everything Plato says of it, or that is said of it in the history of interpretation, comes too late, constituting a retrospective illusion, an "anachronism" (*Khôra* 24–26/ ON 93–94) born of speaking of it in terms borrowed from the things which it contains but from which it itself withdraws. *Khôra* is indifferent to every determination—not serenely or sublimely indifferent, for it is too lowly for that and that is the wrong trope and tropics, but let us say abysmally indifferent. *Khôra* is always "prior" to any mark or imprint, any form or determination that is attributed to it; it has nothing proper, no property of its own. It receives all and becomes none of what it receives, like the air that remains free of the light by which it is suffused (*Khôra* 36–37/ON 99), like a mirror that remains unaffected by the images that come and go across its surface. *Khôra* belongs to a time out of mind, out of memory, to a preorigin older than memory, like the ancient city of Athens that did battle with Atlantis only to disappear without a trace (*Khôra* 96/ON 126).

Of this implacably, impossibly difficult thing, we do not know how to speak or how to avoid speaking; indeed, it is this impossibility that drives the need to say something about it. *Khôra* is not a universal (abstract place in general), nor a particular (a contained place), but something radically singular: place itself—within which multiple places are inscribed. Like every singularity. it bears a proper name— treat *Khôra* as if it were a proper name, like someone you know, capitalized—even though it has no proper name or essential propriety but just takes on the form of whatever inhabits it. For we need, we must, speak of "*something like the khôra*—which is not something and which is not *like* anything" (*Khôra* 26/ON 94), some way to determine this utterly indeterminable somewhat. We need some way to address it: not "the *khôra*" but "Oh, *Khôra*." "Who are you, *Khôra*" (*Khôra* 63/ON 111)? By using the word *khôra* and thus drawing upon the stock of common Greek nouns, Plato picks up a trace left *in* language by something that has withdrawn *from* language (*Psy.* 567–569/DNT 105–108), sinking beneath its surface, like Atlantis sinking into the sea.

The discourse on the *khôra* thus forms an almost perfect inversion of the discourse on the Good. On the one account, things are described from above, in a tropics of *hyper* and *au delà*, beginning with the Good as the supremely real, hyper-essential, sur-real source of sensible things and the inextinguishable light in which they are seen to be the copies of their intelligible paradigms. That would provide an agreeable schema to Christian Neoplatonism, which seized upon it as a way to articulate its experience of the transcendence of God. On the other account, things are explained from below, in a trope of *hypo* and *en deçà*, beginning with an almost perfectly unintelligible or indeterminate origin, or non-origin, or pre-origin, in which sensible things are inscribed according to eternal patterns. On the one hand, a hyper-essential sur-reality for which words fail us, of which words fall short; on the other, a hypo-essential sub-reality, an almost unreal, indeterminable indeterminacy which seems rather to fail words, to fall short of word or meaning. In biblical terms, it was perhaps a little more like the chaos over which the spirit of God bent. On the one hand, hyperbole and the excess of being, essence, and meaning; on the other, defection, less than meaning, essence, and being. On the one hand, a classic philosopheme; on the other, exorbitant textuality—and *différance*.

DIFFÉRANCE: *KHÔRA* IS ITS SURNAME

Derrida is interested in *khôra* for family reasons, not because *khôra* is a mother or a wet nurse, but because she/it is a cousin (*cousin/cousine*) of deconstruction, a kin of the kin-less, of the same non-kind as what he calls *différance*. If *différance* is what deconstruction is all about, in a nutshell, then "*khôra* is its surname" (*Khôra* 95/ON 126). To deploy a famous Platonic image: the story of *khôra* works like an "allegory" of *différance*, each addressing a common, kindred non-essence, impropriety, and namelessness. Just as Plato composed the allegory of the cave to explain the surpassing excess of the *agathon*, so, on the other side of being, Derrida can put Timaeus's story of the *khôra* to work explaining the lowly recessiveness of *différance*, being's humble hinterlands or underside. It also helps us to understand the divergence of deconstruction and negative theology, since *différance* is *khôra's* cousin, not God's. Derrida loves *khôra* the way he loves *différance*, illegitimate children both.

In another work, entitled *Sauf le nom*, the second part of a trilogy "on the name" of which *Khôra* is the third part, Derrida speaks of " 'something' without thing, like an indeconstructible *Khôra*." But something like *khôra* is "indeconstructible" not because she/it is a firm foundation, like a metaphysical ground or principle, or like the eternal form of the Good, that can be "sheltered from deconstruction." Rather, her undeconstructibility arises because she is a "place" that takes place "as the very spacing of de-construction" (*Sauf* 104/ON 80), the space in *which* everything constructible and deconstructible is constituted, and, hence, beyond the reach of construction or deconstruction. *Différance*, like *khôra*, is a great receptacle upon which every constituted trace or mark is imprinted, "older," prior, preoriginary.

Far from bearing a likeness to the God of the great monotheisms, a "super-being" (*hyperousios*) who is affirmed all the more eminently in being negated in the negative theology of Christian Neoplatonism, a God to whom Plato's *agathon* bears a family resemblance, *différance* is better compared to *khôra*, that is, to the incomparable, unmetaphorizable, desert-like place without properties or genus. Rather than of the edifying, uplifting, highly proper, and propitious family resemblance of God and the *agathon*, the father of us all, both above and beyond Being—these are the best families and they travel in the highest circles!—it is perhaps better, more graphic, to think, of *khôra* and *différance* as a couple of bastards. (As an aside, it is also worth asking oneself where the hearts of the prophets and of Jesus would be—with the St. James's street aristocrats, the best and the brightest, or with the Dickensonian bastards.)

Levinas was fond of saying that, although the transcendent God of the Hebrew scriptures was systematically excluded by the totalizing categories of Greek philosophy, still from time to time the utter alterity of God did on rare occasions break out in philosophy—most notably in Descartes's idea of the infinity of God in the Third Meditation, and in Plato's notion of the *epekeina tes ousias*, the Good beyond being. Derrida may be understood to make a counter-move to Levinas, or, better, to offer a counter-part by which the Levinasian gesture is always already disturbed (for it will never be a matter of choosing between these two). For Derrida, *khôra* may be taken as one of those "places" in the history of philosophy where the *différance* by which all things are inhabited wears through, where the abyss in things opens up and we catch a glimpse of the groundlessness of our beliefs and practices. The face of the other person, Levinas says in a very uplifting and beautiful image at the end of *Otherwise than Being*, is the trace God leaves behind as he withdraws from the world.[8]

Khôra, Derrida might say, in a more downgrading and not-all-that-beautiful image, is one of the traces *différance* leaves on Plato, on the Greeks, on philosophy, on us—for "we" are all marked by the Greeks and (their) "philosophy"—as it "retreats" from view. As the spacing in which the traits of our beliefs and practices are inscribed, *différance* is in *re-trait*. That is why Derrida says that, in speaking of the *khôra*, Plato has not simply invented some utterly novel idea; rather, he has borrowed a word from the common stock of Greek nouns, but a word in which a certain formlessness or namelessness has left its mark (*Khôra* 18/ON 90-91), something about which philosophy cannot philosophize, something that resists philosophy, that withdraws from philosophy's view and grasp. Not from above, as in the uplifting and edifying mode of Plato, Levinas, and negative theology, but from below, as if passing beneath philosophy's vision, too low for philosophy to go—"behind and below the assured discourse of philosophy" (*Khôra* 94/ON 125).

In the *khôra*, Plato gives expression to an intractable "necessity" below, an uncircumventable, an achronic "preorigin," which is not to be confused with the Eternal, Originary "Truth" (capital letters for capital fellows!) of the intelligible paradigms above:

> The strange difficulty of this whole text lies indeed in the distinction between these two modalities: the true and the necessary. The bold stroke consists here in going back behind and below the origin, or also

[8] Emmanuel Levinas, *Otherwise than Being, or, Beyond Essence*, trans. Alphonso Lingis (The Hague: Martinus Nijhoff, 1981), p. 185.

the birth, toward a necessity which is neither generative nor engendered and which carries philosophy, "precedes" (prior to the time that passes or the eternal time before history) and "receives" the effect, here the image of oppositions (intelligible and sensible): philosophy. This necessity (*khôra* is its sur-name) seems so virginal that it does not even have the name of virgin any longer [*Khôra* 94–95/ON 126].

In the *khôra* Plato affirms—or concedes—a counter-origin, a non-engendering non-origin, truth-less, intractable and necessary, down below, that in its own way mocks the prestigious, fatherly, originary, truth-making power of the *eidos* (and above all of the Good) up above. As far as Derrida is concerned, Plato is here hitting upon the effect that *différance* always produces, running up against the necessity that *différance* always imposes on any discourse—and "*khôra* is its sur-name." By "necessity," then, Derrida does not mean an eternal or necessary truth but the necessary un-truth that forces itself into every verity. So, Derrida is interested in *khôra* because he regards it as a tip-off, a signal, or a clue that philosophy is in a certain amount of trouble here—like a politician who is asked an embarrassing question for which his advance men did not prepare him. Plato has here run up against an effect of *différance* and may be read as telling us a likely story about *différance*, offering us a mirror image or likeness of that which robs his—the—assured distinction between origin and copy of its security.

So, if you can bear it, if you are not already too dizzy, I propose one last *mise en abîme*: the *khora* reflects *différance* (a play of reflections in a black pool). *Khora* is its sur-name, its over-name, the name we inscribe over an abyss. For just as *khôra*, by providing the space within which the sensible copy of the intelligible is inscribed, precedes and precontains the opposition between the two, so *différance* precedes and precontains all the oppositions that are inscribed within it, including those oppositional distinctions with which philosophy opened for business among the Greeks.

Let us then, like the fool who says in his heart that God does not exist, ask "what" *différance* "is," in a nutshell, having duly noted the impossibility of asking anything that foolish. By *différance*, Derrida does not mean anything mysterious—technically speaking, "*différance*" does not "mean" anything at all, and if it does, "he" (Derrida) does not "mean" it, for the same reason that it does not answer to a "what" or an "is." In the most tentative and general sense, Derrida is describing the code of repeatability, of which language is the most familiar but by no means the only example, within which our beliefs and practices are "inscribed." Rather than thinking of language in the classical way, as a set of exterior signs of already constituted interior thoughts (another defining feature of "logocentrism"), Derrida, following Saussure and modern linguistics, thinks of users of language invoking coded, that is, repeatable, marks or traces that build up or constitute from within certain unities of meaning as "effects" of the code. These traces are not inherently meaningful in themselves but "arbitrary" and "conventional." Thus it makes no difference whether you say "*rex*," "*roi*," or "king" so long as "we"—those who share these conventions"—can tell the *difference* between *rex* and *lex*, *roi* and *loi*, and king and sing. The meaning—and reference—is a function of the difference, of the *distance* or the "spacing" between the traces, what is called, in a perfectly serious way, the "play" of differences or traces. By the "play of differences" Derrida does not mean something capricious, like romping in the nude down the Champs-Elysées (cf. UG 112/AL 289), but the differential spacing, the discerned distance, the perceived (heard, seen) intervals between traces first analyzed in structural linguistics. [9]

That meaning and reference is a function of the play of differences is confirmed in a perfectly serious and quite commonsensical way every time we use a dictionary. The "meaning" and "reference" of a word in a dictionary is set in terms of *other words* with which it is internally related. A word has a "place" in a dictionary, not only the one that you have to "look up," which is a function of its graphic setting (its spelling), but also a semantic place or setting, a position, a range of connotation and denotation relative to other words (places) in the language. The meaning of a word is defined differentially, relative to the meaning of other words. What you will never find in the dictionary is a word that detaches itself from these internal relationships and sends you sailing right out of the dictionary into a mythical, mystical thing in itself "outside" of language, wistfully called the "transcendental signified." A serious dictionary is a good sober example of the "play of differences," of the differential spacing within which, by

---

[9] See Ferdinand de Saussure, *Course in General Linguistics*, trans. Roy Harris (London: Duckworth, 1983); for a helpful commentary, see Jonathan Culler, *Ferdinand de Saussure*, rev. ed. (Ithaca, N.Y.: Cornell University Press, 1986).

means of which, all the users of the language make what sense they are able to make. So when Derrida says of *"khôra"* that it is "the relation of the interval or the spacing to what is lodged in it to be received in it" (*Khôra* 92/ON 125), that is also well said of *différance*, to speak darkly and through a veil (and *never* face to face!) of *différance*.

In classical terms, Derrida is deeply resistant to "essentialism," the notion that there are ideal meanings ("presence") that somehow or another antedate the play of traces to which the play must conform itself (must "represent"). Essentialism is a view that legitimately traces its genealogy back to Plato himself, to at least "one" Plato, the famous, dominant, orthodox, patriarchal, aristocratic, classical, philosophical one, the one you have to know to pass your Plato course. (You will have to attend a course at the Collège if you want to learn about the bastards.) Derrida holds, on the other hand, that presence is always the "effect" of the play of traces, of "representations"—whence his (not all that) paradoxical dictum that presence is the effect of representation (VP 58/SP 52). For meaning and reference are always built up slowly and tentatively from below, from within the networks of codes and assumptions within which we all always and already operate.[10]

Derrida's notion of *différance* results from introducing two improvements on this Saussurean point of departure.

(1) In the first place, Derrida argues that, though rule-bound up to a point—let's be serious: there surely are rules of grammar and of usage, standardized and normalized linguistic practices—the play of traces is not a "closed system" but ultimately an open-ended play (see DLG 42–108/OG 27–73). He argues against the "closure" of the play and holds that the effects of which "iterability," the code of repeatability, is capable cannot in principle be contained, programmed, or predicted. It always possible, *in principle*, as a "structural" matter, to repeat differently; that is built right into the very idea of "iterability" or "repetition." Furthermore, any such "laws" as one would "forge" (formulate/fake) would themselves be effects or subsets of the play of traces, would be inscribed within them "later" and so would not govern over them *a priori* (earlier). The play of differences is always "older" than any of its effects, constituting a quasi-*arche* "before" the archical law the rules would impose. Laws are always deconstructible, but the play of traces, in itself, if it has an itself, is not deconstructible.

---

[10] For a more careful exposition of Derrida's claim, see my *Radical Hermeneutics*, chap. 5.

That is why Derrida will also speak of *différance* as an *archi*-writing, which is reflected here when he calls the *khôra* a "pre-origin." By archi-writing Derrida does not mean that, historically, writing is older than speech, as his careless critics too precipitously claim. Nor is he trying to establish writing as a *still higher principle* of language than any logico-semantical laws. Rather than on a firm foundation or perfectly enclosed system he is trying to pull the plug on any leak-proof system by acknowledging a still lower un-principle, an unsettling, dis-placing "necessity" we are under to labor always under a play of traces, having to cope with an irrepressible iterability that can never be contained or decisively regulated. He does not stake out the ground of a higher principle but concedes a certain *an-arche* at the bottom of our principles. Derrida is not denying that we have "principles" and "truth"—let the word go forth and let there be no mistake about that. He is just reinscribing our truths and principles within the an-arche of *différance*, attaching to them a co-efficient of "contingency." For the only "necessity" he acknowledges is the necessity that precedes all oppositions, including that between the principle and what is based upon the principle, the necessity, the requirement, always to forge truths and principles slowly from below, inscribing them in a vast and meaning-less receptacle called *différance*.

That is why you cannot, *stricto sensu*, ask "what" *différance* "is," or for its "meaning" or "truth." Strictly speaking: it is the condition of possibility of these things, which are so many effects of its play, traces traced on its surface, from which it itself withdraws (*re-trait*). More strictly still: *différance* is a quasi-condition of possibility, because it does not describe fixed boundaries that delimit what can happen and what not, but points a mute, Buddhist finger at the moon of uncontainable effects. Everything from the God of Christian Neoplatonism to rubbish heaps, from the most sublime laws of physics or ethics to the hate-talk on Rush Limbaugh's radio show, from the Declaration of Independence to street-corner rap—everything is inscribed in *différance*, which is its enabling and also slightly disabling quasi-condition.

This notion of *différance* as a quasi-condition provides us with the answer to the question of the analogy or convergence of deconstruction and negative theology. Deconstruction is deeply enamored of the strategic and formal resources of negative theology. Deconstruction loves the way that negative theology has found to say the unsayable, the twists and turns it takes in dealing with the impossible by which it has been struck, with its impossible desire, all of which Derrida deeply admires, so that to be compared with negative theology is no criticism for him, but a high compliment that associates him with the best families. But in the end Derrida must defer this honor and decline this high compliment and 'fess up that deconstruction consorts with bastards. Deconstruction has to do not with the *hyperousios*, the super-being beyond being, but with something like *khôra*, a *cousin/cousine* if there is such a thing, something that is neither a being nor a non-being, but a certain "quasi-condition" within which both are inscribed. So Derrida thinks of negative theology as a kind of "hyperessentialism," faced with the problem of how not to speak of a "transcendent" being beyond being, whereas deconstruction, humbly and from below, has the problem of how not to speak of this quasi-transcendental condition, this necessity or necessary condition, this condition of possibility and impossibility, called *différance*.

To try to make this "necessity" without truth, this necessary untruth, look more edifying, think of the way, after the apple, God sent Adam and Eve packing and imposed upon them the "necessity" of work, sweat, and pain, and, later on, after the tower, disseminated the tongues of the builders at Babel and imposed upon them the "necessity" of translation. Just so, godless *différance* imposes upon us all the necessity to work out meaning and reference by the work, sweat, and pain of the "play" (some fun!) of differences, the necessity to translate among many competing codes, to cope even with incompatible codes, and to hold our head as a sea of iterability washes over us.

Still, this necessity does not cause Derrida to lose heart: "these traits are not negative" (*Khôra* 94/ON 126), but, rather, a way to keep things open, since deconstruction for Derrida is always an affirmation of the other, a precursorial way to make way for the invention of the other. Thus, a good deal of the analyses undertaken by Derrida test the limits, push to the frontiers, transgress the boundaries, that are put in place by the several "-ologies" that would regulate the "an-archic freedom" of the trace. Derrida is constantly interested in the new, unpredictable, unforeseeable, unprogrammable "effects" that are forth-coming, in-coming, in-ventable within a currently prevailing set of conventions. Hence, if Derrida is not an essentialist, neither is he a conventionalist, for conventionalism is just an alternate way of regulating and containing the play of traces. Deconstruction is, rather, an unconventional conventionalism, an *in-ventionalism*, bent on giving things a new bent or twist, on twisting free of the containing effects of both essentialism and conventionalism, in order to release certain unforeseeable effects, looking for "openings," making room for—giving a place to—what is unforeseeable relative to some horizon of foreseeability.

(2) In addition to arguing against closure, Derrida also generalizes what was originally a linguistic model in Saussure so that *différance* is not restricted to language but leaves its "mark" on everything—institutions, sexuality, the worldwide web, the body, whatever you need or want. This does not amount to arguing that these things are all linguistic—an error he calls "linguisticism"—which is true only up to a point. Rather, he is arguing that, *like* language, all these structures are marked by the play of differences, by the "spacing" of which *différance* is one of the names. That is why he speaks of the "trace" and not the "signifier," which belongs to linguistics and would implicate him in a linguisticism with which he would have no part, although that is a mistake of which he is commonly accused by people who must, I am convinced, be going on secondhand accounts of his work.

In the previous chapter, we saw what deep interest Derrida takes in "institutions." In an institution, individuals are distributed across a hierarchized, institutional spacing, a play of places, which define in advance the role, the power, and the voice of the individual, something that is embodied in expressions like the "main office," the "top floor," and "power corridor." To live and work within an institution is to exercise a "differential" function, to be inserted or inscribed within the differential space of the institutional hierarchy. That spacing is true no less of society at large. Contrary to Rousseauism, the young Derrida argued (DLG 149–202/OG 101–40), even the most "primitive" society is marked by this spacing, hierarchy, *différance*, or "archi-writing," even if such a society lacks writing in the strict or narrow sense. Wherever one is, one is placed within a play of differences, "received" or "inscribed" within *différance*—in a family, an institution, a society, a language, a history, an academic discipline, an army, etc.

Or in a sexual relationship—whence all the attention Derrida pays to the gender issues surrounding *khôra*. The debate about homosexuality comes down to a debate about an over-organized, over-regulated, narrowly oppositional space in which there are only two hierarchically ordered places, a "binarity" of male and female, of male over female. For Derrida, the way to break this up is to open up all the *other* places that this binary scheme closes off. In Derrida's view, "male" and "female" are fixed containers, prisons, trapping men no less than women within one place, one role, closing off the possibility of "innumerable" genders, not just two. That is why "feminism," while constituting a strategically necessary moment of "reversal," a salutary overturning that purges the system of its present masculinist hegemony, must give way to "displacement," which is a more radical "gender bender" in which the whole masculine/feminine schema is skewed. So *différance*, the "third kind" or genus, makes it possible to get beyond (or beneath) two kinds, not just to three, but to the "innumerable," that is, to the indefinitely new, because differential, possibilities that are opened up once you acknowledge the contingency of "two." "One, two, three, but where, my dear Timaeus, is the fourth . . ." (*Timaeus* 17A)?[11]

It should not go unnoticed that Derrida describes this dream of innumerable genders as "choreographies," *khôra*-ographies, that is, the joyful, dance-like marking off of places, multiplying the places of sexual spacing (PdS 95–116/*Points* 89–108; cf. OCP 227–228). The effects of a deconstructive analysis as regards the issues of gender cover a wide range. For deconstruction wants to let "straight" men get in touch with their feminine side, and "straight" women with their masculine side, and, hence, to bend up these rectilinear orthodoxies a little. But it is also happy to see men get in touch with men, and women with women, gay and lesbian "rights" (which also means "straight"). *Dilige et quod vis fac.* But in the end, it would "disseminate" the very idea of "masculine" and "feminine" as narrow, contingent, constraining straitjackets, "straight" effects within an indefinite, differential play of traces.

Différance, containing all, including all the genders, all the places, is a *pandekhon*, not as a universal container mothering, nursing, or "holding" all, but, more paradoxically, as an open-ended and porous receptacle of the *uncontainable*, of innumerable and incalculable effects, as an un-principle, an an-arche. *Différance* is an absolutely neutral receptacle—*khôra* is its sur-name—that suppresses nothing, releasing the innumerable, the unforeseeable, the "invention of the other."

Différance is the nameless name of this open-ended, uncontainable, generalizable play of traces.

And *khôra* is its sur-name.

---

[11] For more on Derrida and feminism, see Diane Elam, *Feminism and Deconstruction: Ms. en Abyme* (New York: Routledge, 1994); and the collection entitled *Derrida and Feminism: Recasting the Question of Woman*, ed. Ellen Feder, Mary Rawlinson, Emily Zakin (New York: Routledge, Chapman, and Hall, forthcoming).

4

Community Without Community

> "Pure unity or pure multiplicity—when there is only total-
> ity or unity and when there is only multiplicity or disassoci-
> ation—is a synonym of death."
>
> —"Roundtable," 13

> "I have always had trouble vibrating in unison."
>
> —PdS 358/Points 348

Deconstruction gets blamed for a lot of things—for everything from
undermining the law of gravity to supporting Mormon polygamy and
to starting the wars in Bosnia! At least, it has been suggested that the
nationalist wars in central Europe are a good example of the legacy of
the postmodern advocacy of "difference," of the right to be different.[1]
What else can the Croatian difference, the Bosnian difference, the
Islamic difference, the Christian difference breed than strife not harmony, division not unity, war not peace? Alas, I would say such nationalisms are the *last* thing that Derrida means by "difference" and
the *tout autre*, or by the politics of difference and a democracy to
come. Indeed, the various nationalisms are for him the almost perfect
embodiment of "identity," of identitarianism, of self-affirming, self-
protecting, homogenizing identities that make every effort to exclude
the different. Such nationalist identitarianism does everything it can
to prevent the "other" from crossing over "our" borders, from taking
"our" jobs, from enjoying "our" benefits and going to "our" schools,

---

[1] George Fried, "Heidegger's *Polemos*," *Journal of Philosophical Research*, 16
(1991), 145–195, argues that nationalist difference is an example of postmodern difference (see p. 184); see my response in *Demythologizing Heidegger*, pp. 218–219n14
(where I misspelled Fried's name!).

from disturbing "our" language, culture, religion, and public institutions. They could not be more inhospitable to the coming of the other.

Postmodern difference, let us say, the difference that interests Derrida, is deeply multi-cultural, multi-lingual, and multi-racial, representing what I have elsewhere called a highly miscegenated "polymorphism."[2] Derrida does not dismiss the idea of unity and identity out of hand, for "pure" diversity, were such a thing possible, would spell death no less surely than would a "pure" totalitarian unity. But he advocates highly heterogenous, porous, self-differentiating quasi-identities, unstable identities, if that is what they are, that are not identical with themselves, that do not close over and form a seamless web of the selfsame. What Derrida advocates, in a nutshell, is "democracy," which is supposed to be a very generous "receptacle" for every difference imaginable.

That is why Derrida is troubled by, and wants to make a certain trouble for, the word "community":

I don't much like the word community, I am not even sure I like the thing.

If by community one implies, as is often the case, a harmonious group, consensus, and fundamental agreement beneath the phenomena of discord or war, then I don't believe in it very much and I sense in it as much threat as promise.

There is doubtless this irrepressible desire for a "community" to form but also for it to know its limit—and for its limit to be its *opening* [PdS, 366/Points 355].

What he does not like about the word community is its connotations of "fusion" and "identification" (*Sauf* 38/ON 46).[3] After all, *communio*

---

[2] For an elaboration of this polymorphism, see my *Against Ethics*, chap. 3.

[3] In *Pol.* 338, commenting on Blanchot's remark that the Nazi persecution of the Jews makes us feel that "the Jews are our brothers and that Judaism is more than a culture and even more than a religion, but the foundation of our relations with the other," Derrida, who is troubled by this valorization of the "fraternal" and the Jew, asks himself "why would I never have been able to write that? . . . In the same vein, I ask myself why I have never been able to write the word 'community' (avowable or unavowable, operative or in-operative), if I may say so, on my own account, in my own name." Given Blanchot's definition of Judaism, he asks himself, is he being insufficiently Jewish or more than Jewish? Derrida is referring to the discussion of community in Blanchot and Nancy and distancing himself from the terms of the discussion. See Jean-Luc Nancy, *The Inoperative Community*, ed. Peter Connor (Minneapolis: University of Minnesota Press, 1991), and Maurice Blanchot, *The Una-*

is a word for a military formation and a kissing cousin of the word "munitions"; to have a *communio* is to be fortified on all sides, to build a "common" (*com*) "defense" (*munis*), as when a wall is put up around the city to keep the stranger or the foreigner out.[4] The self-protective closure of "community," then, would be just about the opposite of what deconstruction is, since deconstruction is the preparation for the incoming of the other, "open" and "porous" to the other, which would of course make one poor excuse for a defense system. A "universal community" excluding no one is a contradiction in terms; communities always have to have an inside and an outside. That is why Derrida's comments on "community"—which is otherwise a mom-and-apple-pie word, at the very sound of which every politician's knee must bend—are always extremely guarded, on guard against the guard that communities station around themselves to watch out for the other (see *Pol.* 329–331). That, too, is why it was necessary to put the word "we" in scare quotes in the previous chapter. For the deconstructive "we" is always highly qualified and unsure, always running scared, a certain "we who cannot say we," a "we, if such a thing exists."

I said above, referring to Derrida's theory of meaning and truth, that he is neither an essentialist nor a conventionalist, that he subscribes neither to preexisting meanings and truths to which linguistic practices must conform, nor to deeply but inchoately understood practices that exert a more gentle but no less sure rule. In a similar way, we can say here that, as regards social theory, Derrida is neither a liberal nor a communitarian, that he has no more confidence in

---

vowable Community, trans. Pierre Joris (Barrytown, N.Y.: Station Hill Press, 1988). For commentaries on this discussion, see *Community at Loose Ends*, ed. Miami Theory Collective (Minneapolis: University of Minnesota Press, 1991); David Ingram, "The Retreat of the Political in the Modern Age: Jean-Luc Nancy on Totalitarianism and Community," *Research in Phenomenology*, 18 (1988), 93–124; and Robert Bernasconi, who regards the discussion as a debate, "On Deconstructing Nostalgia for Community Within the West: The Debate Between Nancy and Blanchot," *Research in Phenomenology*, 23 (1993), 3–21.

[4] A *communio* is also a common or shared life, from *com* + *munus*, having common "duties" or "functions," doing one's duty to the whole, mutual service. William Corlett, *Community Without Unity: A Politics of Derridian Extravagance* (Durham, N.C.: Duke University Press, 1993), formulates a Derridean (there is no common agreement about how to spell the adjectival form of "Derrida") notion of community in connection with the "gift," one of the senses of *munus*, when a duty or public office is performed without or beyond duty, so that community turns on gift-giving, extravagance. In this way, Corlett means to steer his way between communitarians and liberals.

Rawls's coldly formal guarantee of procedural rights than in snuggling up, à la Alasdair MacIntyre and Stanley Hauerwas, to the hearth of a communal tradition with deep and connatural intuitions of truths that run deeper than we can say or formalize. He is just as troubled by liberalism as by communitarianism, by essentialism as by conventionalism. That is because he is an *in-ventionalist*, because his eye or ear is always turned to what is to come and because he keeps a constant watch for all those forces that would contain what is coming, that would forestall or prevent the invention of the other. Liberalism for him is subjectivism, a philosophy in which everything turns on the "rights" of the "autonomous subject," whereas deconstruction is a philosophy of "responsibility to the other," where everything turns on the turn to the other. Communitarianism, on the other hand, assumes some sort of deep truth in the tradition upon which the individual draws as long as he remains tapped into its flow; whereas for Derrida one must watch out for the ways tradition and community become excuses for conservativism, for the exclusion of the incoming of the other, and hence constitute "as much threat as promise," as much a trap as a tap.

HOSPITALITY

One helpful way to get at Derrida's views on community and identity is to follow his analysis of "hospitality," which is another mom-and-apple-pie word, but a slightly different one, much more to Derrida's liking and with a better fit to the tendencies and rhetoric of deconstruction, one that he can write in his own name, with which he can associate himself.[5] So, just as a rhetorical matter, if someone tries to make deconstruction look bad by claiming it is against community, one could always drape it in respectable robes by saying it prefers "hospitality," that it is a philosophy, a thought, a writing, a doing of "hospitality." If you were intent on making deconstruction look respectable, it would not be a distortion to say that deconstruction is to be understood as a form of hospitality, that deconstruction *is* hospitality, which

---

[5] I am here following Derrida's lectures, still unpublished, entitled "Questions of Responsibility: Hostility/Hospitality," given at Johns Hopkins University in March, 1996 (and elsewhere). There are references to hospitality scattered throughout his published works; see SdM 272–273/SoM 172.

means the welcoming of the other. Deconstruction would thus mean—again in a nutshell—"Let the other come!" "Welcome to the other." If deconstruction had an international headquarters, say in Paris, it would have a large banner hanging over its front door saying "*Bienvenue!*"

The word "hospitality" means to invite and welcome the "stranger" (*l'étranger*), both on the personal level—how do I welcome the other into my home?—and on the level of the state—raising socio-political questions about refugees, immigrants, "foreign" languages, minority ethnic groups, etc. Derrida's interest is drawn to the fact that, by virtue of its etymology, the word "hospitality" carries its opposite within itself (that's a surprise!). The word "hospitality" derives from the Latin *hospes*, which is formed from *hostis*, which originally meant a "stranger" and came to take on the meaning of the enemy or "hostile" stranger (*hostilis*), + *pets* (*potis, potes, potentia*), to have power.[6] "Hospitality," the welcome extended to the guest, is a function of the power of the host to remain master of the premises. A "host" is someone who takes on or receives strangers, who gives to the stranger, even while remaining in control. There is, thus, a certain stress built into the idea of a host (don't we know it!): the one who offers hospitality to the other must be a proprietor, an owner of one's own property, *major domo, maître chez soi*, a "master of the house," as they sing in *Les Mis*. The *hospes* is someone who has the power to host someone, so that neither the alterity (*hostis*) of the stranger nor the power (*potentia*) of the host is annulled by the hospitality. There is an essential "self-limitation" built right into the idea of hospitality, which preserves the distance between one's own and the stranger, between owning one's own property and inviting the other into one's home. So, there is always a little hostility in all hosting and hospitality, constituting a certain "hostil/pitality."

The notion of having and retaining the mastery of the house is essential to hospitality. There is, after all, only a minimum of hospitality, some would say none at all, involved in inviting a large party of guests to your neighbor's house (especially if you do not let the neighbor in on what is going on), or in inviting others to make themselves at home, say, in Central Park or the Grand Canyon, or any other

---

[6] Derrida is following the etymology of Emil Benveniste, in *Le vocabulaire dès institutions indo-européennes* I (Paris: Minuit, 1969), chap. 7, "*L'hospitalité.*"

public place. A host is a host only if he owns the place, and only if he holds on to his ownership, if one *limits* the gift. When the host says to the guest, "Make yourself at home," this is a self-limiting invitation. "Make yourself at home" means: please feel at home, act as if you were at home, but, remember, that is not true, this is not your home but mine, and you are expected to respect my property. When I say "Welcome" to the other, "Come cross my threshold," I am not surrendering my property or my identity. I am not turning myself into *khôra* which welcomes all as an open receptacle. If I say "Welcome," I am not renouncing my mastery, something that becomes transparent in people whose hospitality is a way of showing off how much they own or who make their guests uncomfortable and afraid to touch a thing.

But this *tension* built into "hospitality," this "aporia" or "paralysis"—how can I graciously welcome the other while still retaining my sovereignty, my mastery of the house? How can I limit my gift?—is not negative. On the contrary, it is the condition of possibility (and impossibility) of hospitality. Like everything else in deconstruction, the possibility of hospitality is sustained by its impossibility; hospitality really starts to get under way only when we "experience" (which means to travel or go through) this paralysis (the inability to move). Hospitality *is* impossible, what Derrida calls *the* impossible (the im-possibility of hostil-pitality), which is not the same as a simple logical contradiction. Hospitality really starts to happen when I push against this limit, this threshold, this paralysis, inviting hospitality to cross its own threshold and limit, its own self-limitation, to become a gift *beyond hospitality*. Thus, for hospitality to occur, it is necessary for hospitality to go beyond hospitality. That requires that the host must, in a moment of madness, tear up the understanding between him and the guest, act with "excess," make an absolute gift of his property,[7] which is of course impossible. But that is the only way the guest can go away feeling as if he was really made at home.

This impossibility, this excess, is just what interests Derrida about hospitality. Hospitality, if there is such a thing, is beyond hospitality. Hospitality, "if there is such a thing": that means it never "exists," is

---

[7] The limit case of hospitality would be the "saints" who gives away their home and all their possessions to the poor, which would not be hospitality any longer but a saintly excess. This remarkable convergence of saintly and postmodern excess is explored systematically in Edith Wyschogrod, *Saints and Postmodernism* (Chicago: The University of Chicago Press, 1990).

not "present," is always *to come*. Hospitality is what is always demanded of me, that to which I have never measured up. I am always too close-fisted, too ungracious, too unwelcoming, too calculating in all my invitations, which are disturbed from within by all sorts of subterranean motivations—from wanting to show off what I own to looking for a return invitation. I am never hospitable and I do not know what hospitality is.

You see, then, what deconstruction is about, in a nutshell. Derrida's interest in exploring the tensions within "hospitality" is not aimed at cynically unmasking it as just more mastery and power, as his very hostile and inhospitable critics might think. On the contrary, he wants to show that hospitality is inhabited from within, inwardly disturbed by these tensions, but he does this precisely in order to open hospitality up, to keep it on guard against itself, on the *qui vive*, to open—to push—it *beyond itself*. For it is only that internal tension and instability that keeps the idea of hospitality alive, open, loose. If it is not beyond itself, it falls back into itself and becomes a bit of ungracious meanness, that is, hostile.

Derrida likes to say that we do not know what hospitality is, not because the idea is built around a difficult conceptual riddle, but because, in the end, hospitality is not a matter of objective knowledge, but belongs to another order altogether, beyond knowledge, an enigmatic "experience" in which I set out for the stranger, for the other, for the unknown, where I cannot go. I do not know what is coming, what is to come, what calls for hospitality or what hospitality is called.[8] The aporia is not conceptually resolved by a bit of intellectual adroitness but strained against performatively, by an *act* of generosity, by a giving which gives beyond itself, which is a little blind and does not see where it is going. Hospitality gives to the other with all the aporetics of the "gift," for gifts likewise bind the other to me in gratitude and the need to reciprocate. What is true of hospitality is true, too, of the gift, and of deconstruction itself: it does not come down to knowing anything, but to doing something. (Hospitality reproduces the aporia of the gift, which Derrida also discusses in the "Roundtable" and which we will discuss in the next chapter.)

---

[8] Derrida is here exploiting the four senses of *heißen* in Heidegger's *What Is Called Thinking?* trans. Fred. D. Wieck and J. Glenn Gray (New York: Harper & Row, 1954), pp. 113–125.

This discussion of hospitality allows us better to situate the question of deconstruction and "community." What alerts and alarms Derrida about the form of association described by the word "community," the promise/threat of community, is that, while the word sounds like something warm and comforting, the very notion is built around a defense that a "we" throws up against the "other," that is, it is built around an idea of *inhospitability*, an idea of *hostility* to the *hostis*, not around hospitality. Thus, a "community" is subject to the same "self-limitation" as "hospitality," and, like the word "hospitality," carries within its etymology its own opposite. For the harmony and peace of community depends upon having adequate "munitions" (*munio*, *munitio*) and a readiness for war. (Being able to show the way in which crucial elements of our vocabulary are subject to "self-limitation" is what deconstruction is, in a nutshell.) In hospitality I must welcome the other while retaining mastery of the house; just so, the community must retain its identity while making the stranger at home. If a community is too welcoming, it loses its identity; if it keeps its identity, it becomes unwelcoming. Thus, *the* impossible, the "paralysis" of community, is that it must limit itself, remain a community while remaining "open," forbidding itself the luxury of collecting itself into a unity (PdS 366/*Points* 355). And the "resolution" of the paralysis is the same: performative not constative, an act of madness, a giving without return in which one makes the other welcome, pressing against the limits of this self-limitation. For, following Kant, Derrida also says that every person has the right to be treated with hospitality when traveling to a foreign land.[9]

IDENTITY WITHOUT IDENTITY

In the "Roundtable," Derrida emphasizes the instability of the notion of "identity," that no so-called identity is, or should take itself to be, "homogeneous" or "self-identical," that indeed it is dangerous to let a group—a family, a community, or a state—settle back down into self-identity. This notion is developed in a piece to which he refers us

---

[9] One of the source texts for Derrida in these lectures is Kant's *Perpetual Peace*. See Kant, *On History*, ed. Lewis White Beck (Indianapolis: Bobbs-Merrill, 1963), "Third Definitive Article for a Perpetual Peace: The Law of World Citizenship Shall Be Limited to Conditions of Universal Hospitality," pp. 102–105.

entitled "The Other Heading" (AC/OH), published originally in a newspaper issue dedicated to the question of "European Identity Today."

Europe "today" is shaken by the tremor of unforeseen events—*perestroika*, the break-up of the Soviet Union, German reunification, in a word the "new world order." This constitutes a scene both of possibility—he has never been an orthodox Marxist—and of violence, of genocidal atrocities breaking out in the name of nationalist and religious "identity" (AC 13/OH 6). Derrida reacts to these dangers not by denouncing the very idea of cultural identity, but by deconstructing it, which does not mean—do we have to keep saying this?—leveling it to the ground or leaving it in shambles but opening it up to difference. He thus wants to distinguish an airtight, impermeable, homogeneous, self-identical identity from a porous and heterogeneous identity that differs with itself. Accordingly, it must be an axiom of our reflection, he says, that "what is proper to a culture is to not be identical to itself," that it must differ from itself, even be "different *with* itself" (as when we say in English that we beg to "differ with" so and so) (AC 16/OH 9).

Indeed, what better example of that than Derrida himself, who addresses the question of European identity as someone who is "not quite European by birth," that is, as someone from the "other shore," a Levinasian image for the "other" which is literally true of Derrida, who was born in Algeria, on the southern Mediterranean coast. A French-speaking Algerian Jew whose family had emigrated from Spain in the last century, Derrida says of himself that he has become, with the years, an "over-acculturated, over-colonized European hybrid" (AC 13/OH 7). He is European without quite being European, French without being French, Jewish without being Jewish, Algerian without being Algerian (and even a little bit American). "I am European," he says, "[b]ut I am not, nor do I feel, European *in every part*, that is, European through and through." He is European "among other things," constituted by a cultural and European identity that is not identical to itself (AC 80–81/OH 82–83; PdS 349–361/*Points* 340–350; PdS 216–221/*Points* 203–207).

Derrida does not renounce the idea of cultural identity—one is French or American, speaks a particular language, has a certain citizenship, operates within certain cultural practices—but he wants such identity to be internally differentiated, so that one is *not* identical with oneself, so marked by a "difference with itself" that the very idea of "we" is destabilized. "We" are those who cannot completely say "we," who cannot settle into being *chez soi*, at home with themselves. Whatever institutes community and identity at the same time "forbids it from collecting itself" together (PdS 366/*Points* 355). All the momentum of Heidegger's self-centering, self-gathering center (*Versammlung*), which was never very far from Heidegger's ferocious nationalism, would be divided from itself and opened up to divergence and differentiation, all this Heideggerian *Heim-lichkeit* would be made a little *unheimlich*.[10] "We" all require "culture," but let us *cultivate* (*colere*) a culture of self-differentiation, of differing with itself, where "identity" is an *effect* of difference, rather than cultivating "colonies" (also from *colere*) of the same in a culture of identity which gathers itself to itself in common defense against the other. The only thing that could be self-identical, he allows in the "Roundtable," is a thing itself, something immobilized that lacks freedom, movement, life, history—"It would be, I do not know what, a stone, a rock, or something like that." To be sure, Derrida is speaking here impressionistically, for a closer geological analysis would show that even inorganic substances do not lack atomic and molecular tensions, self-differentiations, layerings, stratifications, histories, and even fossilized traces of life.

Let us pause over an example. "Our" language, here in the U.S.A., "American English," is not quite English, that is, British, nor is it merely American; very early on in its history, British English received quite a dose of French, which gave it a Greco-Latin flavor, and after a couple of centuries in the New World and of being worked over by various Hispanic-, African-, Asian- and who knows what other "-American" experiences, American English has become something internally divided and differentiated. We are not complaining; this is all to its credit. "Monogenealogy would always be a mystification in the history of culture" (AC 17/OH 10–11)

This is not without political import (nothing ever is), and it raises important political questions. The languages of the immigrants, for example, should be kept alive, allowed to feed into and disturb the dominant tongue, in order to preserve these rich national differences and ancient memories, and also to keep the experience of speaking and thinking *otherwise* alive. At the same time it must be recognized

---

[10] See below, Part Two, chap. 5, "Justice," for a discussion of Derrida's critique of *Versammlung*.

that the surest way to perpetuate the poverty of the immigrants is for them *not* to learn English. To deal with that tension, to make that tension creative, we need sufficient numbers of well-trained bilingual teachers with adequate facilities and books who can move easily back and forth between native languages and English so that it would never be a question of choosing between them. But for that we need to convince the right wing and the elderly not to vote against school district budgets, to renounce the—unhappily quite successful—attack they have launched on children, teachers, and schools in order to fill their own pockets. The question of opening oneself to difference, to the other, will *always* come back to the gift, to trumping greed with generosity, to breaking the self-gathering circle of the same with the affirmation of the other. The elderly will not live to see the future in which they invest and so we ask them to give without return, for a gift, if there is one, cannot be less than that.

To signal the notion of a culture that articulates difference, Derrida makes use of a navigational term, "the Other Heading" (*l'autre cap*) (from the Latin *caput*, head, one of my favorite words), as in the heading of a ship or plane. The expression suggests a mindfulness of the heading of the *other*, which forces us to be a little more accommodating about those who are headed otherwise, headed elsewhere, than are we. Beyond that, the title suggests something "other than" a heading. By this Derrida does not mean an anarchic anti-heading or "beheading"—as an international traveler himself, he would be the last one to suggest, for example, that Air France jettison its navigational equipment—but a delimitation of the idea of "planning ahead" in favor of an openness to the future that does without the guardrails of a plan, of a "teleological orientation." In a culture of identity, which keeps its teleological head, an *arche* heads resolutely or ineluctably—either way, frontally—toward its own, proper *telos* inscribed deep upon its hide (or engraved upon its brow, *frons*), gathering itself to itself all the more deeply in an archeo-teleo-logical unity that "becomes itself." The trick in deconstruction, if it is a trick, is to keep your head without having a heading.

That is why, whatever similarities are suggested between Hegel's notion of a dialectical unity-in-difference and Derrida's notion of an identity that differs with itself, the two ideas are, shall we say, rather different. You might even say that Derridean idea is the deconstruction of the Hegelian. So Hegelians should wipe away their Cheshire cat smile, thinking that they are about to swallow Derrida whole, which is of course what Hegelians tend to think whenever they are faced with "opposition." For Hegel's idea of unity-in-difference is archeo-teleological all the way down, guided deeply from within by the momentum of a *Wesen* that is working itself out, becoming itself, getting to be *bei sich sein*, in and through difference. Hegel is thinking of some "organic ensemble," as Derrida says in the "Roundtable," mediating *itself* into an ever higher and higher, self-spiraling unity that gathers together all these differences into a more complex and differentiated unity. Derrida, on the other hand, is no essentialist; at bottom there is for him no *Wesen* and no *telos* but only *différance*, no deep essence to keep things on course but a certain contingent assembly of unities subject always to a more radical open-endedness that constantly runs the risk of going adrift. That is also why Derrida keeps putting a distance between himself and Heideggerian *Versammlung*. For whatever differences there are between the history of the absolute Spirit and the Heideggerian history of Being, between Hegelian teleology and Heideggerian eschatology, between stepping up (*Aufhebung*) and stepping back (*Schritt-zurück*), the two are one when it comes to trumping difference with a more originary and powerful, a more gathering unity that makes its way through the twists and turns of empirical history. Hegelians and Heideggerians may shout as loudly as they wish about contingency, may pay contingency the highest compliments, but they always have something, a *Weltgeschichte* or a *Seinsgeschichte*, up their academic sleeves. Even Husserl's history of transcendental reason—according to which "European science" is the destiny first set in and by Greek *logos* and *episteme*—falls in line behind this Greco-European, archeo-teleo-eschato-logical heading (AC 31/OH 27).

This is not to say that Derrida lacks a concept of history—a common complaint about him and a common misunderstanding of the *il n'y a pas de hors-texte* notion. On the contrary, by depriving himself of the idea of either a teleological or an eschatological heading, Derrida has developed a more spare and radical idea of historical happening. For a culture to be "on the move" with otherwise-than-a-heading means to hold itself more radically open to a "future" (*l'avenir*), to what is to-come (*à venir*). History, thus, is not a course set in advance headed toward its *telos* as toward a future-present, a foreseeable, plannable, programmable, anticipatable, masterable future. History means, rather, to set sail without a course, on the prow for something "new."

Such an open-ended, non-teleological history is just what Derrida means by "history," which means for him that something—an "event"—is really happening, e-venting (*é-venir*), breaking out, tearing up the circular course of Greco-German time. History is not programmed in advance, for Derrida, not set to work within a pre-set archeo-teleological horizon, kept all along on course, keeping its head and its heading by way of some sort of ontological automatic-pilot (AC 22–24/OH 17–19). That is why when something comes along that nobody foresaw, that surprises the daylight out of us, we say it is very "historical." Everybody—from Ronald Reagan to the most internationally famous "Sovietologists" in all the world's most advanced "advanced institutes"—was left speechless by the "historic" turn of events in the "former" Soviet Union. Who would have believed any of us would have lived to use that phrase—as recently as ten years ago?

The paradigmatic gesture of European "modernity" for Derrida is an "auto-biographical" project in which European thinkers tell the story of Europe as the avant-garde and "promontory" of the West—and on this point Heidegger could not be more modernist—composing a eulogy to a Europe that sets the heading for Western, indeed global destiny. That is the line that Derrida would have Europe drop, so as not to close itself within its own identity, and so as to set out instead for another shore, the shore of the other, of the *tout autre*, "the beyond of this modern tradition" (AC 33/OH 29). That is why the present nationalist tremors in Central Europe ought not to be described as a "crisis" of the European "spirit." For a crisis—of which there are Hegelian, Heideggerian, and Husserlian versions—is a thoroughly modernist idea that has to do with a "dramatic instant of decision" (*krinein*) in which European self-identity is at stake. It was all the hype about a spiritual crisis—of the debilitation of the German and Western Spirit, its *Entmachung*—that fueled the fires of Heidegger's National Socialism (and that of quite a few others, too). Even today Francis Fukuyama can proclaim that the world-historical decision has been made, the crisis resolved, the end reached. Europe has reached its teleological fulfillment as the whole globe has opted—is still opting, the crisis will be over in a matter of weeks, now—for Euro-American "capitalism" and a market economy, and the Evil Empire has come crashing to the ground (*kaputt*).

Derrida would warn us against not one but two "capitalisms" (from *caput*), by which he means two too powerful headings, the one having to do with a cultural hegemony, the rule of European "culture," emblematized by the European "capitals" (*la capitale*, the capital city), and the other the hegemony of economic capitalism (*le capitale*), the one criticized by Marx in *Das Kapital*. If we were to force a "philosophy of history" out of deconstruction, which would be too prestigious a label (heading) for Derrida, we might say that deconstruction can be viewed as an attempt to extricate us from two too dominant headings that are trying to steer everything and thereby to restore the play or slack or chance with which history happens.

(1) In the "Roundtable," Derrida expresses his concern about the current state of "international law" and "international organizations." To be sure, he is not opposed to such notions in principle. His concerns are that such international structures are not very international, that they do not reflect the will of many nations speaking together, but are dominated by the largest and richest nations. Since the collapse of the Soviet Union, they have been dominated by the United States in particular, whose wealth and power, no longer checked by Soviet power, simply overwhelms the voice and influence of smaller, poorer countries. "Internationalism," Derrida points out, has a peculiar way of cooperating with "nationalism" (AC 49/OH 48). That is so in part because it presupposes the existence and sovereignty of the several member nations; in the "Roundtable," Derrida wonders whether a "new International" might actually get beyond nationality and national citizenship to something post-national, post-geographic. It is also true because such international associations have a way of ending up serving the interests of the most powerful member-nations, nations who set the international course. Indeed, such nations mask this power with meta-narratives that show them to have been chosen by History, or the Spirit, or Destiny, or Being to lead the way. One nation decides that its destiny is to set the course for Europe, and thereby for the world, so that the whole planet can become itself, that is, European, with Paris, London, or Berlin at the head of the fleet.

That is what Derrida would have Europe avoid, and this by way of biting the bullet of *the* impossible. That means, on the one hand, learning to cultivate difference while avoiding both "dispersion" and "monopoly." As he says in the "Roundtable," either pure unity or pure multiplicity is a "synonym of death." Pure unity would be totalitarian, and pure multiplicity would be anarchistic; either way, a catastrophe. On the one hand, Europe needs to avoid dispersion because it is in constant danger of deteriorating into a myriad of nationalist idioms and self-enclosed idiolects, into a European "apartheid."[11] On the other hand, Europeans need to cultivate cooperation while avoiding "monopoly," a translation of their differences into a single overarching standardization which circulates across the lines of a transnational tele-technology. That would wipe out national difference by establishing a uniform *grid of intelligibility*, a trans-national cultural capital, a central switchboard, a central power, a capital that is not a particular city or metropolis. Such a world would be generically Euro-American or NATO-ese; it would speak American/English, the new *lingua franca*, and it would be driven by a European science that stretches from Copernicus, Galileo, and Isaac Newton to M.I.T. and Silicon Valley. For this world "politics" is perhaps no longer an adequate term; it would be rather a "quasi-politics" of the tele-techno-scientific world, the virtual world (AC 41–43/OH 38–40).

To move ahead in the midst of such an aporia, to proceed where the way seems blocked, that is to "experience the impossible" (AC 43/OH 41) to pass through, to travel through the aporia of impossibility (AC 46–47/OH 45–46). Only then is there a genuine "responsibility," which means the need to respond to a situation that has not been programmed in advance, to invent new gestures, to affirm an unstable identity that differs from itself. That impossibility is the only possible invention, the invention of the other:

> The condition of possibility of this thing called responsibility is a certain *experience and experiment of the possibility of the impossible: the testing of the aporia* from which one may invent the only possible invention, the impossible invention [AC 43/OH 41].

(2) The other capitalism is the one criticized by Marx and celebrated by the free market triumphalism of Francis Fukuyama, in which all the evils of capitalism, the vast disparity of rich and poor nations, of rich and poor people in the same nation, are swept under the rug of the march of the absolute spirit of economic freedom and the free market:

---

[11] D. F. Malan, South African Prime Minister during the 1950s, defended apartheid in part by saying that viewed as a whole Europe was a good example of apartheid—some twenty-five separated nations, languages, ethnic groups. Cited by Anne McClintock and Rob Nixon, "No Names Apart: The Separation of World and History in Derrida's *'Le dernier mot du racisme,'*" *Critical Inquiry*, 13 (1986), 143. See the discussion of Derrida's controversy with McClintock and Nixon in Niall Lucy, *Debating Derrida* (Melbourne: Melbourne University Press, 1995), chap. 1.

[N]ever have violence, inequality, exclusion, famine, and thus economic oppression affected as many human beings in the history of the earth and of humanity [SdM 141/SoM 85].

All the blatant injustice and manifest suffering of such a world is treated as a temporary blip or empirical shortfall of the absolute progress of an Idea whose time has come, is indeed being fulfilled before our eyes as the Evil Empire comes crashing down. That argument, first broached here, is developed in greater detail in *Specters of Marx*.

In the face of such suffering Derrida calls for a "new International," which does not mean an anachronistic revival of a worn-out Marxist idea, another try at an international association of workers with international headquarters somewhere. This international "community," which would barely deserve the name of "community" (SdM 148/SoM 90), would be forged from forces that have resisted Marxist dogma on the one hand but have been no less resistant to conservative and reactionary tendencies. The new International would form an ethical and moral coalition of all those who are, as he says in the "Roundtable," "secretly aligned in their suffering against the hegemonic powers which protect what is called the 'new order.' " They would constitute a coalition of everyone who is done in or headed off by the dominant heading, every who is left out, de-posed, "de-capitated" by their race, income, gender, nationality, language, religion, or even species (animal rights)—in a nutshell, by their "difference."

An Open Quasi-Community

So, then, to "precipitate," to rush head-on, to a conclusion, what does it mean to have an "identity," or, to come back to the question posed in the "Roundtable," to have a "community," which would always mean having a common identity?

To have an identity, in a sense acceptable to Derrida, is to endure these antinomies without having a rule to resolve them up our sleeve, which is the only chance we have for responsibility. To have a rule in advance to solve the antinomy, one that would settle *ahead* of time the singularity of each decision, as if each were a "case" of a more general rule—that would be:

the most reassuring definition of *responsibility as irresponsibility*, of ethics confused with juridical calculation, of a politics organized with techno-science. Any invention of the new that would not go through the endurance of the antinomy would be a dangerous mystification, immorality *plus* good conscience, and sometimes good conscience *as* immorality [AC 71/OH 72].

We need to avoid both the overtly self-enclosing, isolationist, protectionist nationalisms and also the crypto-nationalism of thinking that "we" are the exemplary case, the central site of a worldwide web, the international paradigm, charged with setting the course that the rest must follow, that we—French or Germans, Americans or Europeans, scientists or philosophers, etc.—*are* the "universal" or "reason" set down on earth in order to set the course, to lead the way, to provide the heading. There would be, at bottom, nothing or no one to charge or authorize anyone to provide the heading. For there is, for Derrida, at bottom, no bottom, no *Geist* or *Sein* or *logos* or Divine Voice (whether it uses Hebrew or Arabic) to legitimate such leadership. There is, at bottom, only the "there is," *il y a, différance, khôra*. That is bad news only if you think you have been given a hot line to Being or God, but for Derrida it is a way to keep things open.

The sense of European identity and community, of any community, that Derrida can live with consists in "opening itself without being able any longer to gather itself" to the heading of the other and, beyond that, to something otherwise than a heading. Any possible future community that Derrida could live with would be opened to an other that is not *its* other, not the other whom one is intent on colonizing, opened and exposed to "that which is not, never was, and never will be Europe" (AC 74–75/OH 75–77).

All of which comes down to affirming "democracy," which is an idea that is at once uniquely Greco-European *and* an idea that, detaching itself from its Greco-European moorings and genealogy, is still to come. That is not because "democracy" is a Regulative Idea to which a lead-footed empirical reality has not yet caught up, a Good so good that we can afford to be a little violent in its name, but because we do not know what democracy is, what it is to become, what the democracy to come calls for, what is coming under the heading of democracy. Democracy calls for hospitality to the Other, but the Other is the shore we cannot reach, the One we do not know. Democracy— the old name that for now stands for something new, a porous, permeable, open-ended affirmation of the other—is the best name we have for what is to come. This is said despite Fukuyama, despite the flag-waving American Right Wing, and their lethal denunciations of the

Other. These people think that democracy has already arrived or is due in any day now; they seem completely blind to the deep distortion of democratic processes by money and the media (AC 103ff./OH 84ff.). Democracy is internally disturbed and continually haunted by the deepest demagogic corruption of democracy, by a crowd-pleasing, hate-mongering, reactionary politics that appeals to the basest and most violent instincts of the *demos*. Democracy is the name for what is to come, for the unforeseeable future, for the promise of the unforeseeable. It might well be part of such a democracy to come, Derrida says in the "Roundtable," to be so truly "international" that it will no longer turn on the current notion of nation at all, of "citizenship" in a "nation," and will require a new notion of hospitality—all of which, today, pushes our imagination to the limit.

That polity to come will represent what Derrida often calls a "new Enlightenment" that will know how to respect both singularity and the universal, both reason and what a too-self-confident reason denounces as "faith" or "irrationality," both a common law and the right to be different and idiosyncratic. But, once again, Derrida is not announcing a regulative ideal, an horizon of foreseeability: for this democracy to come will *always* be to come. It will never be in place, and it would be the very height of injustice to announce that it has arrived, which is the kind of error made in the triumphalism of the new world order. For justice is always what has not arrived and, to the extent that it exists at all, it is to be found, like the Messiah on the *outskirts* of Rome (RT 24), among the outsiders, the ones who have not "arrived." It belongs to the very structure of the democracy to come, or Justice, that it is always "to come," that it keeps the present *open* by way of the promise of the to-come, lest we attribute to ourselves a good conscience in democratic matters, thereby letting the present become an oppressive regime. The affirmation of "responsibility," "ethics," "decision"—even, to use an old name for something new, of "Europe" itself—will never be a matter of knowledge (AC 79/OH 80–81), of a determinable program, a knowable plan, of planning ahead, but of a generosity, a gift that gives itself without return—whenever it is called for, whenever the occasion calls for it.

Thus, while it does not belong to Derrida's rhetoric to emphasize this, because he does not much like the word "community," the same sort of qualifying restriction, or self-limitation, would, if you remain attached to this word, attach itself to the notion of "community."

"There is doubtless this irrepressible desire for a 'community' to form," Derrida says—and the question raised in the "Roundtable" reflects this—"but also to know its limit—and for its limit to be its opening" (PdS 362/*Points* 351). There is an "irrepressible desire" for people of common purpose to join hands, for women and men who have "dedicated," which means "given," themselves to a end or purpose, to come together, *con-venire*. One might even dream of a community of dreamers who come together to dream of what is to come. Responding to this irrepressible desire, we might say that a "community" in deconstruction would always have to be what he calls "another community," "an *open* quasi-community," which is of course always a "community to come" and a "community without community" (*Pol.* 331). A community for Derrida ought always to be marked precisely and paradoxically by an exposure to a "*tout autre* [that] escapes or resists the community," something that "appeals for another community" (PdS 362/*Points* 351).

Such a community, we might say, will have slackened its defense (*munitio*), diminished its communal store of munitions, against the other, become, let us say, a "weak community," in the spirit of the "weak thought" (*pensiero debole*) of which Gianni Vattimo speaks. Such a weak community, of course, demands considerable strength, for it would be required to maintain a sense of a certain community even while welcoming the stranger, to remain master of the house while making the other feel at home. This antinomy of a community that is forbidden to collect into a unity is *the* impossible, the "*experience and experiment of the possibility of the impossible*" (AC 43/OH 41), and the paralysis through which community and hospitality must pass. The community to come calls to us from the future, alerting us to the walls that communities—European, American, and Chinese, Christian, Jewish and Islamic, here as everywhere, today as always, communities as such, by their very structure as community—throw up against the foreigner. The community to come calls up a certain generosity, calls for a gift of a "community without unity," at "loose ends," and invokes another, more flattering idea of community, as com-*munus*, with munificence and extravagance,[12] in a community *without* community, as an identity that begs to differ with itself.

Community. Hospitality. Welcome to the Other. Justice.
Come.

---

[12] Corlett, *Community Without Unity*; see above, n. 4.

5

Justice, If Such a Thing Exists

"[T]he law as such can be deconstructed and has to be deconstructed. That is the condition of historicity, revolution, morals, ethics and progress. But justice is not the law. Justice is what gives us the impulse, the drive, or the movement to improve the law, that is, to deconstruct the law. Without a call for justice we would not have any interest in deconstructing the law."

—"Roundtable," 16

DOING JUSTICE TO DERRIDA

To its critics, who have not always tried to do it justice, who sometimes are just a little unjust to Derrida (FL 14/DPJ 4), deconstruction has seemed like an apolitical aestheticism, an indecisive dallying with texts without concern for the demands and decisions of the real world, dedicated more to analyzing discourse than to power, preoccupied more with puns than with politics. (Or else, it is blamed for starting the war in Bosnia). Even were it tolerable, these apostles of anti-deconstruction seem to think, to propose strange readings of odd poems in graduate literary theory classes, when the sort of anarchy that deconstruction perpetrates threatens to spill over into the streets of ethics and politics, that is serious business and it is not to be taken lightly. We have to put a stop to it; that is our ethical and civic duty, we Knights of Good Conscience.

The proof of that, this criticism would run, is the utter anarchy that deconstruction would sow if ever this wild-eyed literary theory were to spread to legal theory, if ever its lawlessness were to invade the law. How could you have a lawless theory of law? So, add to the list of destructive influences attributable to deconstruction—starting the ethnic wars in eastern Europe, encouraging Mormon polygamy, undermining the law of gravity, and corrupting the curricula of our institutions of higher learning—still one more item: the ruination of the law, ruined legal systems, leveled law schools. Of course, were this to put a cap on the production of lawyers in this country, then deconstruction might yet find a place in the public's heart!

Alas, no one ever said life is fair. Such a line on Derrida is just another bit of injustice in an unjust world, a particularly unfair rap, insensitive to the point of stupefaction, of irresponsibility, like the irresponsibility of the signers of Barry Smith's letter, who, intent more on a lynching than an analysis, cannot possibly have read more than casually the texts they denounced *in toto* in the name of academic responsibility and professionalism.

What is true, I think, is that in his earlier writings, along with a series of important philosophical discussions of Husserl, Heidegger, Hegel, Plato, and Levinas, Derrida showed considerable interest in putting the resources of deconstruction to work in literary analysis, even as his reception in the United States was first extended by literary theorists. (And he has never been able to choose between philosophy and literature [AL 34]). Furthermore, he refused to sign on to the reigning Marxist orthodoxy or to pay dues to the French Communist Party, in a country where the pockets of philosophers are routinely searched for their political credentials. Derrida thus incurred the wrath of those who had appointed themselves the Protectors of the People, the World-Historical Spokesmen of the March of History, and the Defenders of All That is Politically Correct, none of which preserved the French Communists from bottomless stupidity and blindness about the brutality of Stalinism or Maoism. But no sensitive and attentive reader could have missed the ethical and political import of deconstruction, even early on (see, for example, MdP 131–135/MdP 111–114). One need not be a master hermeneut to have noticed the massively political tone of such vintage Derridean terms as "exclusion," "marginalization," "disruption," "transgression," "outlaw," "reversal," and "displacement." It takes no great insight to see in Derrida a non-Marxist or post-Marxist left intellectual who stayed clear of the dogmatism of the Church of Latter-Day Gallic Communists. Indeed, having felt the sting of National Socialism as a Jew growing up in colonial Algeria during World War II, Derrida had been from the start acutely sensitive to the questions of injustice, oppression, and exclusion in a post–World War II Europe to which the dogmatic Marxists were singularly blind.

It is also true that, early on, Derrida had created in the unwary the impression of a certain French, post-structuralist Nietzsche—part of what Allan Bloom called somewhat crankily (given Nietzsche's notoriously reactionary politics) the "Nietzscheanized left."[1] Now, without underestimating the serious debt of Derrida to Nietzsche's critique of metaphysics and of its "faith in opposites," such a characterization misses the profoundly Levinasian affirmation of the *tout autre*, the "wholly other," in deconstruction. As this Levinasian dimension has grown stronger and stronger over the years—"Before a thought like that of Levinas, I never have any objection," he would say in 1986[2]— the ethical and political dimension of deconstruction became more and more explicit. This tendency culminated in 1993 with the appearance, *contre temps*, of *Specters of Marx*. This book, which has nothing to do with the dogmatism of the moribund French Communist Party, goes on the attack against the triumphalism of the "new world order" that thinks that Marxism is dead and buried. The "specter" of Marx haunts Europe today, Derrida says, like a specter of justice, like a memory of suffering not quite repressed, like a call for justice in the midst of the most obscene extremes of wealth and poverty. The ethical, political, and religious questions surrounding "Europe today" have more and more taken center stage in Derrida's work, including a recent piece, "Faith and Knowledge" (*Foi*, 1996), in which Derrida takes up the question of Islamic fundamentalism.

I do not think there is anything like a "reversal" or massive transformation in Derrida's thought, of the sort one finds in Heidegger, say, anything like a Derrida I and a Derrida II. But I do think there is a progression in which this originally ethical and political motif in his work, deeply Levinasian in tone, has worked its way more and more to the front of his concerns in the writings of the 1980s and 1990s. This motif has been given an emphasis that even some of his more sympathetic readers had not quite anticipated (FL 21/DPJ 17), the effect of which has been to turn deconstruction in a more decidedly ethico-political (and even oddly religious) direction, but nothing that any attentive reader of the preface to "The Ends of Man" could not have seen coming (MdP 131–135/MoP 111–114).

---

[1] Bloom, *Closing of the American Mind*, pp. 217–226.
[2] Jacques Derrida and Pierre-Jean Labarrière, *Alterités* (Paris: Osiris, 1986), p. 74.

The misbegotten notion that deconstruction is some kind of random intellectual violence, a merely destructive and negative assault on anything still standing, arises from a failure to see what deconstruction *affirms*, a failure to see that every deconstructive analysis is undertaken *in the name of something*, something affirmatively *un*-deconstructible. For without the undeconstructible deconstruction would be without "impulse" and "drive," as Derrida says in the "Roundtable," without movement, momentum, or motivation. The word "deconstruction" has made its way into high-brow, and even not so high-brow parlance, where it has come to be indistinguishable from a purely negative critique, without any affirmative upshot, so that one would no more want to be "deconstructed" than hit by a truck. But apart from the popular misunderstanding, which we might expect, even its partisans have sometimes shrunk from affirming what is affirmatively undeconstructible. We hear a lot in "po-mo" about "decon," but we never hear about "*un*-decon"!

Derrida's critics, and some of his admirers, too, thought that the very idea of deconstruction excluded the undeconstructible, that undeconstructibility would simply be another version of the "transcendental signified" or the "ascetic ideal," a post-structuralist version of the *Ding-an-sich*, or even, God forbid, of God. I think the undeconstructible sounded to them too much like Yahweh giving Abraham and Moses their marching orders. In short, the notion of the undeconstructible suggested a new "-centrism," a post-structuralist "foundationalism." In fact, however, the undeconstructible is beyond both foundationalism and anti-foundationalism. Beyond anti-foundationalism because the undeconstructible is what gives deconstruction impulse, momentum, and, not centrism, but rather an ec-centric ecstasis toward what is to-come. But the undeconstructible is likewise beyond foundationalism, because the undeconstructible is not knowable or foreseeable or forehavable but hangs on by a prayer, "Come."

Everything in deconstruction is driven by the undeconstructible, fired and inspired, inflamed and impassioned, set into motion by what is not deconstructible. Deconstruction is internally related to the undeconstructible and is incoherent without it. What is undeconstructible—justice, the gift, hospitality, the *tout autre*, *l'àvenir*—is neither real nor ideal, neither present nor future-present, neither existent nor idealizable, which is how and why it incites our "desire," driving and impassioning deconstruction.

Another way to see this and to say this is to say that deconstruction is "affirmative" of something undeconstructible, but that it is affirmative without being "positive." For it is affirmative of something *tout autre*, something to come, without staking out the positive traits of a plannable project or a programmable position, affirmative beyond the distinctions between positive and negative, foundational and antifoundational, faith and reason.

DECONSTRUCTION AND THE POSSIBILITY OF JUSTICE

The most forceful formulation of deconstruction's affirmation of the undeconstructible—and one of the best explanations of how deconstruction works in all of Derrida's writings—is found in "The Force of Law: The Mystical Foundation of Authority," a 1989 lecture to a conference on deconstruction and justice convened by philosopher and legal theorist Drucilla Cornell, to which Derrida refers us in the "Roundtable." In this lecture Derrida had been asked by Cornell to address the question of "deconstruction and the possibility of justice." The "and" in this title sounds like a jab, a challenge, he quips, almost a dare: we dare you to say something, anything, that would show that deconstruction has anything at all to do with justice! We dare you to weave these six words into a defensible assertion! What right (*droit*)— what a nerve!—does deconstruction have to speak of justice (said in a bad temper, say, by Ruth Marcus or Barry Smith) (FL 13–14/DPJ 3–4)!

To this dare, and in the face of this very suspicious attitude to deconstruction, Derrida responds by saying, not without cheek: well, not only does deconstruction have some sort of relation to the possibility of justice, some right to speak of justice, but he will risk the assertion that, all due precautions being noted, deconstruction *is* justice (in a nutshell):

> If I were to say that I know nothing more just than what I today call deconstruction (nothing more just, I'm not saying nothing more legal or more legitimate), I know that I wouldn't fail to surprise or shock not only the determined adversaries of said deconstruction or of what they imagine under this name but also the very people who pass [themselves off as] or take themselves to be its partisans or its practitioners. And so I

will not say it, at least not directly and now without the precaution of several detours [FL 46–47/DPJ 21].

Deconstruction, he makes plain in this important lecture, is a discourse on, indeed a discourse *of* justice, justice's own word, if it had a voice or a word. That (not too) startling claim (if you had taken the time to read slowly instead of trying to organize a hanging) turns on the distinction Derrida makes between justice and the law.

By the "law" (*droit, loi*) Derrida means the positive structures that make up judicial systems of one sort or another, that in virtue of which actions are said to be legal, legitimate, or properly authorized. The law, he says, is deconstructible, and this is because the law is constructed in the first place. The law, whether it admits to being purely conventional or claims to be natural, whether it is actually written down or passed on orally, whether it is Anglo-Saxon, Napoleonic, or something else, whether it is imposed from above by *fiat* or composed from below by consensus, is historically instituted or constituted, forged and framed, ratified and amended. Now, such deconstructibility is not bad news; indeed, it is even a stroke of luck (FL 35/DPJ 14), a way to "improve the law" ("Roundtable"). Before Rosa Parks decided to visit the undeconstructibility of justice upon Montgomery, Alabama, for example, it was legal, legitimate, and authorized to force African-Americans to the back of the bus. So, to "deconstruct" does not mean — how often do we have to say this? — to flatten out or destroy but to loosen up, to open something up so that it is flexible, internally amendable, and revisable, which is what the law should be. Whenever a legal system has been good, whenever it has been something more than a blind and inflexible tyrant, whenever laws have protected the weak against the strong and prevented the winds of injustice from sweeping across the land, then the law has been deconstructible. Deconstructibility is the condition of legal progress, of a perfectible and gradually perfected, a self-revising and self-correcting ensemble of norms that distills the knowledge of the generations. As a legal theorist, Derrida is not a strict constructionist, but a strict deconstructionist.

So, not only is the deconstructibility of the law not bad news; it is great news, a way to "improve" the law. But Derrida goes on:

> But the paradox that I'd like to submit for discussion is the following: it is this deconstructible structure of law (*droit*), or if you prefer of justice as *droit*, that also insures the possibility of deconstruction [FL 35/DPJ 14].

Deconstruction and the law mutually enable each other, mutually support and render each other possible. The thing that makes the wheels of the law turn is deconstruction, *even as* the thing that makes the wheels turn in deconstruction is the possibility of deconstructing the law. The law is constructible in a sense that goes beyond the distinction between convention and nature; it is constructible, whether it is flat out admitted to be constructed by convention or claims to be constructed right out of nature itself. Either way, it has not fallen from the sky. Remember, Derrida is neither an essentialist nor a conventionalist, but an *inventionalist*. But because the law is constructible, it is accordingly deconstructible, which means that deconstruction keeps an inventionalist eye open for the other to which the law as law is "blind." For example, when the right wing jurists in the United States strike down affirmative action laws, or the efforts of states to draw congressional districts so as to give African-Americans a voice in Congress, on the grounds that such lines must be "color-blind," then it is being more blind than possessed of judicial insight; the eyes of justice are fixed on the silenced and oppressed who are being ground under by these laws of "equal treatment."

But this deconstructibility of the law goes hand in hand with the undeconstructibility of justice:

> Justice in itself, if such a thing exists, outside or beyond law, is not deconstructible. No more than deconstruction itself, if such a thing exists. Deconstruction is justice [FL 35/DPJ 14–15].

Justice is what the deconstruction of the law means to bring about. Justice is its father's or mother's business that deconstruction must be about, that upon which the deconstruction of the law has fixed a steady eye, that which gives deconstruction meaning and momentum, "impulse" and "drive," its ec-centric ec-stasy. Justice is not deconstructible. After all, not everything is deconstructible, or there would be no point to deconstruction. While it is true that there is no end to deconstruction, no *telos* and no *eschaton*, it is not true that there is no point to deconstruction, no spur or stylus tip, no thrust, no cutting edge. Everything cannot be deconstructible or, better, every *thing* is deconstructible, but justice, if such a "thing" "exists," is not a *thing*. Justice is not a present entity or order, not an existing reality or regime; nor is it even an ideal *eidos* toward which we earthlings down below heave and sigh while contemplating its heavenly form. Justice is the absolutely unforeseeable prospect (a paralyzing paradox) in virtue in which the things that get deconstructed are deconstructed. Thus, deconstruction is made possible by a twofold, conjoint condition:

(1) The deconstructibility of law (*droit*), of legality, legitimacy, or legitimation (for example) makes deconstruction possible.

(2) The undeconstructibility of justice also makes deconstruction possible, indeed is inseparable from it.

What then, or where then, is deconstruction?

(3) The result: deconstruction takes place in the interval that separates the undeconstructibility of justice from the deconstructibility of *droit* (authority, legitimacy, and so on) [FL 35/DPJ 15].

There is a necessary, structural gap or distance between the law and justice, and deconstruction situates itself there, in that space or interval, in that abyss or *khôra*, watching out for the flowers of justice that grow up in the cracks of the law. In a kind of ongoing Socraticism without a vision of a heavenly *eidos*, deconstruction paces off the distance between justice, if such a thing exists, and the laws of any existing polity. We might think of deconstruction as a practice of its own special version of Socratic irony—which earns it about as many friends as Socrates earned in his lifetime (maybe more, since Socrates lost the vote of the five hundred, while Derrida won the vote at Cambridge). Derrida's irony is not the highly Platonized version of Socratic irony defended by Hegel, according to which Socratic irony is said to be driven by a positive vision of the form. Derrida would never lay claim to having "seen" the "form" of Justice; nor would he say there is anything seeable or foreseeable beyond being (for there we are blind). But neither is Derrida's irony the Socratic irony defended in Kierkegaard's *The Concept of Irony*, according to which the Socratic is an infinite absolute negativity, for deconstruction is through and through affirmative, a *oui, oui*, a yes, yes, to justice.[3] Derridean irony is Socratically on the alert to the gap between every existing order and justice, which, if it does not exist, calls for and solicits existence.

So the way to respond—performatively, not just constatively—to the question about whether deconstruction has anything to do with

---

[3] *Kierkegaard's Works. II. The Concept of Anxiety with Continual Reference to Socrates*, trans. Howard Hong and Edna Hong (Princeton: Princeton University Press, 1989), pp. 198–237, 324–329.

the possibility of justice is to say (and to *do*) "yes, yes." Yes, because deconstruction makes justice possible, makes it possible to punctuate the law with justice, to deconstruct—that is, to open—the law to justice, every time the law tends to fold in upon itself and become legalistic, concerned more with formal legality or legitimation and rectitude than with justice. Yes, again, because justice makes deconstruction possible, because the undeconstructibility of justice conjointly with the deconstructibility of the law makes deconstruction work, is what deconstructors do for a living, how they fill their days, for justice is what deconstruction is. Yes, yes, not only the "deconstruction and the possibility of justice," which is the title put to him by the conference organizers, but also "justice and the possibility of deconstruction."

But there is still more! We can never have enough of deconstruction! For the word "possibility" does not go far enough, is not affirmative enough:

> It [deconstruction] is possible as an experience of the impossible, there where, even if it does not exist (or does not yet exist, or never does exist), *there is* (*il y a*) justice.

Deconstruction does not set its sights on justice as the goal or *telos* within a positive horizon of foreseeability—like a Platonic *eidos* or a Kantian regulative idea—which for Derrida is what constitutes the horizon of "possibility," or possibility as a "horizon," a positive vision of justice. The "possible" is a term of art for Derrida, which means the foreseeable and projectable, the plannable and programmable, what he calls the "future present," the future that can come about with a little luck and a lot of hard work, the sort of thing "role models" and "strategic planning" help us bring about. This "possible" future is "already present" as an ideal before it rolls around in actuality, which it can do—it is possible—at least in principle.

The im-possible, on the other hand, is the *un*-deconstructible, that which exceeds or is more than this future (*futur*) possibility. The impossible exceeds this horizontal possibility with a more radical *à venir*, constituting a more radical *l'avenir*, the more radical verticality and transcendence of the "to come." "The impossible" is not a simple logical contradiction, like *x* and *not-x*, but the tension, the paralysis, the aporia, of having to push against and beyond the limits of the horizon, *passage à frontières*. To desire the impossible is to strain against the constraints of the foreseeable and possible, to *open* the horizon of possibility to what it cannot foresee or foretell. Derrida says that he prefers the word "experience" which means a voyage, a traversal but one without "guardrails," (PdS 373–374/*Points* 362–363), because it pushes against the limits (PdS 386–387/*Points* 372–374), and tries to go where it cannot go. Experience is, above all, an "experience of the impossible," an impossible experience, going where you cannot go, passing or traveling (*perire, periens*) just where it is not possible to go, to *the* impossible (*Sauf* 63–64/ON 59–60). The experience of the impossible is the experience of the aporia of the non-road, the need to act where the way is blocked, the urgency of acting in the midst of paralysis, the necessity to push against paralyzing limits (FL 37–38/ DPJ 16). It was in a similar spirit that Johannes de Silentio, trying to think of a way to praise Abraham to the skies, said that he did not merely the possible, or even the necessary (the rational), but the *impossible*.[4]

But this passage is undertaken not by some heroic act of subjective willing, some Herculean-Heideggerian agent of authenticity or an overachieving, insomniac Nietzschean *Übermensch*, but by a quiet but incessant vigilance about the doors that are constantly being shut by the "possible," by constantly seeking openings here and there so that something unforeseeable might come rushing in. The *im*-possible is undertaken when the unforeseeable take us over, when it "over-takes" us by "surprise" (*sur-prise*), which is the agreeable redundancy, yes, yes, fostered by deconstruction.

So, the right title of this conference ought to have been "deconstruction and *the im*-possibility of justice," deconstruction and justice as *the* impossible, justice as the condition of possibility and impossibility of deconstruction and vice-versa. That is why one should say:

> Wherever one can replace, translate, determine the *x* of justice, one should say: deconstruction is possible, as impossible, to the extent (there) where *there is* (undeconstructible) *x*, thus to the extent (there) where *there is* (the undeconstructible) [FL 35–36/DPJ 15].

Justice does not exist, is nothing present, no thing, is not found somewhere either here, in present actuality, nor up ahead as a foreseeable ideal, a future-present. Rather, "there is (*il y a*) justice, which means:

───────────
[4] *Fear and Trembling* in *Kierkegaard's Works*. VI. *"Fear and Trembling" and "Repetition,"* trans. Howard Hong and Edna Hong (Princeton: Princeton University Press, 1983), p. 1.

justice solicits us from afar, from the future, from and as a future always structurally to come, calls "come" to us, preventing the walls of the present from enclosing us in the possible.

The key to understanding what Derrida is about here is to understand that by "justice" he does not mean a Platonic *eidos*, or a Kantian regulative Idea, a determinable ideal or universal model, an identifiable paradigm to be applied as the universal is applied to the particular. What he means by Justice and its impossibility, in the typically unorthodox, exorbitant style of deconstruction, is the "singular," the Abrahamic exception to the law, the "remnant" and the "fragment" that drops through the cracks of the law, not as a merely factual omission or defect of existing laws, but structurally, necessarily. The singular is not a case that can be subsumed under the universal, not a specimen of a species, but the unrepeatable, unreproducibly idiosyncratic. Derrida's singularity reminds us of Heidegger's "ever-mine-ness" (*Jemeinigkeit*), but with this (big) difference: it does not have to do with my own or mine, but with the other, so that it is more like a kind of ever-thine-ness (*Je-deinigkeit*), if there is such a thing. The singular is what is always and already overlooked, out of sight, omitted, excluded, structurally, no matter what law, no matter what universal schema, is in place. Like Johannes de Silentio, Jacques Derrida can complain: unless the singular is higher than the universal, Abraham is lost (along with all the sons and daughters of Abraham, and a lot of other poor bastards). The heart of justice aches over these singularities with a kind of biblical justice, rather the way the kingdom of God is concerned more with the one sheep that is lost than the ninety-nine safely grazing in the flock.

This notion of justice and singularity is articulated by Derrida in what he calls the "aporias of justice." "There is" justice only if there is *aporia*, only if the way is blocked, only if we have run up against a stone wall. When the way is not blocked, then we are just sailing along on automatic, with cruise control and with our hands barely on the wheel, staying inside the lines, applying the law, remaining securely within the horizon of the possible, of the programmable and applicable. We could let a computer do it. This is exemplified by one of the quick and easy solutions that reactionary, crowd-pleasing politicians have found these days to address the deeper difficulties of "criminal justice": "Three strikes and you're out." The computer can count to three, can calculate the felonies, can pass a life-sentence. You do not need a judge, and you do not guarantee justice with this expedient, demagogic formula; you get only legality, conformity to law—and votes (which is the point of these laws). The lines of justice run deep within the abyss and interstices of singularity, about which there can be no calculation (not to mention votes), only "judgment."

Deconstruction and justice everywhere encounter a single, over-arching aporia—that created by the chiasmic interweavings of *justice* as "infinite, incalculable, rebellious to rule and foreign to symmetry, heterogeneous and heterotropic," and *law* as "stabilizable and statu-tory, calculable, a system of regulated and coded prescriptions" (FL 48/DPJ 22). The infinity, incalculability, and heteronomy of justice, which goes to the heart of deconstruction, suggests a comparison with Levinasian ethics. For Levinas, the face of the other who commands me infinitely and places me in a position of "absolute dissymmetry," is itself comparable to the Hebrew notion of *kadosh*, of "sanctity" (*sain-teté*) as the separate and apart, the transcendent, that whose sacrosanct holiness sets it apart and demands our respect. While this characteriza-tion is reserved for God in Jewish theology, Levinas extends it to the other (*autrui*), both the neighbor and the stranger, whom he says we must "make welcome." To what extent, then, does deconstruction converge with these Jewish, Levinasian motifs? To what extent is de-construction a Jewish science?[5] To resolve that issue here, Derrida says, will involve us in too many "difficult questions" (FL 49/DPJ 22). Let us instead examine three aporias, three examples of a single aporia that distributes itself across three domains, which might also be de-scribed as three axioms of Derrida's "inventionalism." For justice and the law are not supposed to be opposites but to interweave: laws ought to be just, otherwise they are monsters; and justice requires the force of law, otherwise it is a wimp.

(1) *The Suspension of the Law.* A decision is just not merely by conforming to law, which ensures mere legality, but only if the law is, as it were, lifted or suspended, so that the judge "invents" the law for the first time, or, better, "re-invents" the law, not by beginning abso-

---

[5] See *Mal d'archive: Une impression freudienne* (Paris: Galilée, 1995); Eng. trans. "Archive Fever: A Freudian Impression," trans. Eric Prenowitz, *Diacritics*, 25 (1995), 9–63, where Derrida follows the question put by Yosef Yerushalmi in his *Freud's Moses* (New Haven, Conn.: Yale University Press, 1991) as to whether psychoanalysis is a Jewish science. I pursue the transference of this question to deconstruction, which is obvious, in *Prayers and Tears of Jacques Derrida*, §17.

lutely *de novo* but by making a "fresh judgment" (Stanley Fish) in a new situation. Such a decision, then, is both regulated (by law) and not regulated (responsive to justice), stretching the constraints of the law to include the demands of justice in a new, different, and singular situation. For every "case" is different; every case is more than a case, a *casus*—a falling from or declension of universality. The situation is not a case but a singularity. Otherwise, the judge is not a judge but a calculating machine, and we do not need a judge but a computer, and we do not ensure justice but mere conformity to law. Still, neither is the judge free to improvise and leave aside the law. A just decision is found in the distance between a blind and universal law and the singularity of the situation before us (FL 50–52/DPJ 22–24).[6]

(2) *The Ghost of Undecidability.* One of the things for which deconstruction is raked over the coals is the notion of "undecidability," which its hasty critics, all too quick to pass judgment, confuse with simple indecision. Undecidability is taken, or mistaken, to mean a pathetic state of apathy, the inability to act, paralyzed by the play of signifiers that dance before our eyes, like a deer caught in a headlight. But rather than an inability to act, undecidability is the condition of possibility of acting and deciding. For whenever a decision is really a decision, whenever it is more than a programmable, deducible, calculable, computable result of a logarithm, that is because it has passed through "the ordeal of undecidability." One way to keep this straight is to see that the opposite of "undecidability" is not "decisiveness" but programmability, calculability, computerizability, or formalizability. Decision-making, judgment, on the other hand, positively *depends upon* undecidability, which gives us something to decide. Like everything else in deconstruction—here comes a nutshell—deciding is a possibility sustained by its impossibility. So a "just" decision, a "judgment" that is worthy of the name, one that responds to the demands of justice, one that is more than merely legal, goes eyeball to eyeball with undecidability, stares it in the face (literally), looks into that abyss, and then makes the leap, that is, "gives itself up to the impossible decision" (FL 53/DPJ 24). That does not mean it is "decisionistic," for that would break the tension in the opposite direction, by dropping or ignoring the law altogether and substituting subjectivistic autonomy for responsibility to the other.

---

[6] It ought not to be forgotten that, unlike Anglo-Saxon law, the Napoleonic code, which is the basis of French law, has no rule of precedent.

One revealing result of Derrida's line of reasoning is that "only a decision is just." The only thing that can be called "just" is a singular action in a singular situation, and this only for the while that it lasts, in the instant of decision. The warm glow of justice never settles over the law, the rule, the universal, the "maxim" that can be drawn from this singular "event," or still less over the person deciding, who can never say "I am just." (Or else, Abraham is lost!) Justice must be continually invented, or reinvented, from decision to decision, in the occasionalistic and "inventionalistic" time of the moment. That is why Derrida speaks of a "ghost" of undecidability: for the undecidability is never set aside, never over and done with. It hovers over a situation before, during, and after the decision, like a specter of justice, disturbing it from within, divesting it of absolute self-assurance (FL 52–57/DPJ 24–26).

(3) *Urgency.* However difficult, unprogrammable, undecidable the situation, justice does not wait; it is demanded here, now, in the singular situation. Justice cannot wait for all the facts to come in, which they never do. Justice cannot wait for the System to be completed, as Johannes Climacus might have said, which is supposed to happen soon, the final results being expected in a week or two. Even if somehow a situation could be saturated with knowledge, still a just decision would not be programmed by the knowledge, which would reduce it to a calculation, but would require a leap from the accumulation of cognition into the act. However much time is expended in deliberation, a just decision would always require an expenditure without reserve, would require resources other than knowledge and deliberation, would always demand action in a "finite moment of urgency and precipitation," and would always be "structurally finite," that is, compelled to put an end (*finis*) to the deliberation in a moment of non-knowledge. We act in "the night of non-knowledge and non-rule," he says, in which we are "mad about this kind of justice," not because we have simply jettisoned all rules and thrown reason to the winds but because we are forced to *reinvent* the rule under the pressure of the present situation. Justice precedes knowledge, is older than knowledge, and belongs to another order—more performative than constative, if that distinction would hold up—than knowledge.

" 'The instant of decision is a madness,' says Kierkegaard," says Derrida (FL 58/DPJ 26). I have several times, not without having something surreptitious up my sleeve, mentioned Kierkegaard and several Kierkegaardian pseudonyms. I do this partly because Derrida is bringing them up himself, but also because I want to point to another genealogy besides the Nietzschean one for deconstruction. I want to underline a line that runs from Kierkegaard to Levinas to Derrida, which opens up another line on deconstruction. All this talk of decision as a "leap" in an "instant of madness," as an aporia ("paradox") which passes through an "ordeal" of undecidability, which turns on the exception that the "single individual" makes of itself from universality, which requires the "suspension" of the universal, and which cannot wait for the System to be completed—what does that remind us of more than *Fear and Trembling*? But with this difference, that in deconstruction this entire aporetic turns not on *my* "eternal happiness" but on the justice due the other, on "the other's coming as the singularity that is always coming" (FL 55/DPJ 25).

Small wonder that three years after "The Force of Law" Derrida would publish an interpretation of *Fear and Trembling*, now translated under the title *The Gift of Death* (DM/GD). In that text, by following de Silentio's interpretation of the fearsome story of the *akedah*, of Abraham and the binding of Isaac, Derrida argues that the "secret" of the singular decision that is elicited from the subject by the coming of the other, and the "sacrifice" of all the other others that it demands, is the paradoxical paradigm for every ethical decision. For "every other is wholly other" (*tout autre est tout autre*). On this construal of the story, "God" occupies the place of the "other," Abraham the place of the self, and Isaac the place of all the "other others." But that sounds as much like Levinas, to whom Derrida has also directed us in search of a precedent for his view of justice, as Kierkegaard. True enough. One way to crack the nut of deconstruction is to force yourself to bring Levinas and Kierkegaard together, to see how they tend to converge, to disturb the assured distinction between what they call, in their respective moments of biblical madness, the "ethical" and the "religious." That is what is accomplished in *The Gift of Death*, where Derrida's reading of *Fear and Trembling* inches Levinas and Kierkegaard ever closer to each other by showing that the "obligation to the wholly other," which is what Levinas means by "ethics" prior to religion, is just what de Silentio means by the "religious" while making a teleological suspension of ethics (DM 81/GD 84; cf. DM 108n8/GD 77–78n6).[7]

---

[7] I have discussed this Kierkegaardian analogy in a detailed analysis of *The Gift of Death* in *Prayers and Tears of Jacques Derrida*, §§13–14.

All this being said, it remains true, as Derrida says in the "Roundtable," that "[t]his does not mean that we should not calculate. We have to calculate as rigorously as possible." This is necessary in order to forestall critics of deconstruction of a more or less Habermasian lineage, like Nancy Frazer and Tom McCarthy, who think that deconstruction is, if well-intentioned, a little vacuous and self-defeating.[8] None of this heartfelt affirmation of justice is an excuse to avoid detailed "juridico-political battles" (FL 61/DPJ 28), to escape the complex polemics of contemporary legal, political, and ethical disputes. The very incalculability of justice requires that we calculate, that we enter into legal and political battles. Interestingly, the examples that he gives of such debates, like the topics mentioned in the announcement of the Collège International de Philosophie, tend to concern mainly "healthcare" issues like abortion, euthanasia, organ transplant, AIDS, medical experimentation, bio-engineering. It takes a careful and complex calculation to clear the way for the incalculable singularity of what justice demands, here and now. That is why deconstruction requires, among other things, radical legal theorists like Drucilla Cornell,[9] a trained professor of the law, as well as radical theologians like Mark Taylor, radical architectural theorists like Peter Eisenmann, etc., who put deconstruction to work in the particulars of specialized and professional debates for which there is no substitute.

THE GIFT

> [T]he gift is precisely, and this is what it has in common
> with justice, something which cannot be reappropriated.
>
> —"Roundtable," 18

In deconstruction, justice has the structure of the gift; it follows, let us say, not the "logic" or the "law" of the gift, but at least its movement or dynamic. Justice must move through, must "traverse" or "ex-per-

---

[8] Thomas McCarthy, "On the Margins of Politics," *The Journal of Philosophy*, 85, No. 11 (November, 1988), 645–648; Nancy Fraser, *Unruly Practices: Power, Discourse, and Gender in Contemporary Social Theory* (Minneapolis: University of Minnesota Press, 1989), chap. 4.

[9] See especially Drucilla Cornell, *Beyond Accommodation: Ethical Feminism, Deconstruction, and the Law* (New York: Routledge, 1991), and *The Philosophy of the Limit* (New York: Routledge, 1992).

ience" the "aporetics" of the gift, must experience the same paralysis and impasse. For the gift, too, like justice, is *the* im-possible, something whose possibility is sustained by its impossibility. Let us say, in plain English, in a nutshell, that in deconstruction justice calls for a gift even as the gift is a call for justice. As Derrida says in "The Force of Law:"

> This "idea of justice" seems to be irreducible in its affirmative character, in its demand of gift without exchange, without circulation, without recognition of gratitude, without economic circularity, without calculation and without rules, without reason and without rationality [FL 55–56/DPJ 25].

Justice and the gift, we might say, are a couple of "quasi-transcendentals" which, a little like the "transcendentals" of medieval philosophy, might be thought of as convertible with one another *in re* (had they any reality) while each adds a new idea, *in ratione*, to the other (had we any idea of what they mean).

What, then, is a gift? Why does Derrida associate it with justice? And what is so "aporetic" about a gift?

To put it very simply: suppose that A gives B to C. What could be more simple than that? If A gives B to C, then C is grateful to A and owes A a debt of gratitude, with the result that C, instead of being given something, is now in debt. On the other hand, A is more or less consciously and explicitly pleased with herself for her generosity. This is all the more true if C is ungrateful and refuses to say "thank you," or if A has remained an anonymous benefactor, so that C does not know whom to thank. For then A may congratulate herself for an even higher generosity which is so unselfish that it does not even require acknowledgment. This is no less true if everything happens unconsciously, for one may certainly contract unconscious debts or unconsciously congratulate oneself for one's being very wonderful and generous. Thus, the aporetic result of A's giving B to C is that A, instead of giving something, has received and C, instead of receiving something, is now in debt. The result, in short, is that as soon as a gift is given it begins to annul itself, or that the conditions which make the gift possible also make it impossible (DT 23–24/GT 11–12).

Q. E. D. (*Quod erat deconstruendum.*) Or, to add an Anglo-German pun to this Latin one, the gift turns to poison (*die Gift*), *die Gift vergiftet.*

That is why Derrida says in the "Roundtable":

> A gift is something that you cannot be thankful for. As soon as I say "thank you" for a gift, I start canceling the gift, I start destroying the gift, by proposing an equivalence, that is, a circle which encircles the gift in a movement of reappropriation [RT 18].

Gifts tend to form a circular economy, a circle of exchange, of reciprocation and reappropriation, a ring of generosity and gratitude, which links or binds the donee to the donor by means of the donatum. (In French, the word *cadeau*, gift, comes from *catena*, chain.) Gifts are "exchanged," which "limits" the very idea of the gift. As a "self-limiting" concept, the "gift" provides an object for a vintage sort of deconstructive analysis, which proves to be a real gift to deconstruction. The very thing that makes the gift possible also makes it impossible, that is, limits or "de-limits" it, which is what Derrida means by a "quasi-transcendental." That is because an exchange is a more or less economic transaction in which things of equivalent value circulate between the parties.

To be sure, there is a protocol here, a certain amount of finesse, taste, and timing. One waits (defers) a certain amount of time before one "returns" the "favor," before reciprocating. Sometimes there is a calendar (a circle, an *annum*) that takes care of the timing for us, so that when I give you or your children a gift for a birthday, wedding, or graduation, I am patient and know that my day is coming and will roll around soon enough. Also, one must be careful not to give the exact same thing in return but to find something interestingly different, of more or less equivalent value, falling within a price range about which there is an implicit, unspoken agreement. That is what regulates the economy of "exchanging gifts" at Christmas time, which is what puts the American economy in the black every year. The economy of the gift would break down if, for example, upon receiving B from A, C simply gave it back on the spot and said "now, we're even." The gift-giving protocol would break down in the other direction if the exchange turned into a contest and the circle spiraled out of control, one party trying to outdo the other in showing off their lavish generosity, as happens in the phenomenon of "potlatch" observed by anthropologists like Marcel Mauss—whose book *The Gift* precipitated this whole discussion among French thinkers (DT/GT, chap. 2).[10]

---

[10] Marcel Mauss, *The Gift: The Form and Reason for Exchange in Archaic Societies*, trans. W. D. Halls (New York: W. W. Norton, 1990).

In order to avoid setting this circle in motion it would be necessary that the gift not "appear" as such, that it be deprived of all phenomenality. If B does not appear as a gift, then A would not be aware that she was "giving" and so would find no occasion to swell with generosity, while C, knowing nothing of a gift, would not contract a debt of gratitude. The "pure" gift is no gift at all, would never conform to its essence as gift, would never be present as a gift. That gift without gift, without the swelling and contracting of gifting, could take place only if everything happened below the level of conscious intentionality, where no one intends to give anything to anyone and no one is intentionally conscious of receiving anything. Such austere, Grinch-like conditions are hardly met at all anywhere. Not even Heidegger's notion of the *es gibt das Sein* can meet this requirement, for Heidegger at once seizes upon the generosity embedded in the German idiom *es gibt* (*geben, die Gabe*), which is supposed to mean simply "there is" (DT 32ff./GT 18ff.). On this account, the French idiom *il y a* is better and more "value-free," more neutral and indeterminate.

What seems best to meet the demands of this ungenerous and ungrateful gifting is Plato's *khôra*, the absolutely indeterminate and indeterminable receptacle which cannot be determined as mother, nurse or receptacle, which is too un-kind, un-kin, and un-gendered, *a-genos*, to en-gender anything, which emblematizes or embodies (without a body) the pure "taking place" or "spacing" of *différance* itself. By all this Derrida means to point to an anonymous, pre-subjective substratum layered beneath the surface of things, to a play of differences beneath benevolence or malevolence, "within" which the various unities of meaning, the various subjects and objects, presences and absences, are constituted, beyond or beneath the life of the conscious subject.

Still, there are subjects, all over the globe, too many to count, and the very idea of the subject implies the desire for restitution and reappropriation, completion and contentment, satisfaction and fulfillment. The "I" is a principle of making expenditures precisely *in order to* gain a return. The agent, Aristotle said, always acts for its own good, even if it is sadly mistaken, and what it takes to be good turns out to be as bad as can be. (Be careful what you pray for, lest your prayers be answered.) The agent always intends to act for its own good; otherwise, it won't act at all. Making allowances for certain differences, that perfectly reasonable principle of "reappropriation" is what eudaemonistic

Greeks like Aristotle and personal-salvation-seeking Christians in the middle ages mean by an "agent," and it is also what modernity means by a "subject." From Plato to Husserl, the subject/agent signifies a certain "intending," a *"vouloir-dire,"* a wanting-to-say, a meaning-to-say, wanting, meaning, and willing well-being. Otherwise the subject/agent would never do a thing, nothing would happen or eventuate.

So, the "subject" can never—in principle—break out of the circle, never simply lay it aside or step outside the circle, which would be to expect too much of the subject, to expect the impossible. The subject is in an impossible fix, an aporia, a paralyzing bind. For as soon as a "subject" "intends" to "give" a "gift" to someone, the whole thing comes undone, the cycle of reappropriation is set off, and the gift starts to annul itself. The solution, if it is one, of this pollution of the gift, the "way out" of this "aporia" (which means "no way out"), for Derrida is, as we have come to expect, to push against this limit, to transgress this boundary as far as possible, or (im)possible, to make a passage to the limits, to embrace this impossibility, to try to do *the im*-possible, which is not a simple logical contradiction. The gift "calls" upon us for an expenditure without reserve, for a giving that wants no payback, for distribution with no expectation of retribution, reciprocity, or reappropriation. To give a gift requires that one then forget, and asks the other to forget, absolutely, that a gift has been given (DT 30–31/GT 16–17), so that the gift, if there is one, would vanish without a trace. If time is a calendar, a ring or annum, a circle or a cycle, then the gift calls upon us to tear up the circle of time, to breach the circular movement of exchange and reciprocity, and in a "moment" of madness, to do something for once without or beyond reason, in a time without time, to give without return.

But that is impossible. To be sure. The gift is impossible; indeed, "the gift is another name for the impossible." That is why we love it so much, like mad. It is the one thing that is above all *desirable*. What we truly "desire" above all, wildly, in a desire beyond desire, is this impossible thing that can never be experienced, never be met with in the sphere of phenomenal presence. It is what can never present itself that we desire most: "one can think, desire, and say only the impossible according to the measure without measure of the impossible" (DT 45/GT 29). For all the garden-variety possibilities, all the determinate presences, all the determinate objects of knowledge and volition, all the "possibles" that remain within the horizon of the foreseeable and the same, do not so profoundly solicit us. They do not draw us out of ourselves, do not shake us out of the circle of the same, do not call up the coming of the other, the invention, the in-coming of the *tout autre*, which is what we most desire. So then, Derrida says, "let us begin *by* the impossible," not "with" but "by": let us be driven by, impelled by, set into motion by, impassioned by this impossible desire, this desire for the impossible gift, for *the* impossible.

Derrida thus traces out the distance or the "gap" between the *"gift, if there is one"*—that which is never present, which never makes an appearance, which is nothing present, extant, existing, which is what we most deeply desire—and *"economy"*—the domain of knowledge, philosophy, science, and exchange; of entities determined and exchanged, of calculation and balanced equations, of equity and sound reason, of laws and regularities. The gift is what we love and desire, of which we can only "think" or have faith without knowledge. The gift is an "unpresentable" exceeding all presence (and presents),[11] and leading us on, drawing us out of ourselves, like a certain beneficent transcendental illusion. The gift is our passion. "Economy," on the other hand, denotes the domain of presences, of presents, of the commercial transactions, the reasonable rules, the lawful and customary exchanges, the plans and projects, the rites and rituals, of ordinary life and time.

Now, it is never a question of simply choosing between these two, between "economy" and the "gift" (that's something of a rule or a nutshell in deconstruction to be invoked whenever you run up against a distinction that is passing itself off as strict). "We" "agent/subjects" are always to be found somewhere "between" the two, *in medias res*, in the gap or space between the gift, if there is one, and economy, hanging on by our teeth, about to go under. It is never a matter of deciding for one rather than the other:

> On the contrary, it is a matter—desire beyond desire—of responding faithfully but also as rigorously *both* [my emphasis] to the injunction or the order of the *gift* ("give") *as well as* [my emphasis] to the injunction or the order of meaning (presence, science, knowledge) [DT 46–47/ GT 30].

---

[11] Derrida is distinguishing the impossible *don*, gift, from the all too possible *"cadeau"* (from *catena*, chain) or *présent*.

Learn *both* to give *and* to exchange; learn to see that each depends upon, invades, and interweaves with the other, and learn to keep watch, to see what is what, as far as that is possible. Know how impossible the gift is, how much it tears you out of yourself, and know how much you are intruding into your gift:

> *Know* still what giving *wants to say, know how to give*, know what you want and want to say when you give, know what you intend to give . . . [DT 47/GT 30].

Watch, watch out, watch for the circle that cancels the gift as soon as the gift shows itself, that swings around and slams you from behind, but do not let it back you down from the gift:

> . . . know how the gift annuls itself, commit yourself even if commitment is the destruction of the gift by the gift . . . [DT 47/GT 30].

And do not give up on economy, do not write it off but:

> . . . give economy its chance [DT 47/GT 30].

For after all, in the end, there are only various economies of one sort or another, and you are not going to put an end to reappropriation or subjects, you are not, whatever you desire, going simply to step outside the circle, especially not by some heroic act of self-sacrifice. It would never be a question of choosing between inhabiting the circle and finding some spot sitting simply outside the circle:

> For finally, the overcoming of the circle by the gift, if there is any, does not lead to a simple, ineffable exteriority that would be transcendent and without relation [DT 47/GT 30].

It would never be a question of finding some place that is simply outside the circle, but of *interrupting* the circle, transgressing and breaching it, throwing away the security of the circle, if only for the "moment." The gift takes place *in a moment*, in a time without time, in which the agent/subject throws reappropriation to the winds, in an instant of madness in which we know all along that the circle will close over soon enough, that the winds of reasonable expenditure will soon enough send the gift drifting back to the subject. It is not a question of actually falling into a transcendental illusion, of requiring that the gift acquire actual being here below or ideal being up above, but rather of being driven *by* the gift which is what gets things moving:

It is this exteriority that sets the circle going, it is this exteriority that puts the economy in motion. It is this exteriority that *engages* in the circle and makes it turn [DT 47/GT 30].

The gift "as the first mover of the circle" gets the circle going, set it off, puts it in motion (DT 47/GT 31). The momentary breach which momentarily bursts the circle open also opens it up to a wider loop, letting more things in, keeping it in a spiraling motion.

Derrida thus points to a double injunctive, which is a bit of a double bind (that's a surprise), *both* to give *and* to do commerce, to love God and mammon. He is saying at one and the same time: (1) *Give*, but remember how the gift limits itself. Because there never *is* a gift (*don*), the gift is *the* impossible that we all desire; because it annuls itself the instant it would come to be, if it ever does, the gift is what we most want to make present. The gift is our passion and our longing, what we desire, what drives us mad with desire, and what drives us on. That means that we must keep watch over our gifts, which should be ways of exceeding and surpassing ourselves, emptying and divesting ourselves, lest they turn into something less than they (already) are, bits of self-aggrandizing selfishness meant to show the other what we can do, self-serving "presents" (*présents, cadeaux*) belonging to the sensible, rational circle of time in which we are not giving to the other but making a exhibit of ourselves.

(2) Give economy a chance; let a little chance and gift make its way into our economies. Lighten up, loosen up, the circle (which, in a nutshell, is what deconstruction is). For the gift is also what turns the circle, what "drives the economy," so that there never is or can or should be a pure economy, any more than there is or can be a pure gift, and to the extent that there is a pure economy it would be quite terrible — and quite uneconomical. If the wedding "ring"[12] were a ring that binds the spouses in mutually constraining obligations, it would not be much of a marriage. For then every marriage would deteriorate into a pure contract, and one spouse would do for the other only what has been promised in the contract — with nothing "extra" "added on," nothing "more," no generous giving, no expenditure without reserve, no superfluous, extravagant giving to the other. In a nutshell, no mar-

---

[12] In French the word for wedding ring is *alliance*, which also means the "covenant" God made with Israel. Derrida explores the resonances of this word in *Circumfession*; see *Circon*. 145/*Circum*. 154.

riage.[13] Then, too, every job and employment would deteriorate into a pure labor contract, with nothing extra added. Employees would just "work the contract," workers begrudging their employer and their work every minute, never doing anything in order to do it well, never "giving" themselves to the job. Employers, on the other hand, would be as parsimonious and pusillanimous as possible with their employees, never giving them the least break or benefit that is not forced out of them. Any such business or firm as that would be not only a miserable workplace but also a poor excuse of a business that will not turn a profit, at least not for long, not in the long run. We hope not, anyway.

The double bind, the double injunctive is this: give, but know that the gift, alas, inevitably turns back into a circle, and give economy a break, for economies, thank God, turn on the gift.

All of this is a way of saying that, as there is no clean distinction between the gift and economy, that there is also no clean distinction between narcissism and non-narcissism, but only certain degrees, gradations, or economies of narcissism, more or less open and widened narcissisms, that self-love is capable of different forms, some of which are not so selfish. We are all more or less narcissistic, for that is what the agent/subject *is*. The agent, Aristotle and the medievals said, acts for its own good. If the agent expends all its energies on the other without return, that is after all what the agent *wants*, and that is how the agent gets her kicks. If you don't believe that, trying blocking the way of someone who is working for the other. Those people are impossible! If the agent stopped loving its own good, it would stop loving the good of the other, since the good of the other is the good for which the agent acts and by seeking the good of the other the agent is doing what it loves to do. Jesus said to love your neighbor *as* you love yourself, because if you stopped loving yourself you would stop loving God, your neighbor, and mammon too; you would stop loving, period. The whole momentum of agency, subjectivity, and love would just shut down, the circle would stop turning, and there would be nothing anybody could do for you.

So there are only various economies of narcissism, ranging from

---

[13] In *Glas* (Paris: Galilée, 1974); Eng. trans. *Glas*, trans. Richard Rand and John Leavey (Lincoln: University of Nebraska Press, 1986), Derrida provides a running commentary on Hegel's view of marriage and the family in the early theological writings and in the later philosophy of right, showing how everything is regulated by the laws of the dialectic; this law, for Derrida, is continually being interrupted by the gift.

uninterrupted narcissism, which is mean, contemptible, and pusillani-mous, which fills everyone who runs into it with disgust, up to the most frequently *interrupted and ruptured narcissism*. In the latter, the circle of the same is constantly being torn asunder, if only to close over again, resulting in someone quite open-ended and magnanimous, someone who has made herself beautiful by making herself, if not downright good, at least not half-bad:

> There is not narcissism and non-narcissism; there are narcissisms that are more or less comprehensive, generous, open, extended. What is called non-narcissism is in general but the economy of a much more welcoming, hospitable narcissism, one that is much more open to the experience of the other as other. I believe that without a movement of narcissistic reappropriation, the relation to the other would be abso-lutely destroyed, it would be destroyed in advance. The relation to the other—even if it remains asymmetrical, open, without possible reappro-priation—must trace a movement of reappropriation in the image of oneself for love to be possible, for example. Love is narcissistic [PdS 212–213/*Points* 199].

Amen. On that point, Aristotle, Jesus, Thomas Aquinas, and Derrida are all agreed (a formidable procession in which Jacques can somewhat nervously take his place, at the end, at a little distance, so that we are not sure whether he is in it or just watching).

It does not take much to see that the lines we have drawn between the gift and exchange mirror perfectly, are isomorphic with, perhaps indeed converge with, the distinction between justice and the law. For justice calls for a gift even as the gift is a call for justice. Justice is the welcome *given* to the other in which I do not, so far as I know, have anything up my sleeve; it is the hospitality that I extend to the other, the expenditure without return, given without a desire for reappropria-tion, dispensed in a moment of madness, in which I tear up the circle of the law, in a time without time, in a desire beyond desire. Justice and the gift are impossible, *the* impossible, which is my passion, that *by* which I begin and am impassioned. The passion for justice and the passion for the gift come together in and as the passion for the impos-sible.

To think justice as the gift is, if you think about it, to propose an interesting theory of obligation, namely, an obligation without debt and the deadening weight of guilt and compulsion, yet still without simply canceling or annulling the obligation. If I am addressed by the other, overtaken and surprised, traumatized even, as Levinas likes to say, shocked by the blow that the circle of the same receives from the incoming of the other, then I "must" "respond." But this "must" is without necessity, compulsion, or force; it is beyond mere duty or dutifulness. If I respond to the solicitation of the other out of pure duty, that is almost insulting (please, do not bother, if you hate it that much!). If justice is what is "owed" the other, it is at the same time "given" without restraint, not outside but beyond duty, beyond the sheer force that would wring it out of me almost against my will, given in an expenditure without reserve that goes beyond what would be "rightfully" expected, beyond what "duty dictates." Justice is "rendered" (re-dare), given back to the other, which is where it belongs in the first place.

The law as law, on the other hand, is no gift, and hence no guarantee of justice. Insofar as it is only law, the law is pusillanimous and mean-spirited, blind and unkind, unloving, and ungenerous, ungiving and unforgiving, tight-fisted and rigoristic, wooden and "legalistic." The law is a calculated balance of payments, of crime and punishment, of offense and retribution, a closed circle of paying off and paying back. When things are merely legal, no more than legal, then they contract into narrowly contractual relationships with no "give," no gifts. If all we had were the law, if the law were our only recourse, everything would grind to a halt, would be ground up in legalistic, litigious squabbling, littered with lawyers running everything, who would eventually run everything into the ground. That is why Drucilla Cornell, in her inimitable way, says that the law is a "monster." That is a flamboyant but quite precise way of drawing attention to the fact that the law is an economy that will eat you up if you do not watch out for it.[14]

But let us not forget how such distinctions work. There is never a question of finding some place that is simply exterior to the law, that lies purely outside the law, some pure out-law state (although Montana might be a good place to start looking for one). That is (one reason) why Drucilla Cornell is a professor of law, not a Jewish prophet. No such place is to be found; there is, there exists, no pure justice, any more than a pure gift is something that exists. Hence, just as we must

---

[14] Cornell, *Philosophy of the Limit*, p. 167.

learn both to "give" and also to "give economy a chance," so we must also learn to love justice and also to give the law a chance, to open the law as much and as far and as frequently as possible to justice. Just as there are only degrees and economies of narcissism, so there are only degrees and economies of law, varieties of legal systems, which constitute more or less open-ended, porous, welcoming legal codes—lest they turn into outright monsters. Just as we find ourselves always *between* the gift and economy, so we find ourselves always between justice and the law, always trying to interrupt the authoritative voice of the law with the soft sighs of justice, to relieve the harsh strictures of the law with the gentleness of a gift.

DIKE: DERRIDA, HEIDEGGER, AND DIS-JUNCTIVE JUSTICE

The question of justice and the gift raises the question of Heidegger (and of Heidegger's "question"). Heidegger is never far from Derrida's thoughts—here, as elsewhere. While it would be a mistake to underestimate Derrida's debt to Heidegger's delimitation of the "history of metaphysics" as a history of being-as-presence,[15] it would be no less mistaken to overlook the distance that Derrida puts between himself and Heidegger. This is something that I think needs further emphasis, given the link between Derrida and Heidegger.[16] In the "Roundtable," Derrida comes back to one of his most constant complaints about Heidegger, which has to do with the constancy of the theme of "gathering" (*Versammlung*) in Heidegger:

> [O]ne of the recurrent critiques or deconstructive questions I pose to Heidegger has to do with the privilege Heidegger grants to what he calls *Versammlung*, gathering, which is always more powerful than dissociation. I would say exactly the opposite [RT 14].

No matter what tribute Heidegger pays to the "difference" between Being and beings, it remains true that for him beings gather (or are

---

[15] "What I have attempted to do would not have been possible without the opening of Heidegger's questions." But despite this debt, or because of it, what Derrida calls *différance* goes beyond Heidegger's ontological difference. See Derrida, *Positions*, trans. Alan Bass (Chicago: The University of Chicago Press, 1981), pp. 9–10.

[16] For a good treatment of the connection, see Herman Rapaport, *Heidegger and Derrida: Reflections on Time and Language* (Lincoln: University of Nebraska, 1989); I have also explored both the link and the break in *Radical Hermeneutics*, chaps. 6–7.

gathered, in the middle voice) themselves together back into Being where they converge upon a more profound unity and truth, which is likewise the gathering of thinking to being. Thus, when Heidegger delimits the metaphysical idea of "identity," he does so not in terms of something like *différance* but in terms of a higher, or deeper (it doesn't matter much) notion of "belonging together" (*Zusammengehören*). When Parmenides says that being and thought are the same (*auto*), Heidegger says that this is to be understood not as the simple identity of a self-thinking thought, but as the mutual tending toward each other of being and thinking, which belong to each other as to their own most proper element. For being needs thought in order to be manifest, even as thought is always the thought of being. Now, that may be very lovely, very edifying, a poetic improvement upon cold-hearted logical identitarianism. But as a gesture aimed at delimiting metaphysics, it succeeds simply in repeating metaphysics on a higher (or deeper, if you insist), more edifying level, thinking beyond identity to unity, heaving and sighing after some sort of hyper-unity, rather in the way that negative theology goes beyond being to an even higher (or deeper) affirmation of the Being of God as a *hyperousios*.[17]

All the Heideggerian hype about a gathering hyper-unity, the whole Heideggerian axiomatics of gathering, particularly as regards the question of justice, Derrida thinks, spells trouble. As Derrida says in the "Roundtable":

> Once you grant some privilege to gathering and not to dissociating, then you leave no room for the other, for the radical otherness of the other, for the radical singularity of the other [RT 14].

The incoming and transcendence of the other would be closed off and suffocated by this valorization of unity and accord. Now, while Derrida has no wish simply to wash his hands of Heidegger, to denounce him as a Nazi who no longer deserves to be read—on the contrary, the more the tide turns against Heidegger these days, the more Derrida rallies to his defense—it is equally clear that Heidegger would never have been able to associate himself with National Socialism, indeed with any nationalism whatsoever, biological (lower) or spiritual (higher), of whatever altitude, had he shared Derrida's radically "dis-

---

[17] See Martin Heidegger, *Identity and Difference*, trans. Joan Stambaugh (New York: Harper & Row, 1969) for the analysis of identity as belonging together.

sociative," that is, pluralistic and democratic sensibilities, had he been more suspicious of the *Versammlung* that he valorizes and Derrida critiques. On this point of pluralism, of a democracy to come, and, hence, of justice as dissociation and disjunction, as polyvalence and plurivocity, Derrida could not be further removed from Heidegger. Derrida is as far removed from Heidegger on this point of politics as a Parisian, post-Marxist left intellectual can be from a right-wing, reactionary, mountain-climbing anti-Marxist and anti-modernist.

Derrida's critique of Heidegger on this point is developed, appropriately enough, in *Specters of Marx*. Here Derrida pursues the impish paradox that justice happens precisely when "the time is out of joint," that the possibility of justice lies in dis-joining, disad-*just*ment, a point he pursues by way of a cross-reading of Shakespeare's *Hamlet* with Karl Marx, which is itself a peculiar conjoining of the disjoint. The notion that justice has to do with a time that is off its hinges, deranged, a little mad, is a perfect fit in the sense of a perfect foil for Heidegger's famous analysis of the "saying of Anaximander."[18] There Heidegger claims that the emergence of beings into unconcealment, their rising up from and falling back into concealment, takes place according to the rule of *dike*, which is thus to be interpreted as a word of Being and not "moralistically." *Dike* judiciously oversees the unconcealment process, allotting to each entity its apportioned moment, its temporary place in the sun of *phainesthai*, fitting each entity into the transition between concealment and unconcealment. By the same token, *dike* strikes down the tenacious and stiff-necked entity that would resist going under and persist in presence, which persistence is the very stuff of *adikia*, the disjoining of the whole. Providing thus the opportune juncture for the entity, *dike* "harmoniously conjoins" (SdM 49/SoM 23) entity to entity, thereby gathering entities together in an all-pervasive accord, a harmonic (fugal) movement whose name is also *aletheia*. (Justice for Heidegger has Greek, not Jewish names.)

But Derrida complains that, by "translating" (however meditatively) *dike* as *Fug*, fit, joining, juncture, and by treating disjuncture, disloca-

---

[18] See Martin Heidegger, *Early Greek Thinking*, trans. D. F. Krell (New York: Harper & Row, 1975), pp. 13–58, for the interpretation of gathering in "The Anaximander Fragment." For a commentary on Derrida's earlier observations on Heidegger's interpretation of the Anaximander fragment, see John Protevi, "Avoiding a 'Superficial Reading': Derrida's Reading of the 'Anaximander Fragment,' " *Philosophy Today*, 38, No. 1 (1994), 88–97.

tion, being-out-of-joint as *adikia*, Heidegger remains within the horizon of Being as presence that he would otherwise bring into question. For Being is taken to mean the close fit, close to itself, the proper joining of the proper to itself. That means that this Heideggerian *dike* would function for Derrida as *droit*, as a kind of law of association or assembling together that risks repressing the relation to the other. For the latter requires the "irreducible excess of a disjuncture or an anachrony" that, risky as it is, "would alone *do justice* or *render justice* to the other as other" (SdM 55/SoM 27), which requires one to give beyond oneself, to give what one does not have (cf. DT 12–13n1/GT 2n2; 201–202n1/159–160n28; Sauf 83–84/ON 70; 112/84–85). Doing justice to the coming of the other depends upon transgressing the law of gathering, breaking open and disjoining what gathers itself together and closes in upon itself in self-proximity. Justice thus is dis-ad-justment and dis-juncture. For only thus is there an opening up to the future, to what is to come, to the coming of the other and the democracy to come. That opening breaks the spell of the present closure, allowing the present to be haunted by ghosts. Not only ought the living present to be disturbed by the spirits (*revenants*) of the dead, whose suffering justly claims our memory and mourning, but it ought also to be pried open by the ones still to come (*arrivants*), who also lay claim to justice.

Justice is never found in the present order, is never present to itself, is never gathered unto itself. Justice is rather the relation to the other, the dis-juncture that opens the space for the incoming of the other. The essence of justice, thus, is to have no essence, to be in disequilibrium, perpetually disproportionate with itself, never to be adequate to itself, never identical with itself. Justice never exists, and that is essential to justice, for justice, like the gift, is the impossible, our passion, which we desire with a desire beyond desire, what we love like mad. Justice calls, justice is to come, but justice does not exist. Indeed, it would be the height of injustice to think that justice exists, that it existed once in Greece whose true sons are Germans, or that it is here, for example, in the good old U.S.A., in the middle of American apartheid, the National Rifle Association, the unimaginable violence of our streets, the growing extremes of poverty and wealth, and the demoralizing, demagogic degradation and corruption of democracy that we witness with every political campaign. Justice haunts us, disturbs our sleep, stalks us like the specter of old Marx whom we can't quite bury, keeps us up pacing the floors well into the night, has us seeing ghosts. The specter of justice disturbs the assured distinction between what is and what is not, between to be and not to be, which is a bit of sleeplessness over being about which we can be instructed rather better by Hamlet than by Heidegger.

6

The Messianic: Waiting for the Future

"As soon as you address the other, as soon as you are open to the future, as soon as you have a temporal experience of waiting for the future, of waiting for someone to come: that is the opening of experience. Someone is to come, is *now* to come. Justice and peace will have to do with this coming of the other, with the promise. . . . This universal structure of the promise, of the expectation for the future, for the coming, and the fact that this expectation of the coming has to do with justice—that is what I call the messianic structure."

—"Roundtable," 23

THE MESSIANIC TWIST IN DECONSTRUCTION

It is clear to anyone with a Jewish ear, to anyone with half an ear for the Hebrew and Christian scriptures, that this whole thing called "deconstruction" turns out to have a very messianic ring. The messianic tone that deconstruction has recently adopted (which is not all that recent and not only a tone) is the turn it takes toward the future. Not the relative and foreseeable, programmable and plannable future—the future of "strategic planning"—but the absolute future, the welcome extended to an other whom I cannot, in principle, anticipate, the *tout autre* whose alterity disturbs the complacent circles of the same. The messianic future of which deconstruction dreams, its desire and its passion, is the unforeseeable future to come, absolutely to come, the justice, the democracy, the gift, the hospitality to come. Like Elijah knocking on our door! The first and last, the constant word in deconstruction is come, *viens*. If Derrida were a man of prayer—

which he is, as I have elsewhere tried to show—"Come" would be his prayer.

Viens, oui, oui (Parages 116; PdS 70/Points 65). That is deconstruction in a word, in three words. In a nutshell.

Derrida at first avoided the notion of the messianic on the grounds that it entailed the idea of an "horizon of possibility" for the future and, hence, of some sort of anticipatory encircling of what is to come.[1] But after this initial "hesitation," Derrida adopted the term "messianic," evidently under the influence of Walter Benjamin (SdM 95–96n2/SoM 180–181n2).[2] Benjamin spoke of a "weak messianic power" (the "weak" corresponding to what Derrida calls the messianic "without" messianism), which Benjamin associates with historical materialism. In Benjamin's view, the present generation is to be viewed messianically, as those who were all along to come, those who were all along expected precisely in order to "redeem" the past. We today live in a pact with the disasters of the past, inheriting a promise we never made, to recall the dangerous memory of past suffering, which is a pledge not to be taken lightly. The "now," the present time, is precisely a messianic time in which we are responsible for the entire history of humankind. Every present, every "second of time," what Derrida will call the "moment," is "a strait gate through which the Messiah might enter." Every day is a "holy day," a day of "remem-

---

[1] Note the alteration of "The Force of Law," the original lecture delivered in New York City (DPJ 25), that is introduced in the Galilée edition (FL 56), concerning the "messianic promise" or "other horizons of the same type."

[2] Walter Benjamin, "Theses on the Philosophy of History," in Illuminations: Essays and Reflections, trans. Harry Zohn, ed. Hannah Arendt (New York: Schocken Books, 1969), pp. 253–264; cf. SdM 95–96n2/SoM 180–181n2. For a classic discussion of the messianic, see Gershom Scholem, The Messianic Idea in Judaism and Other Essays on Jewish Spirituality, trans. Michael Meyer et al. (New York: Schocken Books, 1971). On the link between Scholem and Benjamin, see Susan A. Handelman, Fragments of Redemption: Jewish Thought and Literary Criticism in Benjamin, Scholem, and Levinas (Bloomington: Indiana University Press, 1991); and Eduardo Cadava, "Words of Light: Theses on the Photography of History," Diacritics, 22 (1992), 98–99n19. For more on Benjamin's "weak messianic power," see Irving Wohlfarth, "On the Messianic Structure of Walter Benjamin's Last Reflections," Glyph, 3 (1978), 148–212; Iseult Honohan, "Arendt and Benjamin on the Promise of History: A Network of Possibilities or One Apocalyptic Moment?" Clio (1990), 311–330; Christopher Hering, "Messianic Time and Materialistic Progress," Journal of the British Society for Phenomenology, 16 (1985), 156–166; and Christopher Fynsk, "The Claim of History," Diacritics, 22 (1992), 115–126. Derrida himself cites the role of Peter Szondi, "Hope in the Past: On Walter Benjamin," Critical Inquiry, 4 (1978), in underlining this theme in Benjamin for him; cf. MfPdM 155n10.

brance," an "all saints" day in which we remember the saints, the dead and their suffering. This Benjaminian motif enters crucially into what Derrida calls "the work of mourning" in the subtitle of the Marx book, the work of remembering the spirit of those who precede us (*revenants*) without assimilating their alterity into the present,[3] where it collaborates with the distinctively Derridean motif of the justice "to come" (*l'à venir*) and the affirmation of the future, of those who are yet to come (*arrivants*).

This messianic motif appears alongside his recent "circumfession" (*circonfession*) of his "alliance" ("covenant") with Judaism, never broken but never kept, by ignoring which he has been "read less and less well over almost twenty years," his revelation of "my religion about which nobody understands anything" (*Circon.* 145–146/*Circum.* 154). The news could not be worse for Derrida's secularizing, Nietzscheanizing admirers. They thought they found in deconstruction the consummating conclusion of the Death-of-God, the final stake in the still-twitching heart of the old God. If the first version of the Death-of-God, in Feuerbach and the young Hegelians, turned into the Birth of Man, then according to this atheistic metanarrative, deconstruction has been sent into the world to proclaim the End of Man, to deconstruct the subject and all metaphysical humanisms, and hence finally to scatter the ashes of the old deity to the four winds of *différance*.[4] However much that line on Derrida may conform to the requisite academic dogmas about religion—if there is one "other" that is just too other, too, too *tout autre* for academics to swallow, it is religion!—it has nothing to do with deconstruction, with its letter or its spirit, or with Derrida, with his eye or his ear, which is deeply messianic and not a little Jewish.

Deconstruction is always more complicated, more plurivocal and heterogeneous than any secularizing, modernist critique of religion, which is, after all, a vintage component in the old Enlightenment. The genealogical lines and links of deconstruction run back, not only to Nietzsche, but also, as I am constantly insisting, to Kierkegaard and

---

[3] Mourning, for Derrida, is another "self-limiting" idea: if it succeeds (in interiorizing the dead other) it fails (in respecting his or her alterity); see MdPdM 49–52/MfPdM 28–32.

[4] I think that in *Erring: A Post/modern A/theology* (Chicago: The University of Chicago Press, 1984) Mark Taylor feeds these secularizing admirers of Derrida the best statement of this death-of-God metanarrative, even though Taylor's own interests in religion and deconstruction run deeper than that, as evidenced by "Denegating God," *Critical Inquiry*, 20 (1994), 592–611.

Levinas, who are arguably the most important religious philosophers, or philosophical men of religion, or thinkers engaged in a philosophical repetition of religion (DM 52–53/GD 49), in the last two centuries. If there is any sense to speaking of deconstruction as "post-modern" (which diminishes with each passing day) or as engaged in the production of a "new" Enlightenment (SdM 149/SoM 90), which I hope is increasing day by day, then deconstruction must likewise be seen as a form of "post-secularization." For deconstruction moves beyond all Enlightenment debunking of religion and chastises the Enlightenment—as Derrida chastises Marx—for having chased away one ghost too many (SdM 277/SoM 174). For without the messianic spirit, which likewise haunted Marx in his most prophetic moments and is indeed part of his legacy (SdM 56/SoM 28), deconstruction (which expects justice, which *is* justice) does not have a ghost of a chance.

The messianic turn in deconstruction, if it is a turn, what is at least a messianic twist recently given to deconstruction, also gives the lie to Derrida's critics, one more time, if this is still necessary, who take deconstruction to be the enemy, not only of institutions, the state, law, order, literature, reading, reason, the good, the true and the beautiful, etc., but also of religion. Deconstruction is a blessing for religion, its positive salvation, keeping it open to constant reinvention, encouraging religion to reread ancient texts in new ways, to reinvent ancient traditions in new contexts. Deconstruction discourages religion from its own worst instincts by holding the feet of religion to the fire of *faith*, insisting on seeing things through a glass (*glas*?) darkly, that is, on believing them not thinking that they are seeing them. Deconstruction saves religion from seeing things, from fanaticism and triumphalism. Deconstruction is not the destruction of religion but its reinvention.

Like an old and wise father confessor, deconstruction helps religion examine its conscience, counseling and chastening religion about its tendency to confuse its faith with knowledge, which results in the dangerous and absolutizing triumphalism of religion, which is what spills blood. Religion is most dangerous when it conceives itself as a higher *knowledge* granted a chosen *few*, a chosen people of God: that is a formula for war. As if God favors Jews over Arabs, or prefers Christians to Jews, or Protestants to Catholics, thereby drawing God into the game of whose theological ox deserves goring. As if God took the side of one people against another, or granted special privileges to one people that are denied to others—to "the other." Religion so instructed, deconstructed, and reconstructed, closely hewn to its messianic and prophetic sources and to the God who said that He does not delight in ritual sacrifice but in justice, religion as a powerful prophetic force which has a dream of justice for *all* of God's children—that is the religion that emerges from an hour on the couch with deconstruction. That religion is good news, for the oppressed and everybody else.

None of this means to say that Derrida is, as he says in the "Round-table," "simply a religious person or . . . simply a believer," that he is a pious Jew, liberal, orthodox, or conservative, or a "believing" Jew, or religious in the conventional sense. Least of all does it mean that he has anything to do with the Book-thumping fanaticism and violence of the several fundamentalisms, Christian, Jewish, or Islamic, which inevitably spell war for the lands they beset, which have been spilling the blood of innocent people from time immemorial. Derrida has, as he tells us in *Circonfession*, married outside Judaism, exposed his sons to the impropriety of not being circumcised, even as he himself "quite rightly pass[es] for an atheist" (*Circon.* 146/*Circum.* 155) He was born into an assimilated Jewish family in the Christianized culture of Algiers (raised on the rue Saint-Augustin, a street named after his "compatriot"), and the Judaism to which he was exposed, the particular religious faith of Abraham and Moses such as he experienced it, did not "take."[5] He did not, would not, could not take it.

That is why Derrida distinguishes the "messianic" as a *universal* structure (like Benjamin's "weak" messianic) from the various "messianisms," which are a little too strong. By the concrete messianisms he means the specific religious beliefs, the historical doctrines and dogmas, of the "religions of the Book," all *three* of them, Judaism, Christianity, and Islam, although Derrida also extends the term to include the "philosophical messianisms," the teleologies and eschatologies of Hegel, Marx, Heidegger. To that list should be added at the last minute the latest, Johnny-come-lately version, Francis Fukuyama's "gospel" of the good news that the free market is the *telos* toward which the West has been groaning and Ronald Reagan is its prophet (SdM 97–100/SoM 56–57). The distinguishing feature of any messianism is that it *determines* the figure of the Messiah, gives the Messiah a deter-

---

[5] Derrida has become more forthcoming about his personal life in two highly autobiographical books, *Circumfession* and *Memoirs of the Blind*, and also in some interviews; see PdS 349–355/*Points* 339–344.

minate characterization and specific configuration, with the result that the Messiah is *identifiably* Jewish, Christian, Islamic, or, God forbid, Capitalistic, where a supply-side, free market Messiah is the latest teleological consummation of History. That contracts the absoluteness of the messianic promise and expectation within the borders of a *people*, so that God is thought to have cut a special deal with Greco-European Christians, or Jews, or Arabs; of a *language*, so that God is said to have spoken Hebrew, Greek—or was it Aramaic?—or Arabic; of a *national history*, so that God is made to take his stand with the destiny of some nation-state and takes up arms within the strife among the nations. The messianisms have all the makings of a catastrophe, that is, of war. This they unfailingly provoke, with merciless regularity, under one of the most grotesque and terrifying names we know, that of a "holy war," which means, alas, killing the children of God in the name of God, who too often really are children, killing the innocent in the name of peace and justice, killing in the name of the promise. Today, Derrida says, the war waged by these messianisms over the "appropriation of Jerusalem" has become a world war (SdM 101/SoM 58).

Nor are the philosophical messianisms innocent of this blood. Hegel thought that war was the way for the Spirit to beat itself into shape, and Marx was in a rush to finish *Kapital* before the revolution made his prophecy redundant. There is nothing accidental in Heidegger's love of war, his love of *Kampf* as the way to beat Being into shape; nothing accidental in his support of the Nazi seizure of power, which afforded the Greco-Germanic History of Being the chance to fulfill its missionary destiny, which is nothing more than a corrupted Heideggerian messianism disguising its biblical sources.[6] Fukuyama is delighted with the outcome of the cold war, which was fueled all along by several hot ones in East Asia and Central America. The several messianisms always take themselves to have an identifiable "mission," a missionary identity, a mission to establish the rule of their messianic vision in a foreseeable and foregraspable future, and they have rarely lacked the nerve to seize the opportunity to give their destiny a little boost wherever the occasion presented itself. That is when the blood begins to flow.

The "messianic," on the other hand, has to do with the absolute structure of the promise, of an absolutely indeterminate, let us say, a

---

[6] For more on "Heidegger's *Kampf*," see my *Demythologizing Heidegger*, chap. 2.

structural future, a future always to-come, *à venir*. The messianic future is not a future-present and is not sparked by a determinate Messiah; it is not futural simply in the sense that it has not as a matter of fact shown up yet, but futural in the sense of the very structure of the future. The messianic future is an absolute future, the very structure of the to-come that cannot in principle come about, the very open-endedness of the present that makes it impossible for the present to draw itself into a circle, to close in and gather around itself. The messianic is the structure of the to come that exposes the contingency and deconstructibility of the present, exposing the alterability of what we like to call in English the "powers that be," the powers that are present, the prestigious power of the present. The messianic future, the unformable figure of the Messiah in deconstruction, has to do with something absolutely unpresentable and unrepresentable that compromises the prestige of the present, the absolutely undeconstructible that breaks the spell of present constructions.

The messianic, Derrida says, is a "structure of experience" (SdM 266/SoM 168), the very structure of experience itself where experience means running up against the other, encountering something we could not anticipate, expect, fore-have, or fore-see, something that knocks our socks off, that brings us up short and takes our breath away.

Vanitas vanitatum, said Qoheleth in his best Latin, *et omnia vanitates*. The whole thing is a vanity, an idol. Everything is deconstructible, the French translation reads, but justice in itself, if there is such a thing, is not deconstructible (translation from "The Postmodern's Bible"). The essential indeterminacy of the messianic future, of the figure of the Messiah, is of the essence of its non-essence. The non-presence of the Messiah is the very stuff of his promise. For it is in virtue of the messianic that we can always, must always, have no alternative but to say, "come." We can and we must pray, plead, desire the coming of the Messiah. Always.

That is part of the force of the story of the coming of the Messiah that Derrida repeats in the "Roundtable" (having cited it in *Politiques de l'amicitié*, 55n1), which is to be found at the end of Blanchot's *Writing the Disaster*.[7] In this story, the Messiah, having appeared outside the city of Rome dressed in rags, is recognized by someone who

---

[7] Maurice Blanchot, *Writing the Disaster*, trans. Ann Smock (Lincoln: University of Nebraska Press, 1986), pp. 141–143.

penetrates this disguise—which is meant to shelter his presence—and who, "obsessed with questioning," says to the Messiah, "When will you come?" The story, Blanchot says, has to do with the relation between the messianic "event" (*événément*), let us say with an event in messianic time, and its "nonoccurrence" (*inavènement*), its non-coming about in ordinary historical time. For the coming (*venue*) of the Messiah, the messianic coming, is not to be confounded with his actual presence (*présence*) in recorded history, with occurring in ordinary time, with actually showing up in space and time, which would ruin everything. The coming of the Messiah has to do with the very structure of a messianic time, as the time of promise and expectation and opening to the future, for the "Come, Come" must resound always, according to Blanchot. The lightness of a messianic expectation, its buoyancy and agility, are not to be weighed down by the lead-footed grossness of the present. The Messiah is the one of whom we are *always* saying "Come," which is what keeps things on the move. The messianic has the structure of what Blanchot punningly calls *le pas au delà*: the step (*pas*)/not (*pas*) beyond, the beyond that is never reached but always pursued. [8]

Were the Messiah ever to show up in the flesh, were, *per impossibile*, his coming ever taken to be an occurrence in historical time, something that could be picked up on a video camera, that would be a disaster. The effect would be to shut down the very structure of time and history, to close off the structure of hope, desire, expectation, promise, in short, of the future. Even if, as some Jewish sages hold, the Messiah has actually come and gone in ordinary time, that would not be the "coming," and it would still be necessary to say "Come." That is why, in Christian messianism, where it is held that the Anointed One has already come, all eyes and all hope are turned, not only to his earthly sojourn, but to the day when he will come *again*, for the Messiah must always be *to come*. The Messiah is a very special promise, namely, a promise that would be broken were it kept, whose possibility is sustained by its impossibility. (Another self-limiting idea.)

Now, the remarkable thing is that all this is not just a bit of esoteric Jewish theology but the very stuff of this postmodern bugbear called

---

[8] See Maurice Blanchot, *The Step Not Beyond*, trans. Lycette Nelson (Albany: State University of New York Press, 1992); for a commentary highlighting its relevance to Derrida, see my *Prayers and Tears of Jacques Derrida*, §6.

deconstruction. Deconstruction turns on the unpresentable and unrepresentable, unforeseeable and unnamable, impossible and undeconstructible promise of something to come, something, I know not what, *je ne sais quoi*, let us say a justice to come, or a democracy to come, or a gift or a hospitality to come, a stranger to come. Deconstruction is messianic all the way down but its Messiah is *tout autre*, a just one who shatters the stable horizons of expectation, transgressing the possible and conceivable, beyond the seeable and foreseeable, and who is therefore not the private property of some chosen people.

FAITH WITHOUT RELIGION

That is why Derrida says in the "Roundtable" that he wishes to distinguish between religion and faith. For deconstruction has to do with something I know not what, about which it is possible only to have faith, to keep the faith, to hold on to by a prayer. What Derrida calls the "promise" is not a personal promise, not a personal covenant made between a determinate divinity, Yahweh, and an identifiable people, the Jews. Derrida wants to credit faith, as he says in the "Roundtable," but without "accrediting," giving special credentials to, some determinate body of religious beliefs, with its associated notions of a chosen people, promised land, sacred language, hand-picked vicar, or institutional commission. For that religion, on his telling, would let all hell break loose. The way to avoid this holy hell is deconstructively to reconstruct, within the parameters of the absolute promise, what Derrida does not flinch from calling in a recent piece a "religion within the limits of reason alone."[9] But he uses this vintage Kantian chestnut from the old Enlightenment *without* opposing reason to faith and without letting reason hold court over faith, which is the defining mark of the old Enlightenment. For the whole point of a deconstructive, postcritical, postsecularizing analysis of what is called reason—that is, the point of a New Enlightenment—would be to show the extent to which reason is woven from the very fabric of faith.

The "promise" that Derrida has in mind is the very *structure* of

---

[9] Jacques Derrida, "Foi et savoir: Les deux sources de la 'religion' aux limites de la simple raison," in Jacques Derrida and Gianni Vattimo, *La Religion* (Paris: Seuil, 1996). See Caputo, *Prayers and Tears of Jacques Derrida*, §11, for a commentary.

the promise, a promise protected in all its indeterminacy and open-endedness, that inhabits and disturbs whatever is present and phenomenalizable. It would be the very essence or presence of injustice to say that justice is present, here and now, that the gift has been made, the Messiah has shown up, for then we would have to go on to identify when, where, and among whom. Has he arrived in the U.S.A. today? In California, perhaps? Or in the "new order" of Heidegger's Greco-Germania? In the New World Order of the Free Market? Is he a supply-sider? That would have the effect of blessing some present order or another, endowing it with God's or History's or Being's favor, and turning whatever differs from it into the devil himself, into an obstacle blocking the way of God, or Being, or History, or the Absolute Spirit. Such an obstacle must be removed by an unconditional war waged in the name of all that is holy against the devil himself, the evil empire, the occlusion of Being, or whatever. An old, familiar, and bloody story.

So, much to the surprise of its critics and to the chagrin of its more secularizing friends, it turns out that deconstruction turns on *faith*, but on faith "without religion" (SdM 102/SoM 59), faith as distinguished from religion in the sense of the several religious messianisms, on faith as non-knowing, on a certain delimitation of the power to determine cognitively a program or an ideal. We are required to proceed by faith alone, which is also what Derrida means by reason, which is a kind of faith, since the only reasonable thing to do most of the time is to believe. To paraphrase Kant's famous saying, Derrida has found it necessary to limit knowledge, to delimit and deconstruct any determinate philosophical or religious vision, any messianism, in order to make room for faith, for an open-ended messianic faith in the coming of something unforeseeable and undeconstructible. This messianic faith, he says, "guides us here like the blind" (SdM 112/SoM 65). That remark gives us some insight into a work Derrida published in 1990 entitled *Memoirs of the Blind*, a text accompanying a collection of Louvre paintings and drawings that depict the various faces of blindness. Having been invited by the Louvre to serve as the first in a series of guest curators, with the freedom to organize their own exhibits from among the Louvre holdings, Derrida had chosen the theme of blindness. The text, one of several that he has cast in recent years in dialogue form, begins and ends with the question "do you believe?" (*croyez-vous?*). The final sentence is, "I don't know. One must believe."[10]

The import and the impulse, the drive and the desire of deconstruction is not cognitive or constative but performative; deconstruction is not a matter of knowing or seeing, but of believing. Deconstruction does not terminate in a vision or a truth; it proceeds as Derrida says *sans vision, sans verité, sans révelation*, without vision, verity, or revelation, without seeing or truth (*Ton.* 95/RTP 167). Indeed, deconstruction does not terminate at all, but keeps starting up all over again, beginning where we are, driven by a faith in the impossible and undeconstructible. Deconstructive faith is very much caught up in what Levinas would call the primacy of justice over truth, the primacy of hospitality and friendship over settling theoretical differences in a discussion. Picking up a phrase from Saint Augustine, Derrida says that truth in deconstruction has to do with doing or making truth (*facere veritatem*), making truth happen, effecting it, forming and forging truth with the fires of justice—not *adequatio* or *aletheia*. The delimitation of truth, the dissemination of Truth into many truths, too many, is not only and not ultimately a Nietzschean gesture, which a one-sided reading of *Spurs: Nietzsche's Styles* might suggest.[11] It is not that the "true world" has become a fable in deconstruction, but that it has been subordinated as a construction to undeconstructible justice. Still less is this delimitation of the "true world" a skeptical one, for truth has been delimited in the name of faith, of a messianic faith in a nameless, unpresentable, undeconstructible justice, or gift. The delimitation of truth is a gesture of welcome to the wholly other which constitutes a certain hyper-ethical, not a skeptical or despairing gesture.[12]

Here is a way to put all this in a nutshell. One day an interviewer asked Derrida where his work was going. His response:

---

[10] *Memoirs d'aveugle: L'autobiographie et autres ruines* (Paris: Éditions de la Réunion des musées nationaux, 1990), p. 130; *Memoirs of the Blind: The Self-Portrait and Other Ruins*, trans. Pascale-Anne Brault and Michael Naas (Chicago: The University of Chicago Press, 1993), p. 129. For a commentary, see *Prayers and Tears of Jacques Derrida*, §19.

[11] Trans. Barbara Harlow (Chicago: The University of Chicago Press, 1978).

[12] See the excellent discussion of this point in Ewa Ziarek, "The Rhetoric of Failure and Deconstruction," *Philosophy Today*, 40 (1996), 80–90; and *The Rhetoric of Failure: Deconstruction of Skepticism, Reinvention of Modernism* (Albany: State University of New York Press, 1995).

I don't know. Or rather I believe this is not on the order of knowledge, which does not mean one must give up on knowledge and resign oneself to obscurity. At stake are responsibilities that, if they are to give rise to decisions and events, must not follow knowledge, must not flow from knowledge like consequences or effects. . . . These responsibilities . . . are heterogeneous to the formalizable order of knowledge [PdS 370/ Points 359].

That is why Derrida emphasizes the primacy of faith in the "Round-table," not the determinable faiths of the various messianisms, but the very structure of faith that inhabits everything we say and do, a faith that, if taken to heart by theology, would open up the various messianisms themselves to a faith beyond their determinate, sectarian dogmas and beliefs. Far from being itself something sectarian, Derrida does not hesitate to say that faith, let us say, his "faith without religion," is something "universal," lying at the root of our most everyday practices, not opposed to but forming the very stuff of what we like to call "reason," that holy name at the sound of which the knee of every *Aufklärer* and analytic philosopher, from Habermas to Ruth Barcan Marcus, must bend.

As soon as I open my mouth, I am going on faith, asking you to believe me, asking for your credit and credence, asking you to believe that I am telling you the truth, that is, telling you what I myself believe to be true. Even and especially when I am lying, it is necessary for you to be believing, for how else will I succeed in deceiving you and abusing your confidence? Whenever what we say lacks full transparency— and when does it not?—we proceed by faith. Whenever what we submit to the consideration of the other lacks demonstrative certainty—and when does it not?—we ask for credit. All the exchanges and transactions of everyday communication take place in the element of faith.

The credit we build up with one another is not forged from the demonstrative certainty that accompanies what we say, but from "testimony" or "witnessing," from the witness that I give to you that I am trying to be foursquare. I give you, if not the truth, at least my testimony to the truth. Testimony, too, presupposes blindness. My ability to give theoretical warrant to my assertions is limited, but there is nothing to limit the gift I give to the other, my standing by what I say, my doing what I say. Testimony is what I give to the other, who is precisely other, on the other shore, beyond my knowledge and ken, *au delà du savoir*, a matter for faith not knowledge. This is not to say that witnessing makes it true, since men and women can give testimony to opposite and incompatible faiths, but it makes such truth as there is. Witnessing takes place in the element of faith and justice, not in the order of knowledge and truth.

Even the hardest, coldest, most calculating men of finance are men of faith, men of credit, who believe in ghosts. They move about in a virtual reality where cash—which is itself, relative to the old mercantile system, but a sign—has all but disappeared, replaced by a stream of molecules, by electronic signals that say that certain monies have been paid or lost, grown or diminished, been transferred or advanced, which everyone believes implicitly. Everyone who is involved in banking, the stock market, in buying options and "futures," in international currency exchange, in commercial transactions of any sort, must simply believe, trust. When the big players and high rollers start to lose *confidence* (which means faith) in the market, then the market contracts. When faith ceases to circulate in the economic system, then the circle draws tight, market values fall, interests rates soar, and the market, held the whole while in mid-air by faith, "crashes." Then the big players, big as they are, sink to their knees and start praying like hell (cf. DT 120–125/GT 92–96).

THE MESSIANIC AND THE MESSIANISMS

Which Comes First?

At the end of the "Roundtable" discussion, Derrida raises a which-comes-first conundrum:

> The problem remains . . . whether . . . the religions of the Book are but specific examples of this general structure, of messianicity. There is the general structure of messianicity, as the structure of experience, and on this groundless ground there have been revelations, a history which one calls Judaism or Christianity and so on. . . . [T]hen you would have a Heideggerian gesture in style. You would have to go back from these religions to the fundamental ontological conditions of possibilities of religions, to describe the structure of messianicity on the groundless ground on which religions have been made possible [RT 23].

That is one possibility:

> The other hypothesis . . . is that the events of revelation, the biblical traditions, the Jewish, Christian and Islamic traditions, have been absolute events, irreducible events which have unveiled this messianicity. We would not know what messianicity is without messianism, without these events which were Abraham, Moses, and Jesus Christ, and so on. In that case singular events would have unveiled or revealed these universal possibilities and it is only on that condition that we can describe messianicity [RT 23–24].

The conundrum is this. (1) Are we to think that the "messianic"—or, sometimes, as in the "Roundtable," "messianicity"[13]—is the ontological condition of possibility of any concrete messianism, the formal, a priori structure relative to which Christianity or Judaism, for example, would be the material instantiation? In that case, no historical messianism is possible without the messianic *a priori*. (2) Or, are we to take the concrete messianisms as "absolute events" or "singular events," that is, irreducible singularities that cannot be subsumed under a general, formal category; as unrepeatable happenings that cannot be taken as "cases" of something more universal? In that case, we would know nothing whatever of the messianic without the historical messianisms, so that the messianic instead of being *a priori* would come later, *a posteriori*. Derrida emphasizes that this is a serious dilemma for him and that he might perhaps one day find that he will be driven by it beyond the very distinction between messianic and messianism.

The same conundrum is described in *Specters of Marx* as a difficulty besetting the "two messianic spaces." On the one hand, the messianic might be seen as a "universal structure," a "structure of experience," which constitutes:

> the historical opening to the future, therefore, to experience itself and to its language, expectation, promise, commitment to the event of what is coming, imminence, urgency, demand for salvation and for justice beyond law, pledge given to the other inasmuch as he or she is not present, presently present or living [SdM 266/SoM 167].

But, then, how is this universal structure to be related to the various "figures of Abrahamic messianism"? Is the messianic an "originary

---

[13] The term *"messianicité"* is used interchangeably with *"messianique"* in FL (see FL 56), but it is not to be found in the Marx book.

condition" of the three Abrahamic messianisms, or are the latter "the only events on the basis of which we approach and first all name the messianic in general" (SdM 267/SoM 168)?

The dilemma calls for a number of comments.[14] In the first place, as Derrida points out in *Specters*, "the two hypotheses do not exclude each other" (SdM 266/SoM 168). I take this as follows. It may well be that, in the order of being (*ordo essendi*), the messianic is the formal condition of possibility of the concrete messianisms, even while, in the order of knowing (*ordo cognoscendi*), of how we actually learn about it, the historical messianisms are the only way we have come to learn about the structure of the messianic in general. What is first in the order of being is last in the order of knowing.

In the second place, there is something deeply unsatisfactory about the dilemma that Derrida has posed, and this because it moves within the most classical distinctions between fact and essence, material and formal, particular and universal, example and originary exemplar, empirical and transcendental, ontic and ontological, that is, within distinctions that Derrida has spent his entire life troubling and destabilizing. To illustrate this, ask yourself where, for instance, deconstruction is to be situated? Are we to believe that deconstruction, in contravention of everything that Derrida has been arguing for three decades, is to be associated with a universal, formal, transcendental, ontological condition of possibility? Or, alternatively, are we to think of deconstruction as one more historically specific, let us say postmodern messianism? That would contravene everything that Derrida says about attaching deconstruction to the absolute, abyssal (SdM 56/SoM 28), desert-like "quasi-atheistic dryness" of the messianic in general that keeps it absolutely free of any determining figure of the Messiah, which would always spell war. Clearly, we need to redescribe this otherwise valuable and provocative distinction, which I would propose to do as follows.

We have been insisting (not without a certain deconstructive *Schadenfreude*) that, by introducing the "messianic" into deconstruction, Derrida is being very Jewish. This is not an entirely new turn of events; it has been going on in one way or another for a long time. Susan Handelman pointed out some time ago how very rabbinical, albeit

---

[14] For further discussion, see *Prayers and Tears of Jacques Derrida*, §10.

with a heretical twist, is the whole problematic of *écriture*.[15] It is by now widely recognized, also, that the first Levinas essay is crucial to everything that Derrida has been saying of late about the other and justice. Again, he has shown a lifelong preoccupation with the thematics of circumcision as a way to emblematize deconstructive analyses. But in his most recent work, and as he has gotten to be an older man, all this Jewishness comes to a head, if I may say so, in works like *Circonfession*—at age fifty-nine, he says, I discover the word "dying" (*Circon.* 193/*Circum.* 208)—and *Memoirs of the Blind*, where he has become more autobiographical, more auto-bio-thanato-graphical. In such works he finds himself going back to his Jewish beginnings, which are not only or not quite Jewish, for his was a very Christianized, assimilated Judaism which was also not a little Arab and Algerian, and his bond with Judaism has been both broken and abided by.

So Derrida has become with the years if not very Jewish, at least very quasi-Jewish, or hyper-Jewish, or meta-Jewish, certainly not Jewish in the conventional sense, for, as we have insisted time and time again, Derrida is not a conventionalist but an *inventionalist* or a *reinventionalist* or even an interventionalist. By giving deconstruction a messianic twist he is engaging in a certain reinvention of Judaism, let us say, a reinvention of Judaism as deconstruction but also, let us insist on this in order to scandalize his secularizing admirers, a reinvention of deconstruction as a quasi-Judaism. Is deconstruction really a Jewish science?[16] Well, almost. He is giving a certain messianic bent to deconstruction, twisting and bending it in a messianic direction, and this by way of giving Judaism a new twist, bending it a bit, to the horror of the rabbis, be they conservative, orthodox, or liberal, in a quasi-atheistic direction. He is making deconstruction into a deviant, slightly heretical Judaism, one that reinvents the prophetic and messianic bent in Judaism, that turns it squarely in the direction of justice, and this

---

[15] Susan Handelman, *The Slayers of Moses: The Emergence of Rabbinic Interpretation in Modern Literary Theory* (Albany: State University of New York Press, 1982); "Jacques Derrida and the Heretic Hermeneutic," in *Displacement: Derrida and After,* ed. Mark Krupnick (Bloomington: Indiana University Press, 1983), pp. 98–129; "Parodic Play and Prophetic Reason: Two Interpretations of Interpretation," in *The Rhetoric of Interpretation and the Interpretation of Rhetoric,* ed. Paul Hernadi (Durham, N.C.: Duke University Press, 1989), pp. 143–171.

[16] See *Mal d'archive: Une impression freudienne* (Paris: Galilée, 1995); "Archive Fever: A Freudian Impression," trans. Eric Prenowitz, *Diacritics,* 25 (1995), 9–63; for a commentary, see *Prayers and Tears of Jacques Derrida,* §17.

without regard for sacrifice and burnt offerings. This he does by insisting upon a certain "desertification" of Abrahamic messianism, by an:

> [a]scesis [that] strips the messianic hope of all biblical forms, and even all determinable figures of the wait or expectation; it thus denudes itself in view of responding to that which must be absolute hospitality, the "yes" to the arrivant(e), the "come" to the future that cannot be anticipated [SdM 266–267/SoM 168].)

Deconstruction is a desertified Abrahamism: again, to the scandal of the rabbis, it has deserted father Abraham and gone out into a *khôral* desert, like an an-khôr-ite, where the flower of no determinable Messiah grows. Deconstruction is, he also says, a slightly "despairing" Judaism, not in the sense of giving up all hope but in the sense of giving up determinable hope, not being able to "count on," and hence to calculate, the coming of some determinable messianic figure. Some will say, the rabbis surely among them, maybe Derrida himself will say, it is even a deadly or deathly Judaism, that "this despairing 'messianism' has a curious taste, a taste of death" (SdM 267–268/SoM 169), for it has let any determinable messianic figure die off.

But none of this is to say, we hasten to add, that Derrida's quasi-Jewish messianic is dead as a doornail, that it is not on the move, not astir with a quasi-Jewish passion for its impossible dream. For whatever parts of Judaism Derrida has deserted (or have deserted him) and let die away, he has been engaged all along in reinventing a certain Judaism, let us say, a prophetic Judaism, the Judaism that constitutes a prophetic call for justice, but not the Judaism of religious ritual and sacrifice or even of specific doctrines. Amos has Yahweh say that He takes no delight in festivals, solemn assemblies, or burnt offerings, but in justice:

> Take away from me the noise of your songs;
> I will not listen to the melody of your harps.
> But let justice roll down like waters
> And righteousness like an ever-flowing stream.
> (Amos 5:21–24)

That is the Judaism that Derrida invokes, the *alliance* to which he has remained faithful, to which he calls "come," which he would let come, let come again—this time as deconstruction. Indeed it is what deconstruction is, in a nutshell. For like the religion of Amos, deconstruction takes no delight in sacrifice and burnt offerings, or in the rites and the rituals, the dogmas and doctrines, of the several messianisms, but burns with prophetic passion for justice, longs to see justice flow like water over the land. Take away from me the noise of your messianisms, he seems to say, and let justice come.

Deconstruction is a passion for justice, for the impossible. For God, "my God." In *Circonfession*, Derrida says that, like his "compatriot" Saint Augustine, he has all along been asking himself "What do I love when I love my God" (*Quid ergo amo, cum deum meum amo*)? For this quasi-atheistic, desertified, denuded Judaism does not do away with the name of God. Indeed, the name of God remains to it of the utmost importance, a name to save (*Sauf le nom*), not as the answer to every question, as in the Heideggerian complaint about onto-theology, but, on the contrary, as the question disturbing every answer, the question of all questions, the question one asks oneself day and night. The question is not whether to love God—who would be so hard of heart?—for that is imposed upon us absolutely, but of what we love when we love our God. Deconstruction is love (PdS 89/*Points* 83), the love of something unforeseeable, unforegraspable, something to come, absolutely, something undeconstructible and impossible, something nameless (cf. *Sauf* 91–93/ON 74). Then what name shall we give to this nameless love, to what in religion is always called God? Shall we call it justice? In deconstruction the constancy of what we call "my God" goes by other names (*Circon.* 146/*Circum.* 155)—names like justice, hospitality, testimony, the gift—and democracy. For God is the name of the other, any other, no matter whom (*Sauf* 90/ON 73).

The particular bent that this Jewish-messianic gives deconstruction, the particular twist that the messianic takes in deconstruction, I would like to suggest, is to become a messian*ism* of the democracy to come. Deconstruction is, I would say, still one more messian*ism*, or at least a "quasi-messianism, so anxious, fragile, and impoverished . . . a quasi-transcendental messianism" (SdM 267/SoM 168), an historically specific—French and late twentieth-century—philosophical, or quasi-philosophical, messianism, or a "postmodern messianism," if that word gives you a charge. Deconstruction takes the specific form of a democratic messianism, by which I mean a thought and practice in which everything is turned toward a democracy to come, which takes the form, as Derrida says, of "absolute hospitality, the 'yes' to the *arrivant(e)*, the 'come' to the future that cannot be anticipated" (SdM

266–267/SoM 168). After all, the open-endedness of the messianic aspiration does not issue in speaking of a "monarchy to come" or an "oligarchy to come." The democracy *to come* is a *democracy* to come, an *à venir* with a determinate historical genealogy. In this messianism of the democracy to come, all eyes and ears are turned to everyone and everything that is ground under by the powers that be, the powers that are present, the powers that preside, which is what the scriptures call "the nations" (*ethne*). By keeping itself free of all prevailing idols, deconstruction dreams of a democracy that keeps itself open, welcoming, to the impossible, to the coming of the *tout autre*.

By a democracy to come he is not associating himself, à la Richard Rorty, with the NATO-ese triumphalism of the Western democracies and "liberal euphoria," but with an ethico-political, I would say a prophetic, "aspiration" (as opposed to a "vision").[17] A democratic messianism turns on a hope and faith in an order that allows disorder ("out of joint"), on a hope in something radically pluralistic, plurivocal, multi-cultural, heteromorphic, heterological, and heteronomic, something that outstrips what we today call nation and national citizenship (the "nations"), nationalism and nationality. In this messianic aspiration, the hegemonic rule of the most powerful nations, who dominate the so-called "United Nations," would be delimited in a new International, one that is attuned to the gratuitous sufferings that ensue from what Levinas called the hatred of the other. This is a quasi-political, quasi-ethical, quasi-prophetic, post-Marxist, neo-democratic, Parisian messianism bent on keeping any prevailing or existing democracy structurally open to a democracy to come, which means painfully and acutely conscious of its own injustice, which is why deconstruction can be a pain.

A democratic messianism is on the *qui vive* about all the ways in which every existing democracy is undemocratic, in which there are no democracies, my friends, not yet, for democracy is still to come.[18]

---

[17] For critiques of Rorty from Derrida's point of view, see Ernesto Laclau, "Community and Its Paradoxes: Richard Rorty's 'Liberal Utopia,' " in *Community at Loose Ends*, pp. 83–98; Mark Taylor, "Paralectics," in *Tears* (Albany: State University of New York Press, 1990), pp. 123–144; John D. Caputo, "In Search of the Quasi-Transcendental: The Case of Derrida and Rorty," *Working Through Derrida*, ed. Gary Madison (Evanston, Ill.: Northwestern University Press, 1993), pp. 147–169.

[18] In "The Politics of Friendship," trans. Gabriel Motzkin, *Journal of Philosophy*, 85, No. 11 (November, 1988), 632–644, Derrida begins by citing Montaigne, "O my friends, there is no friend." Montaigne is himself repeating the attribution of this

This democratic messianism is acutely conscious that the most unjust, the most undemocratic thought of all is that democracy is here, now, in Western Europe or the good old U.S.A., or in the New World Order. Derrida wants to keep the prophetic denunciation in place, always and already, never to silence the shrill voice of the prophetic claim that Israel is unfaithful to the Lord and constantly falls down before idols of presence, that she puts burnt offerings before justice. Such a "prophetic" claim is not, however, excused from the most constant and careful calculation, the most scrupulous and detailed analyses of institutions, laws, and programs that serve the interests of big money, and the most relentless criticism of leaders who pass themselves off as "democratic" even as they concern themselves not with substance but with their media image, not with the common weal but their own reelection. Deconstruction situates itself in the gap between all existing democracies, which are not democratic, and the democracy to come, and this precisely in order to keep alive with prophetic fervor a messianic faith in the unforeseeable and incalculable figure of the Just One, of the democracy, to come.[19]

So, then, to return to our conundrum, I would say that it is impossible for Derrida to sit down to the table with the "messianic" if that is taken as a true or strong universal, a genuine transcendental or ontological condition of possibility. For the whole thrust of deconstruction and its notion of *différance* is to show that such structures are always traces in the play of differences and we do not have access to overarching, trans-historical, transcendental, ontological, universal structures. We are, if there is anything at all to *différance*, always stuck where we are, in the middle of the play of traces, in certain historical

---

statement to Aristotle by Diogenes Laertius, and Derrida has come upon it in the final pages of Blanchot's *Michel Foucault as I Imagine Him*, trans. Jeffrey Mehlman, in *Foucault, Blanchot* (New York: Zone Books, 1987); see *Pol.* 333ff.

[19] The most interesting figures working on a "radical democratic" theory within a Derridean framework are Ernesto Laclau and Chantal Mouffe; see Ernesto Laclau's review of *Specters of Marx*, "The Time Is Out of Joint," *Diacritics*, 25 (1995), 86–97; *New Reflections on the Revolution of our Time* (London: Verso, 1990); and, with Chantal Mouffe, *Hegemony and Socialist Strategy: Towards a Radical Democratic Politics* (New York: Verso, 1985); and Chantal Mouffe, *The Return of the Political* (New York: Verso, 1993). For a discussion of Laclau and *Specters of Marx*, see Simon Critchley, "Derrida's Specters of Marx," *Philosophy and Social Criticism*, 21 (1995), 1–30. Laclau and Mouffe have inaugurated a new book series with Verso entitled "Phronesis," dedicated to an "anti-essentialist" theory of radical democracy and leftist politics. Bennington's *Legislations* appears in this series.

(and social, sexual, political, etc.) webs or networks (DLG 233/OG 162). That means we would always have to do with certain messianisms, certain singular and historical formations that are forged by the circumstances of history. Let us recall that Derrida does not renounce the idea of the "historical," as his most thoughtless critics charge, but rather reconceives it in terms of the "singularity" of the "event," the unique and irreducible moment in which something idiosyncratic happens, something that, if it is truly historical, cannot be saturated with universality, bathed in the light of the general, turned into a token of a type. So, Judaism must be for him, I venture to say, and this ought also to hold for deconstruction itself, an "absolute" event, singular, irreducible to some general form.

What, then, of the dry, desert-like "messianic"? Is it not an abstraction from the various Abrahamic messianisms?

> This critique [deconstruction] belongs to the movement of an experience open to the absolute future of what is coming, that is to say, a necessarily indeterminate, abstract, desert-like experience that is confided, exposed, given up to its waiting for the other and for the event. In its pure formality, in the indetermination that it requires, one may find yet another essential affinity between it and a certain messianic spirit [SdM 148/SoM 90].

To be sure. But I contend that this is a necessarily partial abstraction, aimed at extricating itself from the sectarian beliefs and rivalries of the messianisms, but not from the common, undeniably Abrahamic ground they share. To that extent the messianic represents a failed abstraction, a weak universal, a limited formality that twists free from father Abraham only thus far but not farther, and certainly not in such a way as to leave behind no trail or tracks. We can easily track it down and trace it back to father Abraham, and especially to the prophetic hope in justice to come. That is why anyone with an ear for the Hebrew and Christian scriptures is soon enough led to remark about how very Jewish, or quasi-Jewish, or hyper-Jewish, Derrida and what is called deconstruction is getting to be. Nobody thinks he sounds like a "Buddhist" at *this* point, at this precisely *prophetic* and *messianic* point. That is why I have argued in *The Prayers and Tears of Jacques Derrida* that the "apophatic" element in deconstruction, the instructive convergences of deconstruction both with *Christian* negative theology and with Asian and specifically Buddhist motifs, has a limit and must be reinscribed within this more Jewish "messianic" motif.

If it is the mark of a messianism to *determine* or *identify* the figure of the Messiah, I would say that deconstruction represents a messianism that, if it does not identify the form of the messiah, does retain an identifiably or determinably messianic form, the very form of a Messiah. Deconstruction does not have to do with a determinate future but it retains the messianic determination of futuricity, of the *à venir*. Deconstruction does not give a determinate form to the welcome to the other but it retains the form of the welcome. Deconstruction does not identify the promise or covenant, or constrict them to some privileged people, but it retains the expectant, promissory, and covenantal form. It does not give content to its faith and hope, but it retains the form of faith and hope.

So the "messianic" is a *weak* universal, like Benjamin's "weak messianic force," or Vattimo's weak thought, a quasi-transcendental, an abstraction, to be sure, but one that is historically identifiable, lodged inextricably in an historical language, in the determinate Hebrew word *masiah*, translatable into the Greek *christos*, marked and indexed indelibly by its Jewish, Hebrew, biblical, and religious provenance of which it can never be "denuded," by which it is still partially clothed. Deconstruction, no less than Derrida, did not drop from the sky (ED 233/WD 157), and it cannot lift itself like an *aigle* on Hegelian wings above historical particularities. Derrida has brought his Jewish prayer shawl out of the closet.

I have suggested elsewhere that Derrida might be aided here by employing the notion of a "formal indication" to be found in the young Heidegger, as opposed to the stronger, more Marburgian, neo-Kantian talk to be found in *Being and Time* of a "fundamental ontology" and "transcendental" "concepts," to which Derrida refers in the "Roundtable." So viewed, the messianic would be, not a "universal" "concept" that grasps or "includes" its particulars, but a kind of weak or fragile pointer at the lush complexities of the "factical" messianisms. The key to a formal indication is that it does not subsume or enclose particulars within or under it, does not precontain them, but simply points an indicative finger at "singularities" that are beyond its ken, kind, genus, and generic appetite. The facticity or singularity, on the other hand, is not "conceived" or "grasped" but entered into, given in to, by a certain practical or praxical engagement, which means that you can never "get" it from the outside and you can never "get into" it except by "doing" it, *facere veritatem*.[20]

On that accounting, the "messianic" would be a index pointing at the several messianisms, among which would then be included deconstruction itself, which we would need to add to the list as still one more messianism, as a certain deconstructive messianism, an historically identifiable and determinably late twentieth-century, Parisian, post-Marxist, radically democratic, ethico-political, prophetico-messianic plea for justice and the absolute future. Such a democratic messianism is attuned to the terror and suffering that the twentieth century has produced in its totalitarian excesses of the left and right, which is the historical matrix from which deconstruction was born in the 1960s. Nowadays, its ear is tuned to the triumphalism of the "new world order" which, having had a vision of a free-market Messiah wandering the strip malls and freeways of Los Angeles, has hardened its heart against the victims of capitalist excess. No matter how deep it ventures into the desert, Derrida's "messianic" would always be a certain restricted, relative, or weak formalization of a basically biblical and very Jewish idea. Deconstruction is, in particular, the reinvention of a determinably prophetic idea of the expectation of an everlasting justice to come, of one who comes "to bring good news to the oppressed" (Is. 61:1).

When Will You Come?

Derrida concludes his remarks on the messianic in the "Roundtable" by coming back to the story he found in Blanchot's *Writing the Disaster*—which Blanchot found in the Jewish commentators—about the coming of the Messiah. When the Messiah is recognized, the first thing that is said to him is "When will you come?" Up to now we have

---

[20] See Martin Heidegger, *Phänomenologische Interpretationen zu Aristoteles: Einführung in die phänomenologische Forschung*, WS 1921/22, *Gesamtausgabe* 61, ed. W. Bröcker and K. Bröcker-Oltmanns (Frankfurt am Main: Klostermann, 1985), pp. 33–34, 60–61, and passim; the notion of *formale Anzeige* is discussed throughout GA 61. See Daniel O. Dahlstrom, "Heidegger's Method: Philosophical Concepts as Formal Indications," *Review of Metaphysics*, 47 (1994), 775–795; and the groundbreaking studies of John van Buren, *The Young Heidegger* (Bloomington: Indiana University Press, 1994) and Theodore Kisiel, *The Genesis of Heidegger's Being and Time* (Berkeley: University of California Press, 1993).

understood this question, which Derrida says is "very profound," by pursuing the Blanchotian point, so central to deconstruction, that the coming (*venue*) of the Messiah is not to be confused with actual, historical presence (*presence*), that the messianic "event" is not to be confused with its "occurrence" in ordinary time. For the Messiah is always, structurally to come, so that even were he to show up we would still need to ask when we may expect him to come. Indeed, Derrida tells us elsewhere that it was in Blanchot, not the Bible, that he first came upon the thematics of the "come" (*viens*) that are so central to deconstruction (*Ton.* 87/RTP 162). But in the "Roundtable" Derrida offers us two additional ways to read this story.

In the first place, the question signifies:

a way of waiting for the future, right now. The responsibilities that are assigned to us by this messianic structure are responsibilities for here and now. The Messiah is not some future present; it is imminent, and it is this imminence that I am describing under the name of messianic structure.

So, there is nothing procrastinative about deconstructive expectation. The messianic is not a wistful longing for a future occurrence that is a more or less calculable number of years off, not a dreamy waiting for a future present, but a solicitation, a provocation happening in messianic time, which means a provocation coming from the future to come, from the *tout autre*, from the justice or gift or hospitality to come, that is visited upon us *now*, here and how. The messianic "overtakes" us in the messianic "moment," in a transforming "surprise" that seizes us here and now—in the "present, as the 'time of the now,' " as Benjamin says[21]—and elicits and solicits justice from us, now. Derrida associates this moment, as we have seen, with the moment of madness in *Fear and Trembling* in which we tear up the carefully calculated circle of expenditures and returns and give ourselves to the future without reserve. This is what is called the "aporia of urgency" in "The Force of Law," the notion that justice, if there is such a thing, does not wait, that justice, which is always to come, is needed now, must be brought about here, now, today (FL 57–58/DPJ 26). In *Writing the Disaster* Blanchot says that "Come, come" is not said with your lips alone; what is required is "the efforts of men, virtue, their repentance."[22] The messianic is a call that is whispered in my ear to begin

---

[21] *Illuminations*, p. 263.
[22] *Writing the Disaster*, p. 142.

now, today, working for justice, without delay, even though justice is always to come (structurally delayed). So, Blanchot adds, the Messiah may, if he chooses, answer this impertinent question by saying "Today." The messianic commands us not to wait—to bring about justice today, to change our lives today—even as it puts us under the obligation also to wait—to concede, to insist that justice is never here.

But Derrida mentions in the "Roundtable" still another twist to this story, which is, alas, precisely deferral:

> I would like him to come, I hope that he will come, . . . and, at the same time, I am scared. I do not want what I want, and I would like the coming of the Messiah to be infinitely postponed. . . . [A]s long as I ask you the question, "When will you come?", at least you are not coming. . . . So there is some ambiguity in the messianic structure. We wait for something we would not like to wait for. That is another name for death [RT 24–25].

We wait for the Messiah the way we wait for death, hoping it never arrives. For the coming of the Messiah asks something of us, makes a demand upon us, lays claim to us, fixes us firmly in a place of accusation, obligation, and responsibility, asks us to give. That is something we would, if we could, if it could go unnoticed, forgo, omit, duck, dodge. So, we have an "anxious" relationship to the Messiah, an ambiguous mix of sympathy and antipathy, like the "anxiety before the good" described by Vigilius Haufniensis.[23] For the subject, which is a principle of appropriation and narcissism, prefers good investments, gives in to the lazy drift of ordinary time in which the circle of return is allowed to accumulate gains. The subject prefers the easy circulation of self-appropriation, without rupture and interruption, without all the disturbance of an "event," without all the (noiseless) ruckus of the "moment" which tears up the circle.

So, again, contrary to Derrida's critics, "undecidability" and *différance* do not imply indecision and delay. On the contrary, they serve to underline and expose postponement, to make the retardation of justice look bad, to make more salient the urgency of decision. For deconstruction, if there is such a thing, is a passion, an impassioning, an impatience, for justice.

"When will you come?"

"Today."

That is deconstruction in a nutshell.

---

[23] Kierkegaard, *Concept of Anxiety*, pp. 42, 118ff.

7

Re-Joyce, Say Yes

". . . and how he kissed me under the Moorish wall and I thought well as well him as another and then I asked him with my eyes to ask again yes and then he asked me would I yes to say yes my mountain flower and first I put my arms around him yes and drew him down to me so he could feel my breasts all perfume yes and his heart was going like mad and yes I said yes I will Yes."

—James Joyce, *Ulysses*

"For a very long time, the question of the *yes* has mobilized and traversed everything I have been trying to think, write, teach, or read."

—UG 108/AL 287

The "Roundtable" concludes with a question about Derrida's work on James Joyce, about the back-and-forth movement between Derrida and Joyce, for if Derrida has made a dent in Joycean scholarship, if he has influenced how people read Joyce, that is only because Joyce has flowed deeply into Derrida's pen and been at work on Derrida almost from the beginning of his studies. Derrida's interest in Joyce, which beginning early on has left its mark on many of his works,[1] is not difficult to explain. For Joyce is a writer who practiced, who enacted the "dissemination" of which Derrida dreamed and wrote. Joyce is a writer who raises the question of writing, whose writing is immensely "writerly" and draws attention to the very stuff of *écriture*. Joyce is one of an eminent line of "modernists" who have attracted Derrida's (so-

---

[1] In UG 27–34/PSJ 149–152, Derrida gives us a retrospective of his works as various readings made in the light of Joyce. He singles out *Introduction to Husserl's "Origin of Geometry"* (HOG), *Dissemination*, and *The Post Card*, not to mention *Glas* and "Scribble (writing-power)," *Yale French Studies*, 58 (1979), 116–147.

called "postmodern") attention—along with Kafka, Mallarmé, Blanchot, Celan, Artaud, Genet, Ponge, and others—who raise the very question of literature, writers whose texts call attention to themselves as texts, who push us to the limit, who compel us to ask what a literary text is and what we should do with it (AL 41–42). Derrida's particular interest in Joyce turns on the "yes, yes"—Molly's, Joyce's, Derrida's—and that provides a lovely way to conclude the "Roundtable." For it brings Derrida back to the beginning, to the question of beginnings, of inaugurations, with which he started, for beginnings and inaugurations must constantly be restarted and reaffirmed.

BETWEEN HUSSERL AND JOYCE

It tells us something about Derrida, gives us something of a revealing portrait of him as a young man in the 1950s, to see how he was, at one and the same time, deeply taken by both Edmund Husserl and James Joyce. In 1956–57, after passing the examination for the *aggrégation*, he was awarded a grant to study a microfilm collection at Harvard University of unpublished texts of Husserl. Bennington says that this was a "somewhat fictitious pretext" for seeing Harvard Square and visiting the U.S.A.[2] Why, after all, would a Parisian philosopher come to Massachusetts to study Husserl? Whatever work he did on Husserl that year at Harvard, we know from what Derrida says in the "Roundtable" that he also spent a lot of time reading James Joyce in the Widener Library (he also was married that year, in Boston, in June, 1957). Derrida was taken not by the more engaging Husserl of "life-world" phenomenology, to which Merleau-Ponty had given so much currency in those heady days of "French phenomenology," but by the most rigorous and abstract, the most scrupulous, even tedious analyses of signs, meaning, and ideality to be found in Husserl's *Logical Investigations*. To this Derrida joined a fascination with the explosion of metaphoricity and of multilingual association in Joyce. "It is from the tension between these two interpretations of language," he says in the "Roundtable," "that I tried to address the question of language."

Indeed, his first reference to Joyce occurs in a book on Husserl, his first published work (1962), to which he refers us in the "Roundtable," a French translation of Husserl's "Origin of Geometry" accompanied

---

[2] Bennington and Derrida, *Jacques Derrida*, p. 329.

by a now justly famous "Introduction." Trying to trace the historical genesis or constitution of ideal meaning, Husserl insisted upon "the imperative of univocity" (HOdG 101/HOG 100) that the same words bear the same meaning across time, that later generations be able to repeat and reactivate exactly the same sense, in order thereby to allow communication and, hence, progress among generations of investigators. The opposite conception is Joyce's, which locates history in releasing every buried association in language, in loading every vocable, word, and sentence with the highest possible amount of associative potential, which cultivates rather than avoids plurivocity, so that history lurches forward in a labyrinth, a "nightmare" of equivocation (HOdG 104–105/HOG 102).

Derrida is struck by the self-limitation of both ideas. For unbridled equivocality would breed such confusion that "the very text of its repetition" (HOdG 105/HOG 103) would be unintelligible, even as perfect univocity, were such a thing possible, would result only in paralysis and sterility, in the indefinite reiteration of the same, not in a "history." Joyce would thus have to make some concessions to univocity, even as Husserl would be forced to admit a certain equivocity into history, a certain mutation that is no mere accident or fall but a transformation that must accompany every repetition and transmission, in virtue of which history is not a simple reproduction but a productive self-transformation.

Deconstruction—as usual—situates itself in the distance between these two. It does not renounce the constitution of meaning and the transmission of scientific ideas, even while it inscribes ideality in the flux of writing, for the sphere of ideal meaning is always and already forged from below, as an effect of the play of traces. Deconstruction is a certain Husserlianism, a theory of the constitution of meaning and ideality, but one that is always already exposed to a certain Joyceanism, to the irrepressible anarchy of signifiers, the unmasterable, anarchic event of archi-*écriture*. For textuality or *écriture* sees to it that we are at best able to put together certain unstable and contingent unities of "meaning," certain effects of the differential play of traces that, with a lick and a promise, may get us through the day, that are only as good as the work they do and only for the while that they do it, before they give way to more felicitous effects and more successful convergences, before they are taken up not into "higher" but into different and more felicitous configurations.

Dissemination is an attempt not to decimate meaning but to explain it by exposing its Joycean underside, laying bare the nominalistic contingency of what we call meaning, making plain, in short, the constructedness and, hence, the deconstructibility of meaning. "Joyce" is the name of one of the poles of deconstruction, the name of one of its tropics, the name of a body of texts in which the chance, the contingency, the associative powers, the mobility, the energy, and the "joy" of the trace are almost perfectly summoned. The aim of deconstruction is not to dissolve everything in Joycean excess and let it go up in the smoke of disseminative plurivocity. Derrida expressly warns us against mistaking this talk of the "play of signifiers," which too often results in "inferences" that are "facile, tedious, and naively jubilatory" (UG 111/ AL 289). The aim is to expose what we call "meaning" and "ideality," science and philosophy, to this Joycean operation, to hold the feet of the identity and ideality of meaning to the fire of *différance*. The aim is not to throw meaning to the four winds but to insist upon a more chastened sense of the contingency of sense, of everything that calls itself universal or necessary, transcendental or ontological, philosophical or scientific. The idea is not to jettison these ideas but to redescribe them, for they are not what they say they are, and this by way of reinscribing them in the play of traces:

> But this identity of sense, the ground of univocity and the condition for reactivation, is always relative, because it is always inscribed within a mobile system of relations and takes its source in an infinitely open project of acquisition [HOdG 106/HOG 104].

"Joyce" is thus, early on, a name for an operation, an energy, that is always at work in language, and, hence, in deconstruction. But it is the name of but one operation, for deconstruction is always situated "between," in the "tension" between, these Joycean and Husserlian poles (cf. UG 27–29/PSJ 149).

THE GRAMOPHONE EFFECT

In the more sustained work he published on Joyce in the 1980s (UG),[3] Derrida takes up the question of the "encyclopedic" side of Joyce, thus

---

[3] For help with UG, see the "Introduction" by Derek Attridge and Daniel Ferrer in PSJ 1–14; Carol Jacquet, "Nes, Yo' in Joyce, Oui-Rire Derrida," in *James Joyce*

bringing Joyce into relationship, not with Husserl, but with Hegel. As he says in the "Roundtable,"

> Joyce has represented for me the most gigantic attempt to gather in a single work, that is, in the singularity of a work which is irreplaceable, in a singular event—I am referring here to *Ulysses* and to *Finnegan's Wake*—the presumed totality, not only of one culture but of a number of cultures, a number of languages, literatures, and religions. This impossible task of precisely gathering in a totality, in a potential totality, the potentially infinite memory of humanity is, at the same time and in an exemplary way, both new in its modern form and very classical in its philosophical form. That is why I often compare Ulysses to Hegel, for instance, to the *Encyclopedia* or the *Logic*, as an attempt to reach absolute knowledge through a single act of memory [RT 15].

The irrepressible energy of Joycean textuality is not pure abandon, sheer play, and gambol, but a structured movement of acquisition, an accumulative, in-gathering, en-circling, encyclopedic movement which attempts to summarize the "infinite memory of humanity." What is going on in *Ulysses* is, thus, to be compared to Hegelian "*Erinnerung*," inwardly appropriating and making one's own the entirety of the preceding historical process, not by way of lifting it up (*aufheben*) "vertically" into an ingathering, spiralizing concept (*Begriff*), as in Hegel's *Logic*, but, let us say, by way of releasing "horizontally" the infinitely associative power of signifiers to link on to other signifiers across an endless surface of language. Were one to follow every link in this Joycean "project of acquisition," were one to release every association, eventually—had one world enough and time, in principle at least, it is an "ideal" and an "infinite task"—one would traverse the whole and return home again, like Ulysses. In *Ulysses* signifiers tend to link up in a world wide web, a telecommunicational metaphor that for Derrida is to be taken seriously (phones are ringing all day long in *Ulysses*). In either case, Hegel or Joyce (or "www"), we encounter a logic (*legein*) of Heideggerian gathering (*versammeln*).

That makes Derrida a little nervous. For the prototype of deconstruction is not Ulysses but Abraham, a wandering Jew, a divinely

Literary Supplement, ed. B. Benstock (Miami: University of Miami Press, 1987); Richard Kearney, *Transitions: Narratives in Modern Irish Culture* (Manchester: Manchester University Press, 1988); M. McArthur, "The Example of Joyce: Derrida Reading Joyce," *James Joyce Quarterly*, 32 (1995), 227–241.

displaced nomad sent out into God-knows-where never to return home again (ED 228n1/WD 320–321n20), not a Greek cutting a wide Homeric circle of reappropriation around the Mediterranean, even as the prototype of justice in deconstruction is to cut some slack in all this gathering, to open up the joint. Hence, like Levinas before him, whose "ethics as first philosophy" is, however unlikely this may seem to both the creditors and the discreditors of deconstruction, one of Derrida's most important predecessors, Derrida is always interested in interrupting Ulyssean circles with Abrahamic cuts, in "circumcising" the self-enclosing circle of the same. That is the point, the tip, the cutting edge, if I may say so, of the thematics of circumcision that runs through *Ulysses Gramophone*, which turns out to be another important text for understanding Derrida's more Jewish side and one that prepares the way for reading *Circumfession*. He even considered calling this piece on Joyce "Circumnavigation and Circumcision" (UG 105/AL 285). The problem with circumcision, we shall see, is that it cuts both ways, cutting off from as well cutting open—so that when the Mohel wields his blade he has to be very careful indeed about what he cuts. (Circumcision commands considerable caution.)

Beginning with the famous end of *Ulysses*, Molly's famous end, with the last, capitalized word in the book, which even looks like the signature signing the book—the book of "Yes"—Derrida's analysis of Joyce turns on "yes." True to Joyce's spirit and signature, Derrida amplifies the "yes" multilingually, playing on the polyphony and polyvalence of "yes," "*oui*," and "*ja*." He focuses on the number of *yeses* in *Ulysses*, on the number of times Joyce says yes (*dire oui*), on the yes-saying of Joyce (*l'oui dire de Joyce*) (UG 75/AL 267). That title, in the French, is a play on words that also suggests "hearsay" (*ouï-dire*), an odyssean-circumlocutionary expression implying "what goes around comes around." It also resonates in German, suggesting to him both Nietzsche's "yea-saying" (*Ja-sagen*) and Angelus Silesius's "*Gott spricht nur immer 'Ja'* " analyzed in another piece entitled "A Number of Yes" (*Psy.* 639–650/Number). While he himself found "more than 222 *yeses*" (UG 74/AL 266), and a computer count subsequently upped this number to 369 (AL 266n6), Derrida's interest is focused on "yes, yes," "*oui, oui*," on "two words for Joyce," which is the subtitle of *Ulysses Gramophone*.[4]

---

4 "Two words for Joyce" is also the subtitle of UG and of the first chapter of UG

As the title suggests, Derrida is interested in the telecommunicational motifs in *Ulysses*, for example, in the occurrence of telephone conversations, the first of which occurs on the Passover, just after Bloom had recited the most solemn Jewish prayer of all, "*Shema Israel.*" This, Derrida says, is a long-distance phone call par excellence, "Hello, Israel," placed by God, the "collector of prepuces," to Israel, "person-to-person" (UG 79/AL 269), which is an impish way to allow the serious idea that the very notion of "divine revelation" is inscribed in a communications system and involves the ability to read and translate. The "lines of communication," the "communication networks," the messages, transferences, transportings, and translations, embodied in the elementary technologies (telephones, telegraphs, gramophones, newspapers) found in *Ulysses* (which were already enough to scare Heidegger half to death) embody *différance* in a way that today has become determinative of the very structure of our world. As he made plain in *Specters of Marx*, teletechnology fills the world with the specters of "virtual reality," blurs the lines between what is real and unreal, present and absent. This is the question of what Derrida calls a "postal technology," of the world as a network of messages, and its "babelization," God Himself having disseminated and deconstructed the first attempt of a people to "make a name" for themselves by their architectural and linguistic competence (UG 77/AL 268). Derrida's interest in scrambled messages is not a matter of taking devilish delight—after all, it was God, not the devil, who diss(h)eminated the Shemites—in reducing communication to chaos (*Psy.* 203–235/DiT 165–207). His desire is to keep the lines open, to prevent telecommunicational "systems" and "networks" from becoming scenes of totalization and control, from enclosing senders and receivers encyclopedically, instead of providing opportunities for new events, for novel twists and turns, for unheard-of (*inouï*) messages.

Derrida is interested in what he calls "the gramophone effect," which has to do with the essential "iterability" or repetition built into any signifier, any coded trace. A signifier, like a scientific experiment,

---

(UG 15ff./PSJ 145ff.), which is a shorter piece first delivered at a 1982 conference on Joyce in Paris. In it, Derrida explores the disseminative energy of the phrase "he war" from *Finnegan's Wake*, which illustrates the possibility of "writing in several languages at once" (UG 29/PSJ 148): he wages war; he "was" (German *war*); Yahweh, the name of God, who said he was the one he was (*war*) etc. So these two words amount to a lot more than two words.

is not significant unless it is repeatable; a meaningful message is woven
from repeatable marks. An absolutely singular, unprecedented, and
unrepeatable mark would be unrecognizable and meaningless. The
analysis of repeatability is brought to bear in a paradigmatic way in this
essay on the "yes," because the yes, if it really is a yes, implies repetition, "yes, yes," as Molly teaches us so memorably. To say yes is to be
ready to say yes again:

> In order for the yes of affirmation, assent, consent, alliance, of engage-
> ment, signature, or gift to have the value it has, it must carry the repeti-
> tion within itself. It must *a priori* and immediately confirm its promise
> and promise its confirmation [UG 89/AL 276].

If I say "yes" today and then excuse myself tomorrow, then my "yes"
will not have been a "yes." I cannot be confident about "yes"; I cannot
sit back and rest on the oars of "yes." When I say "yes," I promise to
remember. As Derrida says in the "Roundtable," "We pretend that
today we are inaugurating something. But who knows? We will see."
We are not sure whether we are inaugurating anything today, not sure
whether anything is being commenced, not sure whether this yes
today—or this "I do"[5]—with all this pomp and circumstance today
will be repeated in the quiet, steady beat of tomorrow and tomorrow.
Built right into "yes," which requires repeated affirmation, haunting
it, as it were, is the possibility of a merely rote and mechanical repetition, "which parasites it like its mimetic, mechanical double, like its
incessant parody" (UG 89–90/AL 276). The very thing that makes
"yes" possible threatens it from within, limiting it from within. Like a
gramophone that perfectly reproduces the living voice on the surface
of a phonograph record or a compact disk, in the absence of any living,
intentional presence. If the technological repetition, if the "reproduction" is "faithful" enough, I cannot tell whether the voice is living or
long since dead, a living "yes" or an automaton. So yes must said,
must be constantly repeated, in the face of this threat or internal menace. "That is what I call the gramophone effect" (UG 90/AL 276).

---

[5] Statistics show that about half the time Americans say "I do" it turns out that they
do not; marriage was precisely the example, and what an example, favored by Judge
Wilhelm in *Either/Or*, and of Constantin Constantius in *Repetition*, of a repetition
that "repeats forward," that produces what it repeats, yes, yes. I have examined the
communication between Kierkegaardian and Derridean repetition in *Radical Hermeneutics*.

Derrida in also interested in the occurrence of the name Elijah, Eli-jah, in which is inscribed Molly's "*Ja*." This is not an innocent or arbitrary choice on Derrida's part, since Elijah is the prophet who is to come again, the one for whom every Passover table is set, and also the prophet-patron of circumcision, ordered by God to preside over every circumcision. Elijah is also, it turns out, Derrida's secret name, given to him on his seventh day but never officially recorded, when he sat on his uncle's lap on "Elijah's chair," as he himself had lately discovered much to his surprise (UG 104–105/AL 284–285). Elijah thus is the name of the absolute surprise, the one to come, *tout autre*, the one who summons up in us the paradoxical posture of waiting for the unexpected, of preparing ourselves for surprise.

JOYCE'S SIGNATURE

This brings us to the "double bind" that *Ulysses* poses for Derrida, but no less for the "international establishment" of Joycean scholarship, which is always on Derrida's mind in this piece. The double bind has to do with what Derrida calls the "counter-signature." A "text" for Derrida has a "signature," which is not reducible to the name of an "author" or to signing a proper name. A signature is a matter of the idiomaticity of a text (PdS 365/*Points* 354–55), of the idiosyncratic string of traces that constitute it, not of the psychology of an author. As a structure of writing it invites or solicits repetition, a counter-signing. Texts, if there is anything to them, elicit, call for, and provoke other texts—responses, commentaries, interpretations, controversies, imitations, forgeries, plagiarisms, echoes, effluences, influences, confluences, translations, transformations, bald misinterpretations, creative misunderstandings, etc. (Otherwise they are ignored and forgotten, and serve only the purposes of tenure and promotion.) These textual links, which in more traditional terms make up what is called a "tradition," or a "history of effects" (Gadamer's *Wirkungsgeschichte*), constitute for Derrida an ensemble of "counter-signatures." It belongs to the very structure of the signature to solicit and elicit "counter-signatures," ways of signing on to, ways of repeating the text. For the textuality of a text, of writing, is marked by "iterability"; by its

very structure, a text is repeatable, and this repeatability is irrepressible.[6]

So, the question of Joyce's signature has to do with the possibility
and character of the counter-signatures, with the generosity of Joyce's
signature. Will it make itself an invulnerable fortress, impregnable to
attack and outstripping, endow itself with a kind of omnipotence such
that no one, no commentator to come, can ever get the best of, ever
circumscribe and circumnavigate "James Joyce?" Or will this signature
invite invention, novelty, something new, giving itself up to innumerable, incalculable innovations to come?

It would require an encyclopedic intelligence, or, better, an encyclopedic community of experts from several disciplines bringing to
bear all the competencies and learning of the modern university, in
order to encircle Joyce, to write *on* Joyce (on Joyce's corpus, on the
body of Joyce), to inscribe and circumscribe this corpus. Let us even
imagine a large computer with every word of Joyce keyed in, and several chairs of Joycean studies, to be called—what else?—the "Elijah
Chair of Joycean Studies." But, even so, what can we say about *Ulysses*
that is not already *pre*programmed, not already anticipated in advance
by Joyce? How could we ever raise ourselves to a metadiscursive level,
"neutral and univocal with regard to a field of objectivity" (UG 99/AL
282)? How could we ever establish a scholarly distance with regard to
this encyclopedic event? We are always already caught in Joyce's net,
by the "overpotentialized" text of *Ulysses*. "Yes, everything has already
happened to us with *Ulysses* and has been signed in advance by Joyce"
(UG 98/AL 281). So, then, the double bind in which we find ourselves
is this:

> [O]n the one hand, we must write, we must sign, we must bring about
> new events with untranslatable marks—and this is the frantic call, the
> distress of a signature that is asking for a *yes* from the other, the pleading
> injunction for a counter-signature; but on the other hand, the singular
> novelty of any other *yes*, of any other signature, finds itself already pro-
> gramophoned in the Joycean corpus [UG 99–100/AL 283].)

The very thing that one would most expect from Joyce, the invention
of the other, the singular novelty of another *yes*, an other reading, a

---

[6] For help with the notion of "signature" and "counter-signature," see Derek Attridge, "Introduction," AL 18–20; and Timothy Clark, *Heidegger, Derrida, Blanchot*
(Cambridge: Cambridge University Press, 1992), pp. 150–180.

new counter-signature, new ways to sign on to Joyce, endlessly, joy-
ously discovering new ways to rejoice in Joyce, to re-Joyce, to say *yes*—
all that has been "cut off" in advance, circumcised and circumscribed,
by none other than Joyce. All the hauteur of the several university
competencies that converge in the Joycean institution are laid low by
Joyce himself before they get off the ground. Nothing new can happen.
That is why, Derrida muses, the distinguished scholars assembled at
this Joyce international must have invited external guests, amateurs
like himself, to address this distinguished body of experts. They are
hoping for something new, for a surprise, waiting for the second coming of Elijah, which—to their surprise—is in a way exactly what they
got when they invited Jacques Derrida, a.k.a. "Elie of El-Biar." Of
course, if the truth be told, Derrida thinks, it is not a question of
choosing between these two, between the most rigorous Joycean scholarly competence, which is always required, and the possibility of something coming from the outside and breaking open these scholarly
circles.

   That brings us to laughter. Laughter will be the third term that links
the signature and the "yes." "*who* signs? Who signs *what* in Joyce's
name?" Those questions, according to Derrida's hypothesis, are "married" to "the question of knowing who is laughing and how laughter
comes about *with* Joyce, *in* Joyce, in a singular way, since *Ulysses*"
(UG 113/AL 289). For there is more than one kind of laughter.
But—in French—"yes" itself splits into the visible yes, *oui*, and the
heard yes (*oui ouï*), *ouï* (heard) deriving from the verb *ouïr*, to hear,
whence "hearsay" (*ouï-dire*), which is a chance graphic convergence
without any etymological link to *oui*. His "method," as it were, is to
explore the link between "saying yes" (*oui dire*) and *oui rire*, yes-laughter. In Derrida's view, this yes-laughter constitutes a tonality in Joyce,
what Heidegger would call the dominant mood or tune (*Stimmung*), a
pathos, that marks everything in Joyce's text, that "re-marks" or "over-
marks" it, that leaves its mark on everything without being reducible
to just one element *in* the whole. The hypothesis is that yes-laughter
signs the length and breadth of Joyce's text, like the final "Yes." in
Ulysses, thus constituting Joyce's "signature" (UG 116/AL 291–292).

   But, Derrida claims, there is a "typology" of yes-laughter in Joyce,
turning on two distinguishable, dominant types or keys (at least) in
which yes (*oui*) can be heard (*ouï*), two different yeses heard in Joyce,

the commentary on which, shall we say, constitutes two words for Joyce.

(1) The first is "a reactive, even negative," a "hyper-mnesic" laughter, taking devilish joy in "remembering everything," "in spinning spider webs" that defy mastery, while remaining itself impregnable by precontaining any of the interpretive strategies that the Joycean institution might address to the corpus. That laughter remains in control of all the interpretive strategies, all the "signatures to come," all the counter-signatures, the commentaries or interpretations constituting the way commentators "sign on to" the original, and hence repeats or extends the (so-called) original text, corpus, or signature. "Joyce" would then be a "master signature" which would "precomprehend" and anticipate in advance any possible commentary or counter-signature, allowing Joyce to remain the master of the house, omnipotent as God, sitting in the center laughing at the circles that his commentators cut around him, castrating and cutting them off in advance (UG 117/AL 292). This yes has the last laugh.

However, omnipotence is always an illusion. "Joyce cannot not know this," that his book is just one more book among the millions in the Library of Congress, lost too among all the electronic media that today are outstripping books. Nor can this book be protected from the objection that it is too precious, "overloaded with knowledge," "hyper-scholastic," too subtle, overcultivated, overcalculated; perhaps he even foresaw being censored and calculated that into its success. In short, there is too much control by a subject, too much desire to be a master-name. That allows Derrida to characterize this first version of yes-laughter, which takes on everything, the whole of memory, in terms of the laughter of Nietzsche's Christian-Judaic donkey—the beast of burden which takes on everything, which cries "Ja, Ja" to every task, that wants to circumcise Greek laughter, to cut it off in advance, and then make the Greek laugh with this other, bitter, derisive, and sarcastic laughter. "This yes-laughter of encircling reappropriation, of omnipotent Odyssean recapitulation," puts generations of Joyce scholars in its debt—A.E.I.O.U.—laughing at their futile squirming. It impregnates "in advance its patented signature . . . with all the counter-signatures to come," "ready to domesticate, circumcise, circumvent everything," in the encyclopedic reappropriation of absolute knowledge which gathers everything close to itself. Ulysses then is like the "Logic" of Hegel, who also lived for a while in Frankfurt, where this

International Joyce Conference is being held (UG 117–120/AL 293–94). In this first kind of yes-laughter, "circumcision" is taken as a circumscribing, encyclopedic encircling, a Judeo-Christian castrator, which by precontaining cuts off in advance whatever counter-signature is to come. That is very much the notion of "circumcision" that Derrida found in Hegel's portrait of the Jew in *The Spirit of Christianity*, glossed at length in the left-hand column of *Glas*, and that in one way or another Derrida spent his life contesting.[7]

(2) Over and against, or rather within and inwardly disturbing, this negative and reactive yes-laughter, Derrida locates another laughter, another tone, tune, and tonality, a different music, another signature, a way to sing a different song, not the sing-song of debt, AEIOU, but a song of the "gift." The gift is always without debt, taking the tone not of hyper-mnesic mastery but of a-mnesic abandon, for the gift (*don*) is not a closed circle but an abandoned (*aban-donné*) event, an event of aban-donation. The gift inscribes another signature, one that joyfully gives itself up for lost, that surrenders its "proper name," that drops its defenses and its desire for reappropriation. After all, an "edition" is supposed to be a "gift," a giving out, *e-dare, editio*, with a "dedication," a textual event of giving away that cannot be contained to some particular friend of the author's. When a text is published and dedicated, from that very moment, it is delivered over to the structure of the trace, sent off "above and beyond any determined addressee, donee, or legatee," delivered up "to a dissemination without return" (DT 130/GT 100). A text is supposed to be an event that provokes other events, an occasion for other occasions. A text—above all a text like *Ulysses*—ought "to contrive the breach necessary for the coming of the other, whom one can always call Elijah, if Elijah is the name of the unforeseeable other for whom a place must be kept." This Elijah Derrida contrasts (holds in undecidable fluctuation) with the other figure of Elijah in *Ulysses*, the "great operator," Elijah "the head of the megaprogramotelephonic network" (UG 120/AL 294–295). There would never be, Derrida adds, any way to keep the one Elijah safe from the other, any way to be sure who would show at your door if you set a place at your table for Elijah.

Joyce's "signature," that is, the singular concatenation of traces, the

---

[7] I substantiate this point in *Prayers and Tears of Jacques Derrida*, §15, "Hegel and the Jews."

unique and irreplaceable "event"—the idiom named only from the outside, as it were, in legal shorthand, by the patronym "Joyce" and the name given at baptism or circumcision—is to be thought of in terms of "another" circumcision, in terms of the mark, the in-cising, the cut that *différance* makes in something that pretends to be one and whole. To understand that, Derrida says, it is necessary to examine more closely how the signature is a function of the "yes."

"Yes" is not only, or not merely, a determinate word in the language, written or spoken, an element of language analyzable by linguistics (UG 86/AL 274), but also, more importantly, a word that comes before language, and after language, and traverses the whole of language, being "co-extensive with every statement." "Yes" is like a vast "amen" (UG 122n/omitted from AL) that silently sweeps over every word and gesture, even accompanying a discreet tap on a prison wall. "Yes" accompanies whatever is said or spoken, every word or sentence:

> [Y]es, that's right, that's what I am saying, I am, in fact, speaking, yes, there we are, I'm speaking, yes, yes, you can hear me, I can hear you, yes, we are in the process of speaking, there is language, you are receiving me, it's like this, it takes place, it happens, it is written, it is marked, yes, yes [UG 124/AL 297].

As a determinate word, "yes" is an adverb, a word designating nothing but referring to other words, as a supplement of words, enhancing them, perfuming them (like Molly's perfume). But the "yes" that interests Derrida, whose operations have surfaced and become explicit in Molly, is prior to this linguistic category, prior even to performativity, "a pre-performative force," prior to the distinction between performative and constative, affirmative and negative. "I" always means "yes-I," or "yes-I-say-to-the-other," even when I say "no." Yes, language is happening, you and I, the I and the other, are happening. There can be no metalanguage to encompass or comprehend, to get behind or on top of this "yes," because any language, including any metalanguage, already presupposes this primal "yes." "Yes" is not the self-positing yes of the *ego cogito*, but the responsive "yes" to the other, the anachrony of responding to a structurally prior address that interrupts all narcissism in advance. By the time I say "yes" I have already been addressed by the other, already been taken up in his arms, which is why Molly's "monologue," while it may be a literary "soliloquy," is not truly a monologue but a "yes" addressed to the other. My "yes" is always second, a "yes" to a prior "yes," which "begins by responding" (UG 130/AL 301). The "yes" precedes ontology, the positing of being, and egology, the positing of self, precedes any positing at all, because all positing and posing presuppose response. Yes, I am responding—to the call of Being, of God, of justice, of the gift, of hospitality, of the other, no matter by what name the other goes (or comes).

Derrida proposes that we can think of this in terms of the "postal" technology that he explored in *The Post Card*, of missives, sendings (*envois*), flying hither and yon, the question being whether sending can be gathered together into the circular route of a postal circle so that no mail is lost and every letter reaches its destination (cf. UG 30–34/PSJ 150–152). The postal circle describes a circle of self-possession, of the "same," a subject in control of his/her comings and goings, of what s/he means to say or do, like an "author" who would remain master of what s/he has written and would dominate all future "criticism," which is a little auto-erotic. Now, it is almost an axiom in deconstruction that when you see a circle, you should breach it (or let it be seen that it is always already breached). So the "yes" in this second, more affirmative sense is to be taken as itself a response to what has already been *sent* our way, which interrupts in advance the circle of self-sending, of narcissism, of self-affecting auto-eroticism, of the self-conscious and self-possessed ego. To the extent that "the Ulyssean circle of *self-sending*" is allowed to close, a reactive yes-laughter wins out, and to that extent the illusion of omnipotence triumphs: the "phantasm of the signature wins out, a signature gathering together the sending in order to gather itself together near itself." Or it does not, and then the circle is torn open in the moment of the "gift," beginning by the impossible (giving without return), and "the specular gathering of the sending lets itself be joyfully dispersed in a multiplicity of unique yet numberless sendings, then the other yes laughs, the other, yes, laughs" and that laughter is, yes, affirmative (UG 136/AL 304).

Re-Joyce.

Two signatures parallel and are a function of the two *yeses*. A self-enclosing, protective, self-defensive signature that is intent on protecting its patronymy and paternal-authorial rights, on remaining master of the house of Joyce. That is the signature of a certain Joyce who seems to sneer and laugh cynically, in a spirit of *ressentissement*, at any possible future commentary, or of an International Joyce Circle that might be tempted to circle around Joyce's signature and to close ranks around its own expertise. The only letters in this postal economy are authoritative "encyclicals" which make the rounds of the faithful telling them what to believe. Such a signature is intent on gathering again to itself what it sends out, on reeling back to itself whatever is "given out" (*Ausgabe*), instead of giving it up for lost.

There is no gift, no *Gabe* in this *Ausgabe*, no *dare* or *datum* in this *editio*, because the author/editor wants everything back. But a text should be a gift, and a signature should make a gift of itself, give itself to the other without return, sent out without expectation of pay-back, that solicits and invites countless new and unexpected counter-signatures. That would be a signature that says "yes" to the other, and that is no easy matter; it requires constant practice and repetition, yes, yes:

> [A] *yes* demands *a priori* its own repetition, its own memorizing, demands that a *yes* to the *yes* inhabit the arrival of the "first" *yes*, which is never therefore simply originary. We cannot say *yes* without promise to confirm it and to remember it, to keep it safe, countersigned in another yes without promise and memory, without the promise of memory [UG 136–137/AL 304–305].

The "yes" arises in "the dissymmetry of request," coming to us from the other, of whom, like Molly, we request that s/he ask us to say yes, soliciting the other to ask us again, so that we can say "yes." "Yes" is breathed with the breath of the other who inspires us. But there is nothing, no, to protect the second "yes" from becoming rote repetition, the automaton of mechanical repetition which is only mouthing "yes."

Accordingly, the "yes, yes" of this affirmative yes-laughter means two things (we cannot be surprised by that), count them, two. (1) The second "yes" is the "yes" of "*response*," that is, made in response to the other whose coming, yes, we have already acknowledged; the second "yes" is an *answer* to the first, breathed under the inspiration of the first, of the other. (2) The second "yes" is also—in the same breath—the "yes" of *repetition*, that is, made in confirmation of the first affirmation and just as primal and pristine as the so-called first. The "yes" if it really is "yes" cannot run on automatic but must really be restarted again and again, each "yes" being originarily "yes," still another origin. The "yes" of repetition must already inhabit the first and be laid claim to by the first, lest the first be not first but a hollow cymbal, which only time will tell. The similarities of Derrida's "yes, yes" to Constantin Constantius's "repetition forwards," which produces what it repeats, should not go unnoticed.

So, then, in conclusion, Derrida asks whether we can take account of the "yes" in Joyce's *Ulysses*, to which should be added *Finnegan's Wake*, hence, in Joyce's "signature." Can we count the ways of "yes"? Can we, in the most elementary sense, even count them at all? If not by hand, then with a computer? But computers, quick as they are, are notoriously stupid, bereft of judgment and *phronesis*, unable to move between the universal and the singular, and require constant direction and intervention. What advice shall we give the computer about foreign words, like the German *ja*, the Italian *si* (not to mention the French *oui*)? Or, more difficult still, how shall we counsel the computer when it comes to "categorizing" the *yeses*, to sorting them out into a typology, to having an ear for the tonalities of the "yes"? How can the computer, how can we, how can Joyce himself, be sensitive to the different tonalities of "yes," to the way the two *yeses* invade and disturb each other? How could anyone be sure that the affirmative, joyous yes-laughter of the gift is not being subtly and surreptitiously undermined by the sneering, resentful, hissing, sibilant "yes" that would protect itself and draw itself into a circle, by the "yes" of "recapitulating control and reactive repetition" (UG 141/AL 308) (like the sibilant "yes" of a superstar who has just executed a slam dunk, which salts the wound of the other side)? That would require one unheard-of (*inouï*) computer! Add to all these encumbrances one more, absolutely ineluctable difficulty: any program or computer, any convoking of an International Joyce Symposium, any body of literature collected together, any effort to write on Joyce's corpus that would attempt to count or take account of "yes," would in fact presuppose the "yes," would come in response, yes, as a yes, to a text by which it has, yes, already been addressed.

The idea in reading Joyce (in reading anyone) is to ward off, to prevent "totalization, and the closing of the circle, and the return of Ulysses, and Ulysses himself, and the self-sending of some indivisible signature" (UG 142/AL 308). On Derrida's accounting, the signature is, in a nutshell, incalculable and unenclosable. That is because it is always already divisible, incisable, circumcisable by a "yes," so that "yes" severs, slashes, slices through the signature, sending it off in innumerable directions, opening it up to multiple repetitions, allowing a self-transforming tradition to graft itself upon it, permitting, soliciting innumerable counter-signatures.

But a circumcised Ulysses has become Abrahamic, which is, to be sure, just what was feared by Hegel, whose Christian Spirit of love did not include forgiving the Jew whom he accused of circumcising Greeks. But for Derrida circumcision is to be thought in terms of the cut that severs the circle of the same, as the cut that *opens the same to other*, which cuts a very different figure—not unlike the circumcised ear or heart in Jeremiah. This circumcision cuts the signature open to the call of the other, so that the signature is like a wandering Jew, in diaspora, never to come home again. Now bad as this may seem to Homer, Hegel, Hölderlin, Husserl, or Heidegger, all of whom have aspir(at)ed to Greco-Germanic homecomings, in one way or another, this cut is not a loss but a gain. For by preventing the closure of the signature, the cut provides an opportunity to discover, to invent, to come upon (*invenir*), something new, the coming (*venir*) of the other, yes, to the in-coming of the other (*l'invention d'autre*). Joyce's signature then would be a gift, cut open and overflowing without return, which solicits endless counter-signatures, a kind of open-ended signing, re-signing, and counter-signing, an open-ended re-Joycing that lets Joyce be Joyce again, yes, and then again, yes, yes, lets his signature sign on to and provide the opening or the occasion for unforeseeable rereadings and resignings.

Re-Joyce, say yes.

"Let us laugh, amen."[8]

INAUGURATIONS (*Encore*)

"Yes" is very close to the heart of deconstruction, if it has a heart, close to its core or kernel, if there is either, and would figure significantly in any attempt, however mad, to put deconstruction in a nutshell, which is sometimes helpful. The very idea of the "yes" as still another nutshell is self-limiting, of course, since the idea behind "yes" is to cut through all casings and self-enclosures. But in deconstruction being a self-limiting idea is no objection.

---

[8] The final words of "Two Words for Joyce" are "let us laugh, amen" (UG 52/PSJ 158), to which is added in the Galilée edition, "*sic, si, oc, oïl.*"

At the end of the "Roundtable" Derrida comes back full circle to the "yes" that impels and drives every inauguration. This circling back on Derrida's part is a bit of a literary flourish, a little ornamentation and perfume, not a Ulyssean circle, no, no. For Derrida is coming back to the breach in the circle, to the "yes" that cuts through every circle and opens it to the other. So he comes back to the question with which we started "today"—let us construe this text of some two hundred pages or so as having traversed but a single day—have we inaugurated anything today? Has anything gotten started today? Who knows?

> If, tomorrow, you do not confirm that today you have founded your program, there will not have been any inauguration. Tomorrow, perhaps next year, perhaps twenty years from now, you will know whether today there has been an inauguration. We do not know that yet. We pretend that today we are inaugurating something. But who knows? We will see.

Every inauguration is in no small part a pretense, pretending with a lot of ceremony and a banquet, speaking always in the future perfect, saying (forecasting) that something will have been done today, that something will have begun today, when no one honestly knows whether or not that will have happened or not. Time will tell. It depends upon the promise to remember and the memory of the promise, which is what an inauguration is. Inaugurations depend upon promises, all the way from big promises, like the one that Yahweh made to Abraham, to smaller-scale ones, as when institutions institute programs. But Derrida is reminding the institution that the relevant point for deconstruction is that you cannot program the program, that the program, like the circle, turns on the gift, begins with the gift, and the gift does not run on automatic. When it does, the program runs into the ground, being reduced to a routine, to rote, to the lifeless repetition of practices for which no one can give much of a rhyme or a reason. The easy rhythms and rote rotations of the circle, the gramophone effect of the program, must be regularly interrupted and disrupted by unprogrammable ("grammatological") irruptions, originary events of various scale.

Sometimes such events are major overhauls that are necessary to hew the program to its real purposes, even though to conservatives they look more like its destruction, as the angry, anguished chorus of deconstruction's critics amply testify. But big events, like large-scale heroic revolutions, are not what Derrida chiefly has in mind by the "yes, yes." Deconstruction is not a big, bombastic, Heideggerian, or Nietzschean Greco-Germanic blast. Derrida is thinking of the small and inconspicuous repetitions that weave the precarious fabric of daily life, that produce what they repeat—Derrida is really repeating something Constantin Constantius said in *Repetition*—without which the program will never make it through the year, or even the month, the week, or the day. The program cannot run on automatic, but must be a self-revising, self-correcting, continual *reaffirmation* of itself, taking responsibility from moment to moment for itself, if it is to have a self, a "yes" followed by a "yes" and then again another "yes."

What, then, could be more suitable, more felicitous, than to invite a deconstructive word or two, yes, yes, from Derrida at the inauguration of a program in philosophy? Remember that by philosophy we mean the freedom to raise questions, which involves a certain amount of freedom to raise hell, to ask any question, to worry oneself about whatever has the look of unquestionable authority and hoary prestige. That includes the right to question questioning, so that we come to understand the question to be an answer, a responding and responsibility, a yes, a way of opening up to a prior address, yes.

What could give Derrida more pleasure? (Well, we need not go into that!) What could give a program in philosophy better direction than to be counseled that you cannot program the program, that there are no rules for the application of the rules, that the program cannot run on automatic even though it requires the automaticity of computers, bureaucratization, institutional directives, authorization, administrative structures, and even administrators who tend to think they own it. It would never be a question of choosing between the program and the yes, the circle and the gift, but of allowing the gift to turn the circle.

A Concluding Amen

Without denying that the devil is in Derrida's eye, or that there is a lot of devilishness in deconstruction, or that the devil of deconstruction is in the details, without having to choose among these possibilities, I would say that deconstruction is hanging on by a prayer. Deconstruction is a way of hanging on *by* a prayer, a way of hanging on *to* a prayer, an old Jewish prayer, "amen," by a vast and sweeping "amen," *oui, oui*. Amen is not the end of deconstruction's prayer but its beginning and sustaining middle, yes, yes, something that precedes and follows and constantly accompanies all its works and days.

If I were more responsible, like Derrida, I would not try to put deconstruction in a nutshell. But, alas, nobody's perfect, and besides Derrida himself has said that we can be flexible on this point and occasionally interrupt or transgress the absolute prohibition against nutshells with occasional exceptions. As Derrida says in the "Roundtable," "sometimes it is not a bad thing," and I have pinned everything on this, "at least if you do not do it too often. It is not that bad that we try to encapsulate deconstruction in a nutshell."

That being said, and at the risk of ruining my reputation, if I had one, a risk that I have limited by developing this point more responsibly in *The Prayers and Tears of Jacques Derrida*, I will risk one last nutshell, not in the sense of an entelechy, a nutshell of all nutshells, the end-all and be-all of nutshells that would contain and encapsulate all the other nutshells, but, let us say, a modest, humble, open-ended quasi-nutshell. If one day someone were to put a microphone in my face and ask me—Derrida himself having boarded a jet to who knows where—whether I could put deconstruction in a nutshell, I would reverently bow my head, or maybe I would fold my hands and look up unctuously to heaven, or maybe I would spread my arms facing the palms of my hands heavenward (for better reception), in any case, whatever posture I would assume, I would invoke an ancient Hebrew word:

Amen

Of which I would then offer a modern (or postmodern?) translation: *Viens, oui, oui.*

The Doctoral Program,
Department of Philosophy,
Villanova University,
Villanova, Pennsylvania
Summer, 1996

Bibliography

BIBLIOGRAPHY OF BIBLIOGRAPHIES

For an invaluable and comprehensive bibliography of Derrida's writings and of the secondary literature up to 1991, see William R. Schultz and Lewis L. B. Fried, *Jacques Derrida: An Annotated Primary and Secondary Bibliography* (New York: Garland, 1992). Extremely helpful too is Albert Leventure, "A Bibliography of the French and English Works of Jacques Derrida, 1962–1990," *Textual Practice*, 5, No. 1 (Spring 1991), 94–127.

For an updating of these bibliographies which includes titles that appear through 1995, see *Social Theory: A Bibliographic Series*, No. 37, *Jacques Derrida (II): A Bibliography*, ed. Joan Nordquist (Santa Cruz, Calif.: Reference and Research Services, 1995).

SELECTED RECENT WORKS OF DERRIDA

Bibliographical information on most of Derrida's major works and their English translations, including most of the titles that have appeared in the 1990s, is to be found in the "Abbreviations" and footnotes, above; this includes *Foi*, which is not found in the above bibliographies. What follows here is information on other recent titles that do not appear either in the Abbreviations or the footnotes, or in the above-mentioned bibliographies.

BOOKS

Apories: Mourir—s'attendre aux "limites de la vérité." Paris: Galilée, 1996. Originally published in *Le Passage des frontières: Autour du travail de Jacques Derrida*. Colloque de Cerisy. Paris: Galilée, 1994.

Pp. 309-338. Eng. trans. *Aporias*. Trans. Thomas Dutoit. Stanford: Stanford University Press, 1993.

Mal d'archive: Une impression freudienne. Paris: Galilée, 1995. Eng. trans. *Archive Fever: A Freudian Impression*. Trans. Eric Prenowitz. Chicago: The University of Chicago Press, 1996. This translation originally appeared in *Diacritics*, 25 (1995), 9–63.

Moscou aller-retour. La Tour d'Aigues: Éditions de l'Aube, 1995. Eng. trans. pp. 11–98: "Back From Moscow, In the USSR." Trans. Mary Quaintance. In *Politics, Theory, and Contemporary Culture*. Ed. Mark Poster. New York: Columbia University Press, 1993. Pp. 197–235.

Résistances de la psychanalyse. Paris: Galilée, 1996. Eng. trans. Pp. 55-88: "For the Love of Lacan." Trans. Brent Edwards and Ann Lecercle. *Cardozo Law Review*, 16 (1995), 699–728. Pp. 89-146: "'To Do Justice to Freud': Madness in the Age of Psychoanalysis." Trans. Pascale-Anne Brault and Michael Naas. *Critical Inquiry*, 20 (1994), 227–266.

ARTICLES

"Adieu" [Eulogy at the funeral of Emmanuel Levinas, December 28, 1995]. *L'Arche*, No. 459 (February 1996), 84–90. "By Force of Mourning." Trans. Pascale-Anne Brault and Michael Naas. *Critical Inquiry*, 22 (1996), 171–192.

Preface to Mumia Abu-Jamal, *En direct du couloir de la mort*. Paris: La Découverte, 1996. French translation of *Live from Death Row* (New York: Avon Books, 1996).

FURTHER READING

The best introduction to Derrida, in my view, is his interviews, where he speaks for himself in a particularly clear and unencumbered way. (In the discussions following his lectures, Derrida is often the clearest and most modest speaker in the room.) My favorite interview, which I recommend very highly, is "Deconstruction and the Other," in *Dialogues with Contemporary Thinkers*, ed. Richard Kearney (Manchester: Manchester University Press, 1984), pp. 105–126. That is the best place to start. *Points* is also a superb collection of very helpful interviews and also a very good place to start.

As even a cursory look at the above bibliographies will reveal, the secondary literature on Derrida is immense and ultimately unmanageable. Schultz and Fried record 1,322 books or contributions to books, and 1,152 articles on Derrida (as of 1991). In addition to referring to the works that I cited in context in the footnotes, I provide here a few recommendations for further study that will be more than enough to get the interested reader started.

Derrida was first welcomed to the United States by literary theorists, first at Johns Hopkins University in the 1960s and then in the 1970s at Yale and Cornell; nowadays he travels annually to New York and Irvine. After the philosophers caught on to Derrida and began emphasizing the influence of Hegel, Husserl, and Heidegger on deconstruction, a small war broke out between them about how to read Derrida. The best introduction to Derrida from the standpoint of literary theory is Jonathan Culler, *On Deconstruction: Theory and Criticism after Structuralism* (Ithaca, N.Y.: Cornell University Press, 1982). The link between Derrida and Paul de Man is central to understanding deconstruction and American literary theory; in addition to Paul de Man's own classic, *Blindness and Insight: Essays in the Rhetoric of Contemporary Criticism* (New York: Oxford University Press, 1971), which discusses Derrida, see the readings gathered in RDR. For a self-consciously literary reading of Derrida, see Geoffrey Hartman, *Saving the Text: Literature/Derrida/Philosophy* (Baltimore: The Johns Hopkins University Press, 1981), which is a study of *Glas*, possibly Derrida's most exotic work; it has a lefthand column for philosophers and a righthand one for littérateurs. The classic "manifesto" of this phase of deconstruction is *Deconstruction and Criticism* (New York: Continuum, 1979), which contains contributions by J. Hillis Miller and Harold Bloom, in addition to Derrida, de Man, and Hartmann.

The most aggressively philosophical reading of Derrida, which accuses the literary critics of misrepresenting Derrida, done by someone who knows him quite well, is Rodolphe Gasché, *The Tain of the Mirror* (Cambridge, Mass.: Harvard University Press, 1986); and *Inventions of Difference: On Jacques Derrida* (Cambridge, Mass.: Harvard University Press, 1994). Similarly, Christopher Norris, *Derrida* (Cambridge, Mass.: Harvard University Press, 1987) is an excellent introduction to Derrida. In his various works, Norris, who particularly contests Rorty's depiction of Derrida, can be criticized for pushing Derrida too close to the "old" Enlightenment. For Rorty's story, see his *Contingency, Irony, and Solidarity* (Cambridge: Cambridge University Press, 1989), chap. 6. I tried to mediate this dispute in my "In Search of the Quasi-Transcendental: The Case of Derrida and Rorty," *Working Through Derrida*, ed. Gary Madison (Evanston, Ill.: Northwestern University Press, 1993), pp. 147–169.

The most spirited and informed delimitation of this philosophical aggression, also done by someone who knows Derrida quite well, is Geoffrey Bennington, *Legislations: The Politics of Deconstruction* (London: Verso, 1994). John Llewelyn does a good job, despite some excessive cuteness, of negotiating the difference in *Derrida on the Threshold of Sense* (New York: St. Martin's Press, 1986), while also trying to open up the question of Derrida and analytic philosophy. *Derrida: A Critical Reader*, ed. David Wood (Oxford: Blackwell, 1992) is a first-rate collection of papers sensitive to Derrida's many sides.

Philosophers will find that *Deconstruction and Philosophy: The Texts of Jacques Derrida*, ed. John Sallis (Chicago: The University of Chicago Press, 1987) contains a number of reliable and helpful essays. *Working Through Derrida*, ed. Gary B. Madison (see above), is also an excellent collection of papers that take up dominantly philosophical issues. Harry Staten, *Wittgenstein and Derrida* (Lincoln: University of Nebraska Press, 1984) and *Redrawing the Lines: Analytic Philosophy, Deconstruction, and Literary Theory*, ed. Reed Way Dasenbrock (Minneapolis: University of Minnesota Press, 1989) will be of interest to analytic philosophers who want to read Derrida; the latter also also contains an exchange between Norris and Rorty.

There is a lot of debate about Derrida's relationship to hermeneutics. *Dialogue and Deconstruction*, ed. Diane Michelfelder and Richard Palmer (Albany: State University of New York Press, 1989) is the basic resource for the Gadamer link. Leonard Lawlor, *Imagination and Chance: The Difference Between the Thought of Ricoeur and Derrida* (Albany: State University of New York Press, 1992) is a fine exploration of the Ricoeur connection. The question of Heidegger and Derrida has provoked extensive commentary. See Herman Rapaport, *Heidegger and Derrida: Reflections on Time and History* (Lincoln: University of Nebraska Press, 1992); I myself have not found a reason to renounce my *Radical Hermeneutics: Repetition, Deconstruction and the Hermeneutic Project* (Bloomington: Indiana University Press,

1987); and my *Demythologizing Heidegger* (Bloomington: Indiana University Press, 1993) is a critique of Heidegger from a Derridean standpoint. John Protevi, *Time and Exteriority: Aristotle, Heidegger, Derrida* (Lewistown, Penn.: Bucknell University Press, 1994) is a sensitive reading of a subtle issue.

If you are interested in Derrida and theology, there is a lot of help to be had. I have attempted to draw up a comprehensive bibliography of such titles in *The Prayers and Tears of Jacques Derrida*. But see, in particular, G. Douglas Atkins, *Reading Deconstruction/Deconstructive Reading* (Lexington: University Press of Kentucky, 1983); "Partial Stories: Hebraic and Christian Thinking in the Wake of Deconstruction," *Religion and Literature*, 15, No. 3 (1983), 7–21; Kevin Hart, *The Trespass of the Sign: Deconstruction, Theology, and Philosophy* (Cambridge: Cambridge University Press, 1985); Walter Lowe, *Theology and Difference: The Wound of Reason* (Bloomington: Indiana University Press, 1993); Louis Mackey, "Slouching Towards Bethlehem: Deconstructive Strategies in Theology," *Anglican Theological Review*, 65 (1983), 255–272; Mark Taylor, *Erring: A Postmodern A/theology* (Chicago: The University of Chicago Press, 1987). See also the articles collected in DNT.

For Derrida and Asian religion and thought, see David Loy, "The Clôture of Deconstruction: A Mahayana Critique of Derrida," *International Philosophical Quarterly*, 27 (1987), 59–80; *Deconstruction and Healing: Postmodern Thought in Buddhism and Christianity* (Atlanta: Scholars Press, American Academy of Religion, 1996); Robert Magliola, *Derrida on the Mend* (West Lafayette, Ind.: Purdue University Press, 1984).

There is a growing and important discussion of Derrida and ethics, most of which centers on the question of Derrida and Levinas. Simon Critchley, *The Ethics of Deconstruction: Derrida and Levinas* (Oxford: Blackwell, 1992) sets the standard. I myself have contributed a fragment to this literature in my *Against Ethics: Contributions to a Poetics of Obligation with Constant Reference to Deconstruction* (Bloomington: Indiana University Press, 1993). The question of politics is raised in the essays in DPJ, in Bennington (above), in Madison's *Working Through Derrida* (above), and in the essays cited in the notes to the discussions of SdM/SoM above, chaps. 5–6. The papers collected in DPJ also do a good job of raising the question of Derrida and the law.

The question of Derrida and feminist theory is an important and ongoing concern. See Diane Elam, *Feminism and Deconstruction: Ms. en Abyme* (New York: Routledge, 1994); and the collection entitled *Derrida and Feminism: Recasting the Question of Woman*, ed. Ellen Feder, Mary Rawlinson, Emily Zakin (New York: Routledge, Chapman and Hall, forthcoming). See also Drucilla Cornell, *The Philosophy of the Limit* (New York: Routledge, 1992).

For Derrida and architecture, see Mark Wigley, *The Architecture of Deconstruction: Derrida's Haunt* (Cambridge, Mass.: The MIT Press, 1993).

Gregory Ulmer, *Applied Grammatology: Post(e)-Pedagogy from Jacques Derrida to Joseph Beuys* (Baltimore: The Johns Hopkins University Press, 1985) is an off-beat but highly interesting discussion of the implications of deconstruction for pedagogy and an extremely sensitive treatment of the question of postal technology and "virtual reality."

Index of Names

Index of Subjects

agent, as a principle of appropriation, 144, 146, 148–149; see "subject, the"
Algeria, 19, 20, 60, 114, 126, 160, 171
Amen, 149, 194, 198, 202
American Philosophical Association, 39
analytic philosophy, 39–41
Aufklärer, 40, 52, 54, 55, 59, 167, 169
author, the, 78, 80, 195–196
à venir, see "come"

Buddhism, 176–177

Cambridge University, 16, 31, 38–40, 43, 132
canon, the, 10–11, 65, 75, 81–82, 94
capitalism, 161; of the European capitals, 118–120; Marxist critique, of, 120
Christianity, 10, 21, 22, 43, 160, 168
circumcision, 186, 189, 191, 192, 194, 198
circumfession, 158
come, 22, 24–25, 41–42, 123–124, 128, 135, 154, 156–158, 162, 164, 172, 178–180, 198; see "democracy," "justice," "messianic," "future"
communitarianism, 108–109
community, 11, 13–15, 7–124 (passim); as quasi-community, 123–124; etymology of the word, 107–108, 108n4
conservative, Derrida as, 8, 37; vs. conservatism, 79, 81, 109
conventionalism, 42, 103–104, 108–109, 131
cultural studies, 71

decision, 3; aporias of, 136–139
democracy, 9, 12, 18, 19, 43–44, 58–60, 61, 107, 122, 123, 153, 173–178
dissemination, 184, 193

différance, 96–105, 122, 151n16, 158, 175, 180, 184, 187, 194
dike, 17, 151–155
double bind, 147–148, 189–191
double gesture, 81

economy, and the gift, 142, 145–151
écriture, see "writing"
emancipation, 55
Enlightenment, old vs. new, 50–51, 53–55, 57, 59–60, 69, 123, 158–159, 164; and religion, 164
essentialism, 42, 101, 103–104, 108–109, 117, 131
Europe, 114, 118, 119, 123, 127
experience, 32–33

faith, 21–22, 23, 159; vs. religion, 164–168
feminism, 104–105, 105n11
Finnegan's Wake, 25, 185, 187n4, 197
formal indication, 177–178
French phenomenology, 182
friendship, 10, 14
fundamentalism, 160
future, 22, 24; future-present vs. absolute future, 133–134, 135, 156–158, 161–162, 178, 179; see "come"

gathering, 13, 14, 25, 31–32, 33, 52, 117, 151–155, 185, 196; see "Versammlung"
gender, 104–105, 121, see also "mothers," "feminism"
gift, 15, 18–19, 70, 71, 94–95, 116, 140–151, 193, 195–196, 199–200; and hospitality, 111–113; and khôra, 143
God, 20, 92, 92n7, 93, 96–99, 102–103, 122, 128, 135–136, 139, 147, 147n12,

Perspectives in Continental Philosophy
John D. Caputo, series editor

Recent titles:

Colby Dickinson and Stéphane Symons (eds.), *Walter Benjamin and Theology*.

Don Ihde, *Husserl's Missing Technologies*.

William S. Allen, *Aesthetics of Negativity: Blanchot, Adorno, and Autonomy*.

Jeremy Biles and Kent L. Brintnall, eds., *Georges Bataille and the Study of Religion*.

Tarek R. Dika and W. Chris Hackett, *Quiet Powers of the Possible: Interviews in Contemporary French Phenomenology*. Foreword by Richard Kearney.

Richard Kearney and Brian Treanor, eds., *Carnal Hermeneutics*.

A complete list of titles is available at http://fordhampress.com.